Service-Learning Through a Multidisciplinary Lens

Edited by

Shelley H. Billig
and
Andrew Furco

INFORMATION AGE PUBLISHING

80 Mason Street
Greenwich, Connecticut 06830

Library of Congress Cataloging-in-Publication Data

Service-learning through a multidisciplinary lens / edited by Shelley H.
Billig and Andrew Furco.
    p. cm. – (Advances in service-learning research ; v. 2)
  Includes bibliographical references.
   ISBN 1-931576-80-7 (pbk.) – ISBN 1-931576-81-5 (hardcover)
   1. Student service–United States. I. Billig, Shelley. II. Furco,
  Andrew. III. Series.
    LC220.5 .S476 2002
    378.1'03–dc21
                    2002014174

Printed in the United States of America

CONTENTS

Part III
Service-Learning and the Disciplines

Part IV
The Impacts on Service-Learning Participants

Part V
Future Directions in Service-Learning Research

INTRODUCTION

Shelley H. Billig and Andrew Furco

Service-learning is an approach to teaching and learning that involves having students perform community service as a means for achieving academic goals. By its very nature, service-learning is a boundary spanning activity that is expressed in a myriad of ways. The practice of service-learning typically involves participants from both educational institutions and community agencies or groups. Activities can be focused on an assortment of tasks that are integrated at varying degrees across a broad range of content areas. Participation often involves multiple generations and individuals with varying talents and levels of expertise. Program design can be oriented toward producing a wide range of results that can be manifested through many different types of service-learning activities. Results may vary depending upon contextual, design, and demographic factors, such as age of participants, level of schooling, content of activities, length of experience, and a host of other variables.

Because of its boundary spanning nature, service-learning research can be studied using a wide variety of theoretical and disciplinary frameworks to investigate a broad range of program outcomes. When the research is conducted in rigorous ways, the multiple perspectives can lead to greater understandings about the practice of service-learning and can offer sound

Service-Learning Through a Multidisciplinary Lens
A Volume in: Advances in Service-Learning Research, pages vii–x.
Copyright © 2002 by Information Age Publishing, Inc.
All rights of reproduction in any form reserved.
ISBN: 1-931576-81-5 (cloth), 1-931576-80-7 (paper)

advice for practitioners who wish to increase the quality of their service-learning approaches and the impact on participants.

This book, the second volume in the *Advances in Service-Learning Research* series, explores the multidisciplinary dimensions of service-learning and the implications of these dimensions for the study of service-learning. The chapters in this volume were selected from a juried, blind review of papers based on presentations at the First Annual International K-H Service-Learning Research Conference, held in Berkeley, California.

The book is divided into five sections. The first section, Dimensions in Service-Learning Research, provides an overview of the multitude of perspectives that can be taken to study service-learning and some of the issues that arise for researchers who perform studies in this field. Chapter 1 contains the keynote speech delivered by Janet Eyler at the Berkeley conference. Eyler reviews the state of the research field and discusses the need to improve the quality of service-learning research in order to improve service-learning practice. She emphasizes the need to conduct more studies that employ randomized assignment of students to treatment and control groups, and exhorts researchers to be clear on the independent variables they wish to study. She also points out that because many service-learning studies are atheoretical, new studies should focus on testing theories and competing hypotheses.

In Chapter 2, Andrew Furco and Shelley H. Billig discuss the need to establish norms for scientific inquiry for the field of service-learning. The authors recommend that service-learning researchers align their practice more firmly to the core principles for scientific research, as identified by the National Research Council. They also suggest that service-learning researchers investigate several promising theories from other fields, such as activity theory and ill-structured problems theory, as possible sources for deepening our understanding of the impacts of service-learning.

Section two presents two new theoretical perspectives that may be used to guide research. Mary Sue Ammon, in Chapter 3, provides a thought-provoking way to understand teachers' thinking about service-learning through the use of a developmental constructivist theoretical model. Using an example of a "book buddies" program, Ammon shows the ways in which the same activity can vary broadly across classrooms depending upon a teacher's learning goals, preparation, reflection, collaborative partnering, and program monitoring for learning. She concludes by reminding researchers how important it is to understand teachers' intentions and perceptions about service-learning to be able to assess the efficacy of the approach.

In Chapter 4, Janice McMillan provides a new conceptual framework that addresses service-learning as "boundary work," a form of analysis that requires the researcher to examine processes and relationships between different institutional and political structures, focusing on social development. She applies her theoretical frame to service-learning practice in

Cape Town, South Africa, exploring the relationship between institutions of higher education, community, and service sectors. In her conclusion, she urges researchers to create "rich portraits of practice," finding a new language to reflect the boundary crossing nature of service-learning in order to understand its complexity as a pedagogical practice.

The third section of the book examines service-learning and the disciplines. Chapter 5, by Pamela Steinke, Peggy Fitch, Chris Johnson, and Fredric Waldstein, provides the results of an interdisciplinary study of service-learning predictors and outcomes. The authors used multiple lenses to interpret their results. They found that best practices for one type of outcome were not necessarily related to best practices for another. The authors urge those who design service-learning to become more intentional about the results they seek so that the design of service-learning activities can maximize outcomes in particular areas.

In Chapter 6, Adrian Wurr examines the ways in which service-learning can improve writing for first year college composition students. Comparing analytic and holistic measures of writing quality for service-learning students and comparison groups, Wurr shows that service-learning had a statistically significant positive effect on student writing both in terms of performance and attitudes toward writing. Essays by service-learning students were judged to be more effective in terms of use of rhetorical appeals, logic, coherence, and mechanics.

Rhonda Waskiewicz discusses health care and service-learning in Chapter 7. Using an experimental design to study occupational therapy students, Waskiewicz uses a semantic differential scale and a community service involvement preference inventory to measure occupational therapy students' awareness and sense of responsibility toward community. Service-learning students also kept journals. Results indicate that participation in service-learning had little influence on scale or inventory scores. All groups changed in positive directions. However, analysis of journals and disaggregation of results by course difficulty (200 level versus 400 level) showed some differences between groups.

The fourth section focuses on the impacts of service-learning. Chapter 8 by Andrea Vernon and Lenoar Foster investigates community agency perspectives in higher education service-learning and volunteerism. The researchers gathered data from community agency staff that worked directly with service-learning students, examining how collaborative partnerships were formed, perceived impacts on youth service agencies and youth, and community views about college student volunteers. Results showed that agency personnel strongly support and appreciate the service provided, though they do not always support the service-learning requirements. Agency staff urge stronger commitment and accountability by the college students to the youth being served so that the students are less likely to drop out of the program, leaving younger children feeling deserted.

Beth Covitt, in Chapter 9, discusses the ways in which service-learning can be used to motivate environmentally responsible behavior. Examining a middle school environmental education program, the author compares service-learning to field trips to understand the ways in which these two types of interventions fulfilled students' personal goals and future intentions to engage in environmentally responsible behaviors. Results show that service-learning had less of a positive effect than the field trips. The author concludes that further study is needed to investigate the role of several variables, such as personal goals, that may mediate the results of service-learning.

Chapter 10 presents a study by Kari Knutson Miller, Shu-Chen Yen, and Nicole Merino of service-learning and academic outcomes in an undergraduate child development course. Using a quasi-experimental design, the authors investigate whether service-learning students have a greater understanding of course content than students who do not participate in service-learning. The authors also examine the value of service provided to the recipient. Data did not show that service-learning students learned more, though the recipients greatly valued the service. The authors discuss the possible reasons behind the conclusions that they reported and recommend several other studies to help understand the results.

The final section of the book examines future directions for service-learning research. In Chapter 11, co-editors Shelley H. Billig and Andrew Furco briefly examine the state of service-learning research and the challenges associated with "growing" the service-learning research field. They recommend a set of strategies to attract funders and a variety of mature and younger researchers to improve the quantity and quality of service-learning research.

PART I

DIMENSIONS OF SERVICE-LEARNING RESEARCH

CHAPTER 1

STRETCHING TO MEET THE CHALLENGE
Improving the Quality of Research to Improve the Quality of Service-Learning

Janet Eyler

Excerpts from Keynote Address to First Annual Conference on Service-Learning Research. Audience is challenged to improve the quality of research design, clarify and improve measurement of independent and dependent variables, and design research to test alternative theoretical perspectives in order to provide research evidence for the improvement of service-learning practice.

Today, I would like to challenge us to stretch to meet higher goals and standards for service-learning research, but before addressing the shortcomings of service-learning research, it is important to celebrate the great strides made over the past ten years in empirical support for service-learning. The success of this First International Conference on K-H Ser-

Service-Learning Through a Multidisciplinary Lens
A Volume in: Advances in Service-Learning Research, pages 3–13.
Copyright © 2002 by Information Age Publishing, Inc.
All rights of reproduction in any form reserved.
ISBN: 1-931576-81-5 (cloth), 1-931576-80-7 (paper)

vice-Learning Research, where 350 researchers and practitioners came together to share their research and find out the latest developments, is itself a sign of the vitality of the field. From very little evidence a decade ago, there are now numerous studies, including several national surveys both of K-12 and higher education (Eyler & Giles, 1999; Gray et al., 1998; Melchior, 1998), a national evaluation study of service-learning in the health care professions (Gelmon, Holland, & Shinnamonn, 1998), and dozens of smaller locally focused studies (Eyler, Giles, Stenson, & Gray, 2000). There is also organized attention being paid to the future of service-learning research. National efforts to think about a research agenda have been supported by the W. K. Kellogg Foundation sponsored *Learning In Deed* initiative and by Campus Compact among others. The successful development of the *Michigan Journal of Service-Learning Research*, the first peer-reviewed journal in this field, as well as special issues of other journals and the publication of a number of books that share research findings have left us immeasurably richer in knowledge of the effects of service-learning than we were only a few years ago.

As a result of this increased research attention, there are some things that we can have some confidence in. Studies summarized in two major reviews of the higher education and the K-12 service-learning research literature (Eyler, Giles, Stenson & Gray, 2000; Billig, 2000) indicate generally small but consistent evidence for the impact of service-learning on:

- the personal development of young people;
- engagement in school and avoidance of risky behavior by adolescents; and
- commitment by young people to making a difference in their communities.

The evidence for academic impact is mixed, but there is some evidence that increased school engagement may lead to better performance and persistence to graduation (Billig, 2000) and that high quality service-learning leads to deeper understanding and improved critical thinking (Eyler & Giles, 1999).

While studies of community impact and institutionalization have lagged behind those focused on student outcomes, research that has been conducted shows positive regard by community partners for the contributions of students (Gray et al., 1998), and there is evidence for increased opportunities for students to participate in academic service-learning courses (Campus Compact, 2000).

While it is heartening to have this increased body of research evidence, it is neither precise nor robust enough to guide decision making about practice. Our success at implementation has outstripped our knowledge of what works best. For a field that engenders so much passion in practitioners and that we believe transforms students by engaging their hearts as well as their minds, there is remarkably little evidence of strong impact and even less evidence about the kinds of practices that lead to the effects we desire.

Our goals and our standards for research have been set too low. Perhaps one reason for the failure to build a strong body of useful research is that most of the studies reported are byproducts of other efforts. Typically these are evaluations conducted to meet reporting requirements of funders or to justify local efforts. Many of the research studies that do exist are one-shot efforts completed as dissertations by practitioners who do not go on to conduct further research. There are few researchers who have developed a sustained research plan, with multiple studies building on previous work. The field has not set high goals for either the quality of methodology or the purpose of research. This is a field more grounded in passion for service, service-learning, and students than in theory or research.

We need to set our sights higher, to stretch further and to undertake more thoughtful, sustained, and focused research programs. One more survey, with more reports from students testifying to loving service-learning and learning a lot from it, will not give us what we need to convince policy makers of the value of our work or to provide evidence to practitioners to improve our practice. While the focus of my remarks here will be on improving the quality of our research to ascertain the impact of service-learning practice on student outcomes, the need for better and more ambitious research applies to understanding community outcomes, faculty involvement, and institutional development as well. While different questions must be addressed in these areas, the same attention to well-conceived, tightly coupled, carefully implemented research is needed in all our domains of interest.

We have set our goals for service-learning research too low in several ways:

- We have not paid enough attention to rigorous research design.
- We have not clearly specified our independent variables.
- We have not given adequate attention to defining and measuring appropriate outcomes of service-learning.
- We have not tested theory and rarely provided competing hypotheses.

IMPROVING RESEARCH DESIGN

Neither the quantitative or qualitative research designs used in much of the service-learning research literature gives us confidence that we know either what impact this practice has on students or how this impact if registered does occur. There may be many reasons for this lack of rigor, including lack of resources, the reliance on evaluation studies of single projects, the difficulties of studying phenomena in the field, and/or the lack of research expertise of practitioners involved in many of these projects.

Although most of the research reported uses quantitative data, there are almost no experimental studies in the literature. Selectivity may well account for most of our findings in survey studies of service-learning. While attempts are made to control statistically for differences among groups in quasi-experimental survey designs, the fact remains that those who choose to perform service or service-learning may differ in many ways from those who do not engage in those activities.

Indeed there is some evidence to suggest that these differences exist prior to the service-learning experience (Eyler, Giles, & Braxton, 1997). Given the consistently found rather small differences in outcomes between those who participate in service or service-learning and those who do not, it is fair to suspect that the differences result from who selects these activities rather than from the experiences themselves. Additionally when some studies find that differences in outcome measures between service-learning students and others result from declines in the scores of the control group, one can also wonder if the findings are not the result of indifference and test fatigue by the control group that is not engaged in the service-learning experience and is thus less patient with completing repeated survey measures of dubious relevance to them. Without random assignment of students to different pedagogical experiences, the power of service-learning to affect desired outcomes cannot be confidently asserted.

A second drawback in most of the research on service-learning is the attempt to assess impact over a short time such as a semester course. Many of the desired outcomes involve personal and cognitive development that take place over a long time. Perhaps the most important goals involve expected behavior after the student has left school. We do not have much information about sustained service-learning experiences over many years of schooling and we also have very little longitudinal data to show long-term impact on attitudes, understanding, and behavior. Since many of the most important goals for service-learning involve citizenship behavior, there is a tremendous need for well-designed studies that follow students through school and into their adult lives in the community.

Many service-learning practitioners advocate qualitative studies of service-learning, arguing that the essence of service-learning is better studied through deeper, more nuanced descriptions of what can be highly idiosyncratic experiences and outcomes. The notion is that qualitative study echoes the integration of heart and head that is at the core of service-learning pedagogy and that the most important effects of service-learning cannot be measured on a survey form, a standardized test, or a final exam. There is certainly an important role for qualitative research in deepening our understanding of processes of service-learning and how students experience them. Better descriptions of actual practice, and exploration of these processes, may also yield more insightful hypotheses for further testing. But what is sometimes presented as qualitative research is simply sharing of anecdotes and stories. There is a great danger of selective perception in sloppy qualitative research and this is magnified when practitioners also interpret journals, essays, and other material produced by their own classes. Strong qualitative research is systematic and contains procedural rules for analysis that mitigate building arguments from selecting anecdotes to fit one's point of view. The field is in need of such studies to give us a better idea about how students develop over time through service-learning experience and to give us greater insights into the experiences that students have in our programs.

The field needs carefully designed, focused studies that can provide information to practitioners and policy makers to guide their work. To develop these studies, we need to be much clearer about specifying the critical elements of service-learning experience and pedagogy and in identifying the outcomes, particularly the academic outcomes that can be expected from this approach.

SPECIFYING THE INDEPENDENT VARIABLE

The independent variable in most studies of the impact of service-learning is, of course, service-learning. Most studies of student impact attempt to contrast service-learning experience with some other educational experience; often that is the same course without a service component. While most practitioners probably have a rich image of their ideal service-learning experience, studies of service-learning impact rarely provide clear descriptions of the experiences that students are having. It may well be that the relatively small impact of service-learning in the literature occurs because what is actually experienced bears little relationship to the kind of experiences described in the best practices literature. It is common to find courses described as service-learning courses where there is little or no explicit continuous reflection and where students sign up through a volunteer center to do something only vaguely related to the academic content of the course. While some service-learning engages students with diverse community members, other programs provide tasks in which they never leave the classroom. Some students are active in service-learning that continues over the course of the year and is central to their academic study; others do disconnected projects of short duration. It should not be surprising that an experience so variable and so poorly specified would have weak impact in large, multi-site surveys or would vary in impact dramatically from one small study to another. The impact of some service-learning experiences may be masked by the lack of impact of other experiences in a large survey sample of students who participate in widely varying activities and classes.

Even where attempts are made to ensure that the experiences studied represent quality service-learning, what happens for students may differ dramatically from what teachers envision. It is not unusual to find students in highly touted programs who see no connection between what they are doing in the community and what is being studied, or who report far less reflection and integration than faculty. When students are asked to tell about their experiences, they may tell what they think their teachers want to hear rather than what they are experiencing. Faculty who are passionate about the value of service-learning may find that their enthusiasm curbs dissent from their students (Eyler & Giles, 1999). Testimonials are very weak data.

It is not clear that all permutations of service-learning will have an equal impact on all desired outcomes. Before we can even begin to ask about impact, we need to describe the experiences that might lead to those impacts. This means clearly defining the characteristics that are thought to make service-learning a powerful pedagogy and then making sure that these components are actually part of the experience that students being studied are having. There have been some attempts to measure quality of service-learning rather than simply contrasting service-learning with its absence and to successfully link it to outcomes. Application, quality of placement, reflection, diversity, and community voice are all associated with positive outcomes. But these studies have generally relied on student reports of the qualitative elements of their experience and the qualities are rather broadly defined (Eyler & Giles, 1999; Mabry, 1998). Future studies need to build on this work on quality and focus more clearly on precisely what aspects of service-learning pedagogy make a difference to varied outcomes.

It would be a valuable contribution to the field for qualitative researchers to conduct observational studies to assess what students actually experience during service-learning programs and to identify the particular needs that students with different characteristics and experiences with service might have. A model might be the one being used by Moore (1999) and others to observe and describe the learning experiences of adolescents in School-to-Work programs. The gap between what faculty envision for students and the actual learning experiences that have been observed in these studies makes clear that part of understanding the impact field-based learning may have on students is to be able to know what is actually experienced during service-learning and how closely that tracks with what is expected. Thick descriptions of service-learning would have many uses, one of which is to create stronger measures of quality service-learning for subsequent hypothesis testing studies.

It would also be a valuable contribution for researchers to move away from large-scale surveys where the experience cannot be clearly observed or controlled to smaller scale studies in which the central features of service-learning, including such elements as reciprocity, reflection, sequencing of learning activities, interaction with diverse others, and so forth, can be managed and clearly observed. It is not possible to have much confi dence in outcomes that depend on quality dimensions that are assumed, but not observed, or rely solely on student report.

CHOOSING AND MEASURING OUR OUTCOME VARIABLES

Just as studies of service-learning have been loose in their attention to defining and measuring the experience to be tested, so too has little attention been given to identifying and measuring outcomes. Because, in a sense, service-learning can be 'all things to all people,' it is tempting to use any measure that is at hand for assessing its impact. Service-learning engages the heart and the head; students are engaged in ways that practitioners believe will lead to increased personal self awareness and confidence, reduced cultural stereotyping and prejudice, increased commitment to and connectedness with community, and improved learning. Oftentimes too little thought is given to matching the expected outcomes or their measurement with the actual experiences planned for students.

While personal and social outcomes of service-learning need to be better defined and carefully measured, great strides have been made in recent years in developing valid measures and making them available to the field. The greater challenge has been to identify appropriate learning outcomes and their measures. The unique value added by schools and colleges or universities is academic learning. It is crucial for the institutionalization of service-learning in the curriculum for practitioners to have a clear set of academic goals for this pedagogy. Because of political pressure and tradition, standardized test scores and grades have often been used to assess learning and yet these may not be sensitive to the most important outcomes for which service-learning is particularly well suited. Service-learning is about doing, about action, about learning from experience, and using the knowledge and skills learned. It is about having assumptions challenged through confronting new perspectives or puzzling experiences and learning to sort out complex, messy real-world situations. It is about knowledge in use, not just about acquiring and being tested on facts. This suggests that educators need to identify aspects of academic learning and cognitive development that are enhanced by this process. This might include assessing the quality of understanding of complicated information, the ability to identify complex or ill-structured problems and come up with strategies to pursue solutions, or the quality of transfer of learning in the application of skills and knowledge to new problems. It certainly includes advanced levels of cognitive development including the ability to make sense of ambiguous conflicting information.

These are important academic goals; few would disagree with the idea that learning to apply what is learned in new situations and cope with complex problems was not central to being well-educated. The current crises faced by citizens attempting to make sense of and steer a course amidst conflicting values and interests makes these capacities even more important. Academic learning goals must include preparing students to apply their knowledge and their capacities to think through problems and learn continuously.

Measuring these outcomes is also a challenge. The field has relied heavily on student self reports, often just single items, of their commitments, their personal growth, and their academic learning. Some attempts are being made to develop and use more fully-developed scales with known psychometric properties. But at their heart, even better developed scales still are about students telling us about themselves and their learning. Service-learning is about doing, not telling, and as a field we should be moving towards observable performance; that is, demonstrated academic competence. This may mean testing using simulated tasks or embedding measurement into the authentic tasks that are at the heart of service-learning. The students who develop an evaluation plan for a community agency have demonstrated their learning. Students who critically analyze a problem have provided evidence of their capacity for analysis. We need measures that allow students to do more than say they can, but allow them to show us that they can.

TESTING THEORY OR COMPETING HYPOTHESES

When research does not clearly specify either the independent or dependent variables, it is not surprising that it tends to be largely atheoretical. Although theoretical concerns are sometimes discussed as frameworks for studies of service-learning or drawn on to interpret findings, there are no examples of theory testing in the literature. It is even rare to find research which tests an alternative hypothesis. Dwight Giles and I attempted to explore an alternative hypothesis in our national survey study of service-learning in higher education. While a modest effort, the results suggest the potential utility of this approach for strengthening our confidence in the results of our research. We were mindful of the fact that given the small effects of service-learning on personal development and attitudes towards civic engagement, it is easy to dismiss these results as the product of some unmeasured factor such as closeness to faculty. Close relationships to faculty have been identified in the higher education literature as a strong predictor of many of the positive outcomes of higher education including persistence and academic success. In our study, we attempted to find out if this might account for positive results related to service-learning; perhaps service-learning students are also those students who seek out and form close interpersonal relationships with other students and faculty. By testing close relationships with faculty as an alternative hypothesis to service-learning experience on our outcomes, we were able to show that each has an independent effect giving us confidence that the measured impact of service-learning was what it appeared to be. Because there are few attempts to test theory or alternative hypotheses, the field is not developing a strong integrated body of evidence to understand or support service-learning.

When there is not a clearly articulated logic behind the predictions made for the research, it is not surprising the results are often not achieved. For example, researchers who study moral development have created a body of research about the conditions under which moral development occurs; but one sees measures of moral development used as outcome measures with little justification in occasional service-learning studies where these conditions are not present. As one would expect, rarely do such studies show results. Service-learning researchers might draw on theory developed in related disciplines to begin to look more closely at how and under what conditions service-learning may contribute to expected outcomes. Service-learning researchers can draw on theories of identity development as they craft studies of personal growth, or on theories of cognitive science to inform careful studies of strategies of service-learning instruction that facilitate learning. Studies of community impact can be framed by social capital theory and institutionalization by change theory.

Studies that test the impact of service-learning vaguely defined on self reported outcomes of personal and social development and learning do not provide much information for either practitioners or policymakers. These studies cannot explain why the process works, what strategies are most effective, or even see very clearly what outcomes flow from the process. Well-designed studies, that clearly define the elements of service-learning being explored and test alternative explanations for effectiveness, provide information that can be used to improve the quality of service-learning. Studies can be conducted that will tell the field what kinds of preparation helps students learn the most from their experience or that will suggest strategies that help students monitor and sustain their own learning. Studies can be conducted that will help teachers balance the amount of didactic information they need to provide along with the experiential learning activities of their students to assure the most sustained learning. Well-designed studies can help us shape service-learning practices that facilitate multicultural understanding rather than continuing to reinforce bias and prejudice. Because we do not have fine-grained, careful, well controlled and theory driven studies on these topics, practitioners currently are left to their own trial and error.

Service-learning research, like much service-learning practice, has been done with high commitment and few resources. Just as practitioners have spent countless hours and personal resources to create service-learning programs for their students and communities, so too have those conducting research done it as overload and with inadequate support. It is essential that future research move beyond this rather haphazard approach. What we need to do is to set our sights higher and insist on quality of research design, whether quantitative or qualitative. We need to move away from large-scale surveys with poorly specified measures of service-learning and service-learning outcomes towards smaller focused studies designed to give us clear direction on the kinds of service-learning experience that will lead to various desired outcomes. Surveys have been useful in sketching out the terrain, but it is now time for more focused study that gives us deeper understanding to direct our practice. And an infrastructure needs to be built to support well developed programs of research that allow scholars to build on their previous work and advance the field in a thoughtful and coherent way. We also need to work with research scholars from related fields and to bring some theoretical rigor to the design of our research programs.

Service-learning research has come a long way over the past decade. We have reason to be encouraged. It is now time to stretch ourselves to provide the kind of empirical evidence we need to construct stronger programs for students and communities.

REFERENCES

Billig, S. H. (2000). Research on K-12 school-based service-learning: The evidence builds. *Phi Delta Kappan, 81*(9), 658-664.

Eyler, J., & Giles, D. E., Jr. (1999). *Where's the learning in service-learning.* San Francisco: Jossey-Bass.

Eyler, J., Giles, D. E., Jr., Stenson, C., & Gray, C. (2000). *At a glance: Summary and annotated bibliography of recent service-learning research in higher education* (3rd ed.). San Diego: Learn & Serve America National Service-Learning Clearinghouse.

Eyler, J., Giles, D. E., Jr., & Braxton, J. (1997). The impact of service-learning on college students. *Michigan Journal of Community Service Learning, 4,* 5-15.

Gelmon, S. B., Holland, B. A., & Shinnamon, A. F. (1998). *Health professions schools in service to the nation: Final evaluation report.* San Francisco, CA: Community Campus Partnerships for Health.

Gray, M. J., Ondaatje, E. H., Fricker, R., Geschwind, S., Goldman, C. A., Kaganoff, T., Robyn, A., Sundt, M., Vogelgesang, L., & Klein, S. P. (1998). *Coupling service and learning in higher education: The final report of the evaluation of the Learn and Serve America Higher Education Program.* San Francisco: Rand.

Mabry, J. B. (1998). Pedagogical variations in service-learning and student out-comes. *Michigan Journal of Community Service Learning, 5,* 32-47.

Melchior, A. (1998). *National Evaluation of Learn and Serve America School and Community-Based Programs.* (Final Report). Washington, DC: Corporation for National Service.

Moore, D. T. (1999). Behind the wizard's curtain: A challenge to the true believer. *N.S.E.E. Quarterly, 25,* 1-3.

CHAPTER 2

ESTABLISHING NORMS FOR SCIENTIFIC INQUIRY IN SERVICE-LEARNING

Andrew Furco and Shelley H. Billig

Because researchers from different disciplines ascribe to different norms for research, the multidisciplinary nature of service-learning has made it difficult to establish a set of norms for service-learning research. The National Research Council's principles for scientific inquiry provide a foundation for guiding scientific research in all disciplines. The authors suggest that by applying these principles to the study of service-learning, the quality of service-learning research can be improved and norms for service-learning research can be established.

SERVICE-LEARNING AND THE NATURE OF SCIENTIFIC INQUIRY

According to the National Research Council, all scientific inquiry, regardless of the field of study, is based on the same set of core principles (Shavelson & Towne, 2002). Although the principles for scientific inquiry are operationalized differently across disciplines and fields of study, they

Service-Learning Through a Multidisciplinary Lens
A Volume in: Advances in Service-Learning Research, pages 15–29.
Copyright © 2002 by Information Age Publishing, Inc.
All rights of reproduction in any form reserved.
ISBN: 1-931576-81-5 (cloth), 1-931576-80-7 (paper)

reflect a set of basic standards that differentiate scientific research from non-scientific inquiry. As a field grows and advances through the accumulation of scientific knowledge, the norms for scientific inquiry that guide the research within the field begin to take shape. The validity of a field's scientific research is dependent upon the presence of these norms, which are continuously self-regulated by a field's scientific community (Shavelson & Towne). As the National Research Council suggests, the development of a field's norms for scientific inquiry occurs over time through the exploration and use of designs and methodologies that are successful in advancing the field's knowledge base.

Service-learning is still a relatively young field with a limited research base that extends back a little more than ten years. In many ways, the norms for service-learning research are only now beginning to emerge and take shape. For the most part, the research base for service-learning is comprised of a patchwork of small, independent, and disconnected studies that have sought to fill very large gaps in knowledge about service-learning impact, implementation, and institutionalization. Reviews of service-learning research (Andersen; 1998; Billig; 2000; Billig & Waterman, 2002; Furco; 2002; Eyler, Giles, Stenson, & Gray; 2001; Root & Furco; 2001) reveal a fragile, far flung research base that has presented a broad range of research questions, relied on a multitude of theories, utilized a plethora of methodologies, and produced an expansive array of results.

Because the norms for service-learning research have not yet been established, service-learning researchers have generally relied on conjecture or experience to determine the critical questions for investigation. Further, since service-learning researchers represent different disciplines and fields of study, they have tended to rely on the particular norms of scientific inquiry with which they are most familiar and comfortable.

Perhaps the greatest criticism of the research in service-learning has focused on the general lack of quality of the investigations. Several sessions at one of the largest gatherings of service-learning researchers ever held—the 2001 First Annual International Conference on K-H Service-Learning Research—focused on the need to improve the quality of service-learning research. These sessions, including the keynote address (see Chapter 1), made a case for why better service-learning research is needed and explored the standards of research that should be followed in order to advance the knowledge base in service-learning. While common questions, theories, and methodologies are desirable, the fact that service-learning research traverses a vast, multidisciplinary terrain makes it more difficult to ascertain which research questions are most significant or which theories or methodologies are most appropriate to guide the investigation. In some instances, research questions or theoretical frameworks that are ideal for a service-learning study in one discipline might be considered quite peculiar in another discipline, even when the focus of the inquiry is similar. For example, as shown in this volume, a composition professor's use of written discourse analysis to study the ways in which service-learning students in English classes reflect on local social issues might not be a preferred methodology among psychologists who seek to study developmental factors in the way service-learning students verbalize their feelings about local social issues.

Establishing norms for service-learning research will require a strategic coalescence of the various norms that guide research in the different disciplines. The set of core principles for scientific inquiry that are applicable to all scientific investigations suggested by the National Research Council (NRC, 2002) represents a promising approach for developing these norms.

THE CORE PRINCIPLES OF SCIENTIFIC INQUIRY

In a recent report on scientific inquiry, the National Research Council (2002) identified six core principles for research, presented in Exhibit 1. The NRC believes these principles underlie all scientific inquiry. Although the ways in which each of these principles are operationalized across the disciplines vary, adherence to each principle is critical for ensuring that the investigation maintains sufficient scientific rigor. Thus, regardless of the disciplinary lens through which service-learning is studied, these core, guiding principles apply.

EXHIBIT 1
Guiding Principles of Scientific Inquiry[1]

Scientific Principle 1:	Pose significant questions that can be investigated empirically
Scientific Principle 2:	Link research to relevant theory
Scientific Principle 3:	Use methods that permit direct investigation of the question
Scientific Principle 4:	Provide coherent, explicit chain of reasoning
Scientific Principle 5:	Replicate and generalize across studies
Scientific Principle 6:	Disclose research to encourage professional scrutiny and critique

[1]Adapted from Shavelson & Towne (2002). Scientific research in education. Committee on Scientific Principles for Education Research. Washington, DC: National Academy Press.

THE NATURE OF THE RESEARCH QUESTIONS

The first guiding principle of scientific inquiry is centered on the nature of the research question(s). Successful scientific inquiry, regardless of the topic studied, investigates significant questions that are posed to test or refute hypotheses and theories within the field. In discussing the nature of research questions for scientific inquiry, Shavelson and Towne (2002, p. 55) state, "Questions are posed in an effort to fill a gap in existing knowledge or to seek new knowledge, to pursue the identification of the cause or causes of some phenomena, to describe phenomena, to solve a practical problem, or to formally test a hypothesis." Such questions are formed based on existing knowledge in the field and/or new information that is needed to advance the field's knowledge base.

In more established fields of study, reviews of prior research provide the basis for determining the significance of the question(s) under investigation. However in newer fields, such as service-learning, the existing research base is likely to be thin. Therefore, the research questions posed are likely to be based more on thoughtful conjecture than on previously researched findings or existing theories. Regardless of the basis for their development, research questions developed for the purpose of scientific inquiry must be stated in ways that allow for the implementation of an empirical investigation. According to the Shavelson and Towne (2002), studies based on questions that do not lend themselves to empirical investigations (e.g., studies that do not explore observable phenomenon) do not constitute scientific inquiries. Stanovich and Stanovich (in press) take the argument one step further, writing, "Empiricism, pure and simple, is not enough; however...Observation itself is fine and necessary, but pure, unstructured observation of the natural world will not lead to scientific knowledge....Scientific observation is termed *systematic* because it is structured so that...depending upon the outcomes of the observation, some theories of the causes of the outcome are supported and others are rejected."

Publicly verifiable knowledge will help to address both the issue of subjectivity and idiosyncrasy that currently plagues the field. Converging evidence on important questions will give confidence to those who are making important decisions based on the research.

The nature of the research question, then, contributes mightily to the rigor in the field. Currently, too few studies in the service-learning field have investigated questions of broad significance. Reviews of service-learning research reveal that the majority of service-learning studies have been based on narrowly-focused research questions that have not had broad utility for the field. Many service-learning studies have studied the effectiveness of particular programs; for example, Does buddy reading impact the literacy rates of tutees? or Does participation in a particular environmental stewardship program lead to change in attitude about the need for policies to protect the environment? While such investigations might reveal important findings for those involved in such programs, the research questions posed in these studies have limited significance to the broader service-learning field. Recently, there have been a number of calls for more service-learning studies that produce findings that have broader generalizability (Billig & Waterman, 2002).

As the norms for service-learning research begin to take shape, researchers in the field should target their limited resources for research on studies that investigate important, significant questions that garner information that can substantially advance the field. Many of the significant questions to be researched have already been articulated in several service-learning research agendas (Billig & Furco, 2002; Campus Compact, 1998; Eyler & Giles, 1998). For the most part, these questions are broader in scope than those that have been posed in most previous investigations. Comparative analyses of service-learning with other pedagogies, investigations of outcomes across a broad range of service-learning experiences and programs, and studies of developmental processes and longitudinal aspects of service-learning's impact are some examples of the kinds of investigations that would focus attention on more significant research questions. Such investigations are likely to produce findings that are significant because of their broader applicability to service-learning research and practice across the disciplines.

TIES TO RELEVANT THEORIES

The second core principle for scientific inquiry focuses on the importance of linking the inquiry to an overarching theory or conceptual framework (Shavelson & Towne, 2002). The goal of scientific inquiry is to generate "cumulative knowledge by building on, refining, and occasionally replacing, theoretical understanding" (Shavelson & Towne, p. 3). In fields of study that have a strong theoretical basis, the theories often serve to guide the scientific inquiry by suggesting significant questions and hypotheses to be posed and appropriate methods to be used. In fields that have yet to establish overarching theories and conceptual frameworks, the findings from a scientific inquiry may result in the formation of a new theory to explain a phenomenon or the refinement or revisions of existing theories. Either way, a clear linkage to theory is a critical component of all scientific inquiry.

In service-learning, the disciplinary affinity of the researcher influences the particular theories that are brought to bear on the research. Even when studying the same outcome (e.g., students' self-esteem) researchers with different disciplinary orientations will utilize different theories to investigate outcomes. For example, in the 1999 Ferrari and Chapman volume of service-learning research, a group of psychologists used a broad range of theories from social psychology, community psychology, and developmental psychology to study the effects of service-learning on young people's internalization of prosocial values and attitudes (Stukas, Switzer, Dew, Goycoolea, & Simmons, 1999); motivations to serve (Switzer, Switzer, Stukas, & Baker, 1999); and development of self-knowledge (Primavera, 1999). Although similar effects of service-learning were investigated by Parker-Gwin and Mabry (1998), they, as sociologists, relied on sociological theories of social capital and social responsibility to guide their inquiry.

In his review of theoretical frameworks for the study of civic outcomes across the disciplines, Battistoni (2002) describes the ways in which different disciplines shape and define the concepts of civic education and citizenship, two popular areas of service-learning inquiry. For example, through a political science lens, civic development is seen primarily in terms of constitutional citizenship, participatory democracy, and public work. In contrast, in sociology, civic education and citizenship are viewed through a conceptual framework that focuses on social capital. Other service-learning studies, such as those by Westheimer and Kahne (2000), use a social justice framework to investigate service-learning effects. Thus, while a group of studies may all focus on assessing the impacts of service-learning on students' civic education, the particular disciplinary lens through which the study is viewed will determine which set of theories will be applied to the investigation.

Further, because most of the discipline-based theories have not been well-tested in the context of service-learning, there is not a well-developed, interdisciplinary theoretical basis on which service-learning researchers from different disciplines can build off of each other's work. For example, few of the studies in the Ferrari and Chapman (1999) service-learning volume, completed by the aforementioned group of psychologists, made any reference to relevant service-learning studies published in other disciplines. For the overall field of service-learning, the end result has been the completion of a set of disconnected, independent studies that rely on many disparate theories to explain the effects of service-learning on teaching, learning, and schooling. Since most studies in the field have not built off of one another, the establishment of a solid, core theoretical basis for understanding the service-learning phenomenon is elusive.

Service-learning researchers, therefore, need to focus more attention on detailing the theoretical aspects of their work, connecting their work more fully to appropriate, existing theories both in their disciplines and in others. In addition, service-learning researchers need to replicate higher quality studies, conduct more studies that build on previous study findings, and test the strength of a defined set of theories more rigorously. Perhaps, most importantly, service-learning researchers need to focus more investigation on the formulation of new theories that help explain the service-learning phenomenon.

USE OF APPROPRIATE METHODS

The third core principle for scientific inquiry focuses on the skillful implementation of methodologies that are appropriate for the question(s) under investigation. As the NRC representatives state, the methods used must "permit the development of a logical chain of reasoning based on the interplay among investigative techniques, data, and hypotheses to reach justifiable conclusions" (Shavelson & Towne, 2002, pp. 62-63). In this regard, the instruments, data collection approaches, and data analysis techniques used in the inquiry are selected based on their ability to maximize the confidence of the outcomes of the investigation.

Over the last few years, the methods used to study service-learning have steadily improved. This is due to a number of factors, including the availability of more instruments that are appropriate for studying service-learning, publications on the challenges and successful strategies for conducting service-learning research (Billig & Waterman, 2002; Waterman, 1997), and a growing number of highly trained researchers in the field. However, there remain several methodological practices in service-learning research that continue to compromise researchers' ability to develop the "logical chain of reasoning" (Lesh, Lovitts, & Kelly, 2000) needed to produce high quality service-learning inquiry. First of all, many of the concepts that are studied in service-learning (e.g., the development of student civic responsibility) are ill-defined and consequently, the instruments that are produced to measure these concepts have minimal internal or external validity. In addition, there are too many examples of data over-analysis whereby a variety of fairly sophisticated statistical procedures, such as hierarchical linear modeling, are applied to studies that have relatively small sample sizes (e.g., less than 50). [1] There is also a tendency to over-report and over-generalize data, particularly when the findings are positive, as for example, when results from a non-randomized study of a service-learning course that showed significant differences in academic learning between service-learning and non-service-learning student groups are generalized to *all* students and to *all* service-learning programs.

Scientific inquiry demands that regardless of the type of methods used (e.g., qualitative or quantitative), the methods must be appropriate for the focus and scope of the study. Using a battery of instruments that have been used previously in service-learning studies might sound good, and in fact, many service-learning researchers seek out such instruments. But unless the purposes and intentions of those instruments are reviewed—What exactly do the instruments measure? For which population were they designed? How valid and reliable are the instruments? For which types of service-learning activities are the instruments most applicable?—The instruments might be inadvertently applied inappropriately. In the end, the study would produce invalid findings and only muddy our understanding of the true essence of service-learning.

Because of the multidisciplinary and multidimensional nature of service-learning, detailed explication of the methods used in the study and the rationale for their use is especially important. Different disciplines prefer particular methods for research, some of which can be highly specialized and unfamiliar to other disciplines. In the field of service-learning, it is probable that a study will be read and reviewed by researchers (and practitioners) who are not from the discipline in which the study is rooted. Because these researchers (and practitioners who may use the information) might not be steeped in the preferred methods and approaches of the discipline, reports from service-learning investigations need to include full details on why particular methods were used, how the methods used are linked to the research questions, and how the methods were operationalized in the study. The detail provided should be substantial enough to allow other researchers to replicate the study. Service-learning researchers should not automatically assume that other researchers will be familiar with specific research methods, especially if the methods used are highly specialized or idiosyncratic to the discipline. Ultimately, norms for service-learning research cannot be established if researchers in the field cannot fully understand, interpret, and review each other's work.

THE LOGICAL CHAIN OF REASONING

The fourth principle of scientific inquiry focuses on the development of a logical chain of reasoning. As the National Research Council (2002) suggests, the chain of logical reasoning is achieved when all of the following elements are addressed:

- The observations made in the study are formally linked to a set of underlying theories;
- The theories and observations are linked to the research question(s) being investigated;
- Assumptions underlying the inferences made are stated and justified;
- Potential biases are acknowledged;
- Estimates of error are made; and
- Alternative and competing explanations to the research questions are identified.

The responsibility of the researcher is to detail these factors explicitly enough so that other researchers can clearly see a logical chain of reasoning among the various aspects of the inquiry.

In many regards, this aspect of scientific inquiry has been given cursory attention by service-learning researchers, both in practice and in general discussions about research. Among the service-learning studies that have been completed, there are very few that exemplify the development of a logical chain of reasoning. Although many studies in the field contain some aspect of the chain—a discussion of potential biases or a discussion of alternative explanations—very few include all the links. Although this problem is not unique to the service-learning field, it has particular importance for advancing the quality of service-learning research. Because service-learning casts a wide net in terms of definitions, programmatic features, purposes served, and disciplines involved, the establishment of a clear, logical chain of reasoning is especially critical to building the knowledge base for service-learning.

For example, too few studies provide adequate descriptions of the nature of the service activities students performed, the degree to which these activities were integrated with curriculum, the amount and type of reflection students engaged in, and the academic learning objectives of the service-learning activity. Because of the highly contextualized and idiosyncratic nature of the service-learning experience, not having the details on the particular aspects of the service-learning experience makes it difficult conduct cross study comparisons. As Furco (2002) suggests, it is difficult to determine from previous research what the outcomes of service-learning are because not all studies that appear in the service-learning literature are studies of "service-learning" programs. Literature reviews of "service-learning research" (Billig, 2000; Eyler et al., 2001) include studies of community service, field education, and youth service programs. Because of the lack of description regarding the programs studied, it is difficult to determine the underlying assumptions and purposes of the programs and ultimately, to what extent many of the studies in the field are truly representative of "service-learning."

Bringing the various assumptions, underlying issues, and potential biases to the fore can allow researchers to understand more fully the context of the service-learning inquiry. In turn, this full disclosure allows researchers to both draw more accurate conclusions about the service-learning phenomenon and to strengthen the field's knowledge base. Ultimately, improving the logical chains of reasoning in scientific inquiries of service-learning will substantially raise the quality and legitimacy of service-learning research.

REPLICATION AND GENERALIZATION

According to the National Research Council, "Scientific knowledge advances when findings are reproduced in a range of times and places and when findings are integrated and synthesized" (Shavelson & Towne, 2002, p. 4). Findings from an individual study do little to advance knowledge in a field unless the findings can be generalized to the broader population. Ascertaining the generalizability of findings and validating findings through the replication of studies in similar or different contexts help strengthen a field's knowledge base.

Unfortunately, most of what is known today about service-learning is based on single assessments of particular aspects of the service-learning phenomenon. Although a number of issues (e.g., the effect of service-learning on students' personal development) have been studied by several researchers (Billig, 2000; Eyler et al., 2001; Furco; 2002; Root, 1997), no single study of service-learning has been replicated fully to date. In many instances, positive findings from service-learning studies have been widely touted, yet many of these findings have not been fully validated. Several researchers have called for the replication of some of the better studies in the field to determine the extent to which the findings hold up across different contexts and situations (Billig, 2000; Furco, 2002; Waterman, 1997). As Stanovich and Stanovich (in press) go so far as to state, "Scientific knowledge does not exist at all until it has been submitted to the scientific community for criticism and empirical testing by others." Replication ensures that the study was not subject to an investigator's bias or the peculiarities of a particular investigation. Although service-learning's knowledge base is becoming more robust with the recent increase in research activity, the lack of validation and replication of the research has restricted the field's ability to strengthen and deepen its knowledge base.

One of the ongoing challenges of service-learning research has been the ability to generalize findings of individual studies to the broader service-learning settings. Most service-learning studies have investigated specific service activities (tutoring, planting trees, serving in a health clinic) integrated with a particular curriculum (science, social studies, psychology, nursing) that involve specific groups of students (middle school students, preservice teachers, college freshmen, and the like) who engage in service-learning in different community contexts (rural communities, urban centers, and so forth). The idiosyncratic nature of the service-learning experience within each study calls into question the generalizability of individual study findings. Furco (2002) suggests that the diversity of programmatic intentions and features among service-learning experiences requires the application of broader and more sophisticated designs that can more fully capture the interplay of the complex programmatic features of individual service-learning experiences. As Furco explains, the use of more comprehensive methodologies in the service-learning field is an important first step both to systematize the current scattershot approach to service-learning research and to help garner more validated and generalizable findings that can strengthen the field's knowledge base.

Overall, the legitimacy of service-learning as an educational practice hinges on the validity of its research findings. Although the situation continues to improve, the service-learning field could benefit from a stronger dose of self-scrutiny when it comes to reporting research findings. Overstating and overgeneralizing findings do a disservice to the field, and only incite further skepticism from those who are quick to dismiss service-learning as fluff. There are many promising, positive findings that have emerged from service-learning research. But these findings need to be more fully validated, and they need to be based on designs that allow them to be generalized from the specific contexts in which they were found to the broader service-learning field.

DISCLOSURE OF RESEARCH FOR PEER REVIEW

The health of scientific inquiry is dependent upon ongoing public critique that is achieved through the wide dissemination of the research and the professional scrutiny of peers. In their summary of the National Research Council's principles for scientific inquiry, Shavelson and Towne (2002, p. 5) state, "Indeed, the objectivity of science derives from publicly enforced norms of the professional community of scientists, rather than from the character traits of any individual person or design features of any study." The broad dissemination of the research allows for study findings to be communicated to the broader field in ways that "open the study to examination, criticism, review, and replication [sic] by peer investigators" with the goal of incorporating new knowledge in the field (Shavelson & Towne, p. 72).

The dissemination and peer review of service-learning research have improved significantly over the last few years. The establishment of a peer review journal for service-learning (*Michigan Journal of Community Service Learning*), the recent establishment of the *Advances in Service-Learning Research* volume series (edited by Shelley H. Billig), the inauguration of an annual conference focused exclusively on service-learning research (*International Conference on Service-Learning Research*), the development of service-learning research agendas (e.g., Billig & Furco, 2002; Campus Compact, 1998), and the establishment of service-learning research networks (e.g., *Learning In Deed* Service-Learning Research Network) are some of the ways in which the field has sought to build a community of service-learning researchers who can review and discuss each other's work. Over the years, the editors of several disciplinary and professional journals (e.g., *Journal of Social Issues, Journal of Public Affairs, Journal of Adolescence*) have commissioned special issues on service-learning as a means of disseminating information about service-learning research and practice to specific research communities. The broader dissemination of service-learning research is an indication that the multidisciplinary and somewhat amorphous field of service-learning is beginning to take shape. Interestingly, with the wider dissemination of service-learning research has come more intense scrutiny of the research. This scrutiny, in turn, has provided an impetus to improve the quality of service-learning research.

Despite this progress, the service-learning field can benefit from broader dissemination of its research. There are many people in educational and community settings who have never heard of service-learning, including some who unknowingly practice it. As more K-12 schools, teacher education programs, and colleges and universities adopt service-learning, there are increasing calls to the research community to share findings on particular impacts of service-learning (e.g., the effect of service-learning on student retention). In addition, the venues for disseminating and critiquing service-learning research are not evenly distributed across the sectors of the field. For example, while a peer reviewed journal for service-learning exists (*Michigan Journal of Community Service-Learning*), the journal only publishes articles on issues related to service-learning in higher education. Very few venues exist for disseminating research related K-12 service-learning issues. The service-learning field can benefit from having more venues to publish and disseminate research and more forums to debate and critique new studies that are completed. (See Chapter 11 for further discussion on strategies for advancing the dissemination and peer-review of service-learning research.)

ESTABLISHING NORMS FOR SERVICE-LEARNING RESEARCH

As the service-learning field continues to mature and the field's research is further systematized, the norms for service-learning research are likely to take shape. Regardless of the form they take, the development of the norms should be driven by the six core guiding principles that undergird all scientific inquiry. A more concerted effort on the part of service-learning researchers to adhere to these principles will help raise the overall quality of the research that is produced in the field. The adherence to these principles is especially important in a multidisciplinary field like service-learning where there are broad and varied approaches to research.

In other fields relevant to K-12 education, teacher education, and higher education that draw from a variety of disciplinary perspectives (e.g., instructional technology, problem-based learning), norms for research have been established. In the field of instructional technology, for example, activity theory has emerged as the primary theory that guides much of the research (e.g., Barab & Duffy, 2000). These theories address conditions for optimal learning that are not bound by time or space, and where communities of learners are formed to collaborate and resolve authentic problems. Similarly, in problem-based learning, the theoretical framework for the research has concentrated on the medical school model of the ill-structured problem approach that views every authentic problem as unique. Learning from research that the ill-structured problem approach provides an essential contextual framework for problem-based learning has helped shaped the direction and nature of research in that field. In the case of both instructional technology and problem-based learning, scientific inquiry has allowed for valid and generalizable findings to be produced through replicated studies. It is through this ongoing replication of studies and building on prior findings that the norms for research within these fields have been formed. Researchers in the service-learning field might benefit from looking at how other multidisciplinary fields have gone about establishing their norms for research.

Careful attention must be paid to the development of these norms for service-learning research. Otherwise, the field runs of risk of not only stagnating, but possibly factionalizing itself into overly specific theoretical, methodological, and programmatic compartments. By adhering to the core principles for scientific inquiry, the service-learning field can rally around a common framework to which all service-learning researchers can ascribe, regardless of their research preferences or goals. It is through this scientifically-based approach that service-learning researchers can come to learn about the value of different theories and methods for studying service-learning. It is through the development of a mutual appreciation and respect for each other's work that the norms for service-learning research can be established and the quality of service-learning research can be improved.

NOTE

1. For example, see Ferrari & Chapman (1999) for the application of various statistical procedures to service-learning studies with sample sizes of 50 or less.

REFERENCES

Andersen, S. M. (1998). *Service-learning: A national strategy for youth development.* New York: New York University.

Barab, S. A., & Duffy, T. M. (2000). From practice fields to communities of practice. In D. Jonassen & S. M. Land (Eds.), *Theoretical foundations of learning environments* (pp. 25-26). Mahwah, NJ: Lawrence Erlbaum Associates, Inc.

Battistoni, R. M. (2002). Civic engagement across the curriculum. Providence, RI: Campus Compact.

Billig, S. H. (2000, May). Research on K-12 school-based service-learning: The evidence builds. *Phi Delta Kappan, 81*(9), 658-664.

Billig S. H., & Furco, A. (2002). Research agenda for K-12 service-learning: A proposal to the field. In A. Furco & S. H. Billig (Eds.), *Service-learning: The essence of the pedagogy, Vol. 1, Advances in service-learning research* (pp. 271-279). Greenwich, CT: Information Age Publishing.

Billig, S. H., & Waterman, A. S. (2002). *Studying service-learning*. Mahwah, NJ: Lawrence Erlbaum Associates, Inc.

Campus Compact. (1998). Special report: Advancing our knowledge of the impacts of service learning. Providence, RI: Campus Compact.

Eyler, J. S., Giles, D. E., Jr., Stenson, C. M, & Gray, C. J. (2001). *At a glance: What we know about the effects of service-learning on college students, faculty, institutions, and communities, 1993-2000* (3rd ed.). Washington, DC: Corporation for National Service.

Ferrari, J. R., & Chapman, J. G. (Eds.). (1999). *Educating students to make-a-difference: Community-based service-learning*. Binghamton, NY: Haworth Press, Inc.

Furco, A. (2002). Is service-learning really better than community service? A study of high school service program outcomes. In A. Furco & S. H. Billig (Eds.), *Service-learning: The essence of the pedagogy, Vol. 1, Advances in service-learning research* (pp. 23-50). Greenwich, CT: Information Age Publishing.

Furco, A. (2002). Issues of definition and program diversity in the study of service-learning. In S. H. Billig & A. S. Waterman (Eds.). *Studying service-learning*. Mahwah, NJ: Lawrence Erlbaum Associates, Inc.

Giles, D. E., Jr., & Eyler, J. S. (1998). A service-learning research agenda for the next five years. In R. Rhoads & J. P. F. Howard (Eds.), *Academic service-learning: A pedagogy of action and reflection* (pp. 65-72). San Francisco: Jossey-Bass Publishers.

Lesh, R. A., Lovitts, B., & Kelly, A. E. (2000). Purposes and assumptions of this book. In A. E. Kelly & R. A. Lesh (Eds.), *Handbook of research design in mathematics and science education* (pp. 17-34). Mahwah, NJ: Lawrence Erlbaum Associates, Inc.

National Research Council. (2002). *Scientific research in education*. Committee on Scientific Principles for Education Research. R. J. Shavelson & L. Towne (Eds.). Center for Education, Division of Behavioral and Social Sciences and Education. Washington, DC: National Academy Press.

Parker-Gwin, R. P., & Mabry, J. B. (1998). Service-learning as pedagogy and civic education: Comparing outcomes for three models. *Teaching Sociology, 26,* 276-291.

Root, S. C. (1997). School-based service: A review of research for teacher educators. In J. A. Erickson & J. B. Anderson (Eds.), *Learning with the community: Concepts and models for service-learning in teacher education* (pp. 42-72). Washington, DC: American Association for Higher Education.

Root, S. C., & Furco, A. (2001). Service-learning in teacher education: An overview of the research. In J. Anderson & K. Swick (Eds.), *Strengthening service and learning in teacher education*. Washington, DC: American Association of Colleges for Teacher Education and the ERIC Clearinghouse on Teaching and Teacher Education.

Stanovich, P., & Stanovich, K. (in press). *Research and reason-based practice in education: What educators need to know*. University of Toronto.

Stukas, A. A., Switzer, G. E., Dew, M. A., Goycoolea, J. M., & Simmons, R. G. (1999). Parent helping models, gender, and service-learning. In J. R. Ferrari & J. G. Chapman (Eds.), *Educating students to make-a-difference. Community-based service-learning* (pp. 1-18). Binghamton, NY: Haworth Press, Inc.

Switzer, C. L, Switzer, G. E., Stukas, A. A., & Baker, C. E. (1999). Medical student motivations to volunteer: Gender differences and comparisons to other volunteers. In J. R. Ferrari & J. G. Chapman (Eds.), *Educating students to make-a-difference: Community-based service-learning* (pp. 53-64). Binghamton, NY: Haworth Press, Inc.

Waterman, A. S. (1997). *Service-learning: Applications from the research.* Mahwah, NJ: Erlbaum Publishing Company.

Westheimer, J., & Kahne, J. (2000). Report to the Surdna Board-D.V.I. New York: Surdna Foundation.

PART II

THEORETICAL PERSPECTIVE ON SERVICE-LEARNING

CHAPTER 3

PROBING AND PROMOTING TEACHERS' THINKING ABOUT SERVICE-LEARNING
Toward a Theory of Teacher Development

Mary Sue Ammon

Data from a study of service-learning partnerships in K-12 school districts in California are used to describe dimensions of variation in teachers' thinking about service-learning, as well as relationships between teachers' goals and their implementation strategies. More specifically, the study suggests that the design and quality of teachers' service-learning activities may be substantially affected by: (a) the clarity and specificity of teachers' goals, (b) the degree to which these goals are discussed with students, (c) the roles established for teachers and students, and (d) the degree to which concepts targeted in service-learning are interconnected with content and activities in other curricular areas. A constructivist model of teacher development is proposed as a potentially useful way to understand qualitative differences and changes in teachers' conceptualizations and actions regarding service-learning.

Service-Learning Through a Multidisciplinary Lens
A Volume in: Advances in Service-Learning Research, pages 33–54.
Copyright © 2002 by Information Age Publishing, Inc.
ISBN: 1-931576-81-5 (cloth), 1-931576-80-7 (paper)

BACKGROUND AND RATIONALE

Service-learning, though not a new teaching methodology, is a reform strategy that gained considerable momentum during the past decade. According to a 1999 study, it is currently employed in nearly one-third of all K-12 public schools and nearly half of all high schools in the country (National Center for Education Statistics [NCES]). In contrast to this evidence of an increase in the number of teachers reporting the use of service-learning, establishing the quality of implementation of this teaching strategy has been more difficult, primarily because of the fact that it can assume so many forms across a wide range of grade levels and subject matters.

Efforts to define service-learning have yielded various lists of general features which have not always fully overlapped (Kraft 1996; Shumer, Berkas, & Murphy, 1992). Moreover, characteristics and qualities cited in these definitions do not seem to mean the same thing to all people. Shumer and his colleagues (1992) have suggested that the variables used to describe service-learning vary according to the particular project. Though this contextual variation explains the difficulty of specifying a universal set of features that characterize well-implemented service-learning, such "definitional relativism" is neither theoretically satisfying nor helpful when it comes to planning evaluation or professional development. For example, studies aimed at evaluating the outcomes of well-implemented service-learning for students, schools, and communities need to specify a set of criteria for including programs in their samples. Previous evaluation efforts of this type (e.g., Melchior, 1998; Weiler, LaGoy, Crane, & Rovner, 1998) have usually established a set of external features to define quality implementation, such as the inclusion of regular journal writing, personal contact with the service recipient, a minimum specified number of service hours, linkages to curriculum, and so forth. But these criteria neither seem to capture the essence of service-learning philosophy embodied in the various sets of general definitional principles nor have they always been shown to be related empirically to targeted student and community outcomes.

Currently, then, service-learning seems somewhat like the elephant described by the six blind men in the poem by John Godfrey Saxe (see Appendix). In this parable, each blind man argued for his conception of the elephant based on the external features he encountered. The situation resulted in six different descriptions of the elephant, all partially correct but all essentially wrong. Although one moral of both stories might be that one cannot ignore the multifaceted nature of these objects of study, another conclusion might be that it is critical to construct more functional characterizations if one is to really understand either the elephant or service-learning.

Previous studies of educational reform initiatives have shown that teachers enact reforms in diverse ways because they bring different knowledge, commitments, and dispositions that influence their understanding of the reform message (Spillane & Jennings, 1997). Consequently, one goal of a recent intensive study of teachers and students in seven districtwide service-learning partnerships (Ammon, Furco, Chi, & Middaugh, 2002) was to examine not only the external features of the service-learning projects and various student outcomes but to explore teachers' goals, priorities, understanding of service-learning, and general pedagogical thinking that affected the details and nuances of implementation and resulting student attitudes and perceptions. This paper will focus on describing what was learned about these more "internal" features of service-learning implementation and will outline a theoretical framework for viewing developmental changes in teachers' conceptualizations of service-learning. The goal of this theorizing is eventually to provide a more useful vision of what service-learning implementation is like at its best.

METHOD

This study of teachers was one component of a three-year statewide evaluation of 34 K-12 service-learning partnerships funded by the California Department of Education through a grant from the Corporation for National and Community Service. Data for the study were collected from two sources: (a) three sets of yearly evaluation reports submitted by local school district subgrantees participating in the state's service-learning program (known as the CalServe Initiative), and (b) an intensive study of a subset of seven local partnerships carried out by the staff at the University of California-Berkeley's Service-Learning Research and Development Center (SLRDC) during the 1999-2000 school year. The data collected by the local district partnerships and reported to the CalServe office were intended to be used to develop a statewide profile of service-learning participation and impacts on students, teachers, schools, and communities. All partnerships were required to report on two types of student impacts, the growth of academic knowledge and skills and the development of civic responsibility. In addition, partnerships were given the choice of evaluating either school district, community, or teacher outcomes for their second focus of study. Although methods for evaluating the first impact area were fairly prescribed by the state, local partnerships were allowed to design their own methods for evaluating their second impact area. Consequently, not all partnerships chose to study teacher impacts. Moreover, the data collected relevant to teacher impacts differed in form and content across those partnerships that did focus on this area and were reported with varying amounts of detail. The decision to gather more uniform and detailed

descriptive information about motivations, goals, implementation practices, and impressions of teachers employing service-learning in some of
these partnerships was, in part, spurred by the desire to obtain a clearer
picture of how and why service-learning was being adopted by teachers as
an instructional practice.

As part of the intensive study carried out during 1999-2000, focus
groups and individual interviews were conducted by SLRDC with participating students, teachers, administrators, service-learning coordinators,
and community partners from seven of the 34 partnerships funded by
CalServe. The content of the interview protocols and two teacher questionnaires was, to some extent, guided by information supplied by the local
partnerships about student and teacher outcomes during the first two
years. During the site visits to the seven "intensive" partnerships located in
varied types of communities throughout the state, 31 teachers from 25 different schools, Grade 3 through high school, were interviewed about the
history, rationale, and implementation of their service-learning plans.

Initial questions on the interviews probed the reasons for and history of
teachers' involvement with service-learning and their working definition of
this teaching methodology. Implementation features such as the roles
given to students and community partners, the training and preparation
provided to students, and techniques used to prompt reflection were then
individually discussed. Teachers were queried about support from other
faculty and administration and about evidence they had gathered on various types of impacts. Finally, teachers were asked about their future plans
regarding the use of service-learning. Special attention was paid to using
multiple, variously worded questions to try to obtain a clearer picture of
teachers' goal priorities for service-learning activities and an account of
how these goals and objectives were communicated to students.

In the questionnaires administered at the beginning and end of the academic year, teachers were asked to supply background information about
themselves and brief answers to planning, implementation, and evaluation
questions about their service-learning activities. The content of the two
questionnaires partially overlapped some of the topics discussed in the
interviews conducted in the middle of the school year. This feature of the
design allowed the research team to review teachers' goals and experiences
at three different times during the year. In all, 34 teachers provided questionnaire data in the fall of 1999, 31 teachers were interviewed in the middle of the year, and 30 teachers completed questionnaires in the spring.
Four additional "comparison" teachers who were not using service-learning filled out the two surveys, and three comparison teachers were interviewed. (Two of the five comparison teachers contributed both types of
data.)

Classroom observation supplemented the interview and questionnaire
data in a number of the site visits. At least three randomly selected students
from each of these teachers' classrooms (110 in all) were individually inter-

viewed about their perceptions of the purposes of service-learning and about details of the experiences that were salient to them. All teacher and student interviews were fully transcribed and checked for accuracy, and the responses from the teacher questionnaires were coded according to categories derived from a preliminary analysis of the responses provided within this data set. The three sets of responses from each teacher were compared for consistency, categorized, and contrasted with those of the other teachers in the intensive study sample and with information reported in local evaluation reports during 1997-98 and 1998-99.

The focus of this paper primarily will be on the information about teacher goals and thinking about service-learning implementation that was contained in partnership reports (1997-2000) and in the teacher interview and questionnaire data from 1999-2000.

TEACHERS' MOTIVATIONS FOR TRYING SERVICE-LEARNING

Previous to the 1999-2000 intensive study of seven partnerships, data were collected from local partnership reports about teacher motivations for using service-learning. Information from these reports suggested that teachers attribute their initial interest in service-learning to a variety of types of experiences and interactions. Rationales provided by teachers for trying service-learning sometimes were personal, referring to teachers' own needs, interests, experiences, and rewards. For example, teachers said such things as "It makes my own learning real," or "It allows me to give back to my community." Many teachers linked their interest in service-learning to professional issues, referring to their educational philosophy and goals for students (e.g., "It fits with student-driven learning," and "I want to promote social consciousness"). Some teachers reported that they were influenced by others (administrators, other teachers, students, or community members) to try service-learning, and some pointed to expectations or mandates established by the state, district, or school (see Ammon et al., 2002, for frequencies of the various responses and other details of these analyses).

Although the information about teacher motivations provided in these local partnership reports provided a useful starting point in addressing this topic, it was not possible to determine the relative frequency, stability, or details of these various teacher motivations from the information supplied in the partnership reports. The data collected from teachers in the intensive study, however, was designed to address these topics.

On the questionnaire administered by the seven "intensive partnerships" at the beginning of the school year, teachers primarily focused on the student outcomes they wanted to foster as teachers. Most often teachers mentioned their belief in the benefit of hands-on, experiential learning with applications to the real world (educational philosophy); their desire to motivate, interest, and empower students (motivation); or their conviction that students should connect with, and be active participants in, their communities (civic responsibility). Teachers less frequently mentioned adopting service-learning in order to improve students' understanding of particular curricula. However, some did mention using this methodology because it was a mandated part of a course or the district's curriculum.

GOALS ADOPTED FOR SERVICE-LEARNING

When teachers were asked what they hoped to accomplish by using service-learning as a teaching strategy, a majority focused on their goals for students. Data from the partnership reports and the intensive study surveys and interviews (see more details in Ammon et al., 2002) brought home the variability of goals adopted for service-learning by teachers. This diversity of goals can be seen in the classification of objectives provided on 29 local partnership evaluation reports about service-learning conducted in 77 classrooms in 1999-2000 (see Exhibit 1). Most teachers voiced more than one objective, usually within two or more of the four general categories of our goal classification system (that is, Personal/Social/Life Skills, Career Development Skills, Academic/Cognitive/Creative Skills, and Civic Participation Skills.) This finding was not surprising, given that service-learning is supposed to involve the coordination of service and learning activities and the incorporation of a number of elements such as youth voice and reflection. But the diversity and differences among teachers in the particular goals verbalized for service-learning projects made overall assessment of quality in outcomes extremely difficult. How does one make relative comparisons of the quality of programs that are attempting to accomplish so many different things?

THE LINK BETWEEN TEACHER GOALS AND GRADE LEVEL, SUBJECT MATTER, AND SERVICE ACTIVITY

The question then arose whether comparisons regarding program quality could be made within subsamples of classrooms that might be more similar with one another in terms of their goals for service-learning. This amounted to asking if the goals and objectives of teachers within grade levels or within subject matter areas or within service activity types might show a greater degree of overlap. After listing and classifying student outcome objectives reported by teachers for their service-learning activities, an

EXHIBIT 1
Classification System for Teacher Objectives and Frequency of Their
Identification in 1999-2000 Teacher Sample

Categories of Service-Learning Objectives	Frequency of Identification in Descriptions by 77 Teachers
Personal/Social/Life Skills	
Communication Skills	22
Interpersonal Skills	19
Intrapersonal/Judgment Skills	13
Interpersonal Understanding	11
Self-Efficacy, Confidence, Self-Concept	8
Resilience/Coping Skills	4
Career Development Skills	
Technical/Practical Skills	18
Career Exploration	4
Educational Aspirations	2
Job Skill Development	1
Academic/Cognitive/Creative Skills	
Application of Disciplinary Knowledge	40
Learning of Disciplinary Knowledge	35
Writing Abilities and Skills	22
Problem-Solving or Decision-Making Skills	19
Academic Motivation, School Adjustment, Attendance	13
Creative Expression	10
Reading Abilities and Skills	8
Broadening or Extending of Disciplinary Knowledge	5
Metacognitive Awareness	2
Civic Participation	
Awareness of Social or Civic Issues, Problems, or Needs	39
Providing Volunteer Services	36
Involvement in Addressing Community Problem or Need	33
Attitudes about Citizenship	14
Connection With or Feeling Part of a Community	13
Feelings of Social or Civic Efficacy	9
Prosocial Feelings	5
Political Knowledge or Knowledge of Social Institutions	3
Awareness of Ethical or Moral Issues	3
Participating in Community Policy-Making	2

examination was made of the objectives listed for programs categorized by features such as grade level, subject matter area, or service activity.

These analyses revealed that there were, in fact, some differences between sets of most common goals of programs grouped according to some of these demographic variables (see Ammon et al., 2002). For example, the frequency rankings of outcome goals listed for students at the K-5, 6-8, and 9-12 grade spans differed slightly from one another. Elementary teachers more often emphasized their desire to enhance the civic efficacy of their students, and high school teachers more frequently emphasized community issues or skills the students needed in the work world. Elementary teachers were more apt to emphasize giving students opportunities for the application of particular disciplinary knowledge or for creative expression. Middle school teachers appeared more concerned that students gain problem solving, technical, and reading skills, and acquire academic motivation and confidence—perhaps, those skills, abilities, and attitudes that they thought would prepare their students for the high school years ahead. Still, there was considerable variability within each of the grade spans in the objectives for service-learning stated by teachers.

In core academic courses or subject areas, service-learning goals and objectives having to do with the acquisition of disciplinary knowledge, writing, awareness of community issues and needs, and connectedness to the community were more frequent. Four personal or life skills goals—interpersonal skills, self-efficacy and confidence, intrapersonal skills, and resilience—were more frequently cited when service-learning was implemented in relation to non-core academic or extra-curricular classes. But again, these groupings of classrooms were on the whole more dissimilar than similar in terms of their service-learning objectives.

Also examined separately were the goals of teachers implementing the same type of service activity, such as school gardens or buddy reading or oral history projects. Again, though there were some similarities within project type, teachers often differed considerably in the goals they emphasized and the way they implemented their programs.

As an example of the way that goal priorities and consequent implementation details may vary even for service projects of the same type, consider the description of three "buddy reading" programs implemented in the intensively studied partnerships (Exhibit 2). Though these three programs might at first glance appear similar because they all involved older students reading with younger students, on deeper examination we found that they differed greatly in terms of their underlying goals, justifications, emphases, and implementation structures.

Teacher A's buddy reading project was primarily designed to affect students' interpersonal understanding and skills, their conceptions of themselves as helping individuals, and their sense of civic efficacy in discovering that "one person can make a difference." Teacher B focused primarily on her students' learning about illiteracy as a social issue and on improving

EXHIBIT 2

Description of Three Contrasting "Book Buddy" Programs

Project Dimensions	Teacher A	Teacher B	Teacher C
Teacher's Primary Learning Goals	**Personal/Life Skills:** Interpersonal Skills and Understanding **Civic Skills:** Civic Efficacy Prosocial Feelings	**Civic Skills:** Awareness and Addressing of Social Issue or Need Attitudes about Citizenship	**Academic Skills:** Reading and Writing Skills Metacognitive Skills
Secondary Goals	**Academic Skills:** Application of Disciplinary Knowledge (importance of literacy in a culture)	**Academic Skills:** Academic Motivation Reading Skills	**Academic Skills:** Academic Motivation **Civic Skills:** Connection to a Community (school)
Who are the students?	Underachieving suburban tenth grade students	Seventh graders in an urban setting	Third/Fourth graders in an urban setting
What is said to students	Buddy reading is a way for you to "make a difference" (and fulfill the community service requirement).	Being a book buddy is one way to address the problem of illiteracy that affects many people.	Learning how to read is very important, and so is being a teacher.
Preparation	Training on how to read books to children by reading resource teacher. Class orientation and task presentations by receiving teachers.	Definition of and discussion about active citizenship by teacher. Discussions about why literacy is important.	Month-long unit by teacher on reading to young children (how to hold and introduce a book, ask questions, select an appropriate book, and so forth). Practice with classmates before trying procedures with little buddies

(continued)

EXHIBIT 2
Continued

Project Dimensions	Teacher A	Teacher B	Teacher C
Reflection Questions	How did it go today with your buddy? What do you need help with?	After reading *Nightjohn*, essays written on following: Why was learning how to read important to Nightjohn? How was he an active citizen? How have I been an active citizen?	What did you notice your buddy could read or could do? What does your buddy still need to work on to be a better reader? How have you seen your buddy improve?
Evaluation/ Assessments	Final essay: How did you feel about helping your buddy learn how to read? How did this experience affect your understanding of literacy and democracy?	Test for facts about illiteracy	District writing assessment
Collaborative Partnering	Team planning between the participating teachers, discussions of interpersonal difficulties and issues to be problem solved by students	Logistical planning with partnering teachers at the local elementary school	Team planning: Receiving teacher helps teach mini-lessons (e.g., how to teach vocabulary) midway through project.
Focus of Adjustment Process	Continuous monitoring of interpersonal relationships in the pairings by both teachers.	Continued emphasis on helping students make the connection between their experience as a book buddy and the idea of being an active citizen.	Monitoring what literacy skills the older students need to improve or be conscious of to teach their buddies how to read.

the school's sense of community and active citizenship. The improvement of the older students' reading abilities was clearly a secondary focus. Teacher C's buddy reading project was centered predominantly on improving the older students' reading fluency and comprehension through their work with younger students. These three examples of buddy reading clearly illustrate the study's conclusion that important features of the goals, implementation, and outcomes of service-learning cannot always be predicted from a simple categorization of program forms or demographic characteristics.[1]

This analysis also underscores the previously noted heterogeneity and variability that exists in teachers' goals for service-learning. As suggested earlier in the chapter, teachers adopt particular service-learning goals (or configurations of goals) for a variety of personal, professional, and practical reasons. Thus, by itself, listing teachers' particular goals for service-learning will not provide a measure of quality of service-learning implementation. Nor would it be practical to try to work out the features of quality implementation within particular types of service-learning goals (such as within programs attempting to improve students' interpersonal skills), because the number of goal-types or goal combinations would be impossibly large. Luckily, the rich body of information obtained about service-learning activities in the intensive classrooms suggested a different analytical direction—a direction that focuses on teacher's thinking about goals.

DIMENSIONS OF VARIATION IN TEACHERS' THINKING ABOUT SERVICE-LEARNING GOALS

The information obtained through the teacher and student interviews and classroom observations suggested a different way to describe teacher goals and their influences on service-learning implementation. What emerged was the idea that a more functional set of variables related to goal-setting might be better for differentiating teachers' thinking and actions regarding service-learning than specific information about particular desired outcomes. Specifically, data from the intensive study suggested that the design and quality of execution of teachers' service-learning activities might be substantially affected by the following dimensions:

- The clarity and specificity of teachers' goals;
- The degree of articulation or discussion of goals with students;
- The roles established for teachers and students; and
- The degree to which concepts or ways of thinking targeted in service-learning were interconnected with content and activities in other curricular areas.

Clarity and Specificity of Goals

Some teachers appeared to struggle when they were asked to describe their goals and ended up specifying goals that were not centrally related to the activities engaged in, or described different goals at different times across the interview and the surveys. Teacher A in Exhibit 2, for example, started out by stating that she wanted her students to understand the possible relationship between the revolutions they were studying in history and illiteracy. A little bit later she maintained that she wanted students to learn how they acquire and use reading skills. But most of her activity descriptions of coaching and class debriefings and individual reflection activities as well as her suggestions for ways to evaluate the outcomes of the program revolved around her desire for students to learn how to establish and maintain close interpersonal relationships with their reading buddies.

Some teachers talked about goals only in very global terms, limiting their statements to phrases such as "active learning" or "civic responsibility." At the other extreme, some specified very particular "direct" goals that were actually realized within the activity itself, such as "interacting with adults." In contrast with what might be seen as overly general or overly specific goals, some teachers designated more indirect or higher order goals but could clearly articulate how these would be manifested in the particular service-learning activities. For example, one teacher described various activities such as organic gardening, maintaining the storm drain, and recycling and not wasting water, and then concluded, "...if I taught anything else, I wanted to teach stewardship."

Discussion of Goals With Students

Teachers differed considerably in terms of how much and how explicitly they discussed with students the reasons for participating in service-learning activities. One teacher reported that she intentionally avoided explaining what she hoped students would get out of the service-learning activities because she feared that such connections to her school-related goals would negatively affect students' motivation and enjoyment of service-learning. She felt that students would benefit just as a result of performing the activities so she did not need to explain her rationale to them. Other teachers appeared to think that the reasons for engaging in service-learning activities would be obvious to students and thus did not need to be discussed. However, a majority of teachers spent at least some time, especially at the beginning of the service-learning unit, discussing the reasons for engaging in particular service-learning activities. The interview data suggested that teachers who reiterate goal(s) for a service-learning activity using consistent phrasing influence the wording that students use in their explanations of their service. In other words, when teachers repeat a particular rationale to students for participating in service-learning, these views and their wordings tended to be incorporated into students' explanations.

In still other classrooms where students were given repeated opportunities to reflect on and construct their own rationales for performing particular service-learning activities, students appeared to adopt the teacher's enthusiasm for the goals as well as being able to talk about them in a flexible and personally meaningful way. For example, in a classroom where the service involved rehabilitating a county azalea preserve, one student described the class' efforts as a type of war between the native plants and the invading exotics. When the class was encouraged to identify native and exotic plants around their school, they ended up deciding to spend two Saturdays clearing brush from their school campus. One student also suggested eradicating the invading pampas grass by encouraging students to ride their bikes over it. When asked in a discussion to evaluate whether they were performing a service, the students were able to generate a long list of "who and what they were helping."

The Roles of Teachers and Students

Teachers varied in their conceptions of the roles that teachers and students should play, both in setting goals and in determining how these goals should be accomplished. Some teachers expended most of their own efforts in planning and arranging service activities for students to perform. These teachers seemed to assume that simply giving students the opportunity to be exposed to adults acting in a socially responsible way, or giving them the opportunity to act in a new way or in a new context, would result in their learning the desired behavior or concept. Other teachers viewed their role more as one of being a model or an interpreter of the service activities for students. Still others conceived their role to be more like a guide or facilitator. Though many teachers talked about the fact that service-learning allows active learning, this phrase can be interpreted by teachers to mean many different things in terms of the student's role—ranging from the student being a performer of physical activities in the community to being an independent investigator of community problems and possible solutions, to being an equal collaborator with classmates, community partners, and the teacher.

Possibilities for Interconnections Among Subject Matter Areas

Some targeted service-learning goals were relevant to only one situation or one specific activity. For example, goals conceptualized as particular subject matter distinctions, such as the learning of the various parts of a seed, were of limited generalizability. Teachers who talked about goals conceptualized in a more abstract way, such as students improving their ability to express their own point of view, to listen to others' divergent ideas, and to seek compromises, could focus not only on activities in the current area of application, but in many other contexts and periods throughout the school year. One teacher talked explicitly about the general applicability of one concept underlying his project of creating a "Migration Marker" display of the wildlife within the nearby coastal area at different times of the year:

> In this particular class and in my biology class as well, we take an ecological perspective in which everything is connected to everything else, not only in the natural world but in our actions and our effects...I say, "OK, we're doing this. What are some of the connections here? What is going to benefit from this? What may not benefit?"

THE EVOLUTION OF TEACHERS' THINKING ABOUT SERVICE-LEARNING

In addition to the dimensions that created differences between teachers in the quality of service-learning goals and related implementation activities, there also appeared to be changes within teachers across time and experience in their vision of service-learning. The intensive study interviews suggested that teachers only gradually construct their understanding of what they are trying to accomplish via service-learning. That is, service-learning does not just automatically become fully understood and implemented once teachers decide (or are strongly urged) to try this methodology. In their interviews, some teachers struggled to articulate their goals and priorities or required some time to make their thinking explicit. It is possible that, for many teachers, implementation issues initially assume priority over conceptualization or reflection about goals. They first seem to need to find out what they are able to do and to observe what happens, and then they can think more clearly about the outcomes these activities are promoting. A number of teachers in the study seemed to enjoy the interviews and the time they were afforded to think about what they were trying to accomplish. One teacher shared her own reconsideration and refinement of goals for her service-learning activities and suggested that it is important for teachers to be ready to modify their perceptions of their particular service projects as these activities develop and new insights emerge.

> My perception of it has changed. When I first conceived the idea, I thought, "Well this allowed the students to do a service, a *physical* service at the senior center"... Initially, they actually served lunch and cleared it and did everything. Then we found out that that was too awkward, because the seniors

were uncomfortable eating their lunches while the students didn't have anything. So then we worked out this other thing [an oral history project]... I've
seen this evolve into that being much more what is happening with it...we
have the opportunity to build bridges in gaps in our communities. Because a
lot of the seniors are Anglo and they tend to have...fears... And now they're
having an opportunity to meet them on a one-to-one basis.

Not only did teachers talk about reconceptualizing the goals they had
for an ongoing service-learning activity, but they often indicated that there
were additional goals they wanted to realize through service-learning but
had not yet had time to incorporate through modification of the activities
that were already in place. This admission was most frequent with regard to
the features of student voice, community input, and reflection, but also
occurred with regard to the elements of authentic service or academic
integration. For example, one teacher, in describing her school's efforts to
implement service-learning, characterized the first year's efforts as "hit or
miss" and then went on to explain:

Because we were learning what service-learning was. We were learning how to
make the contacts; we weren't really into the student voice and this community voice. We were into deciding what would be done ourselves and then
going with it...so it's taken us a while...[So do your students have choice in
what they do?] Not as much as I would like them to do...Yeah, it's kind of
hard.

Another possibility that this teacher had not yet considered was that
implementing student voice and community voice might imply roles for
participants that would be in conflict with her efforts to spell out the curricular content and subject matter standards that would be met through
her set of teacher-designed and directed service-learning activities. She
appeared to foresee changes in the implementation of service-learning as a
process of gradually *adding in* essential elements rather than *reconceptualizing* relationships among participants and planned activities to avoid possible conflicts between goals.

It may be possible for teachers to tack on some superficial version of a
missing essential feature of service-learning without changing the fundamental nature of the existing activities. But it is likely that incorporating
authentic versions of features like student voice or community voice
requires an entire reconceptualization and reorganization of project activities on the teacher's part. The way teachers conceptualize service-learning
projects or activities may depend on their beliefs about learning and teaching and on ways these beliefs can change during their careers. There is,
therefore, a need for a framework in service-learning that helps us better
understand qualitative differences in teachers' pedagogical thinking and
how their thinking changes over time.

A FRAMEWORK FOR UNDERSTANDING
DIFFERENCES IN TEACHERS' PEDAGOGICAL THINKING

An alternative to an additive view of development in teachers' pedagogical thinking is the developmental constructivist framework developed by Paul Ammon and his colleagues at the University of California-Berkeley (Ammon & Black, 1998; Ammon & Hutcheson, 1989; Levin & Ammon, 1996). Developed first to examine changes in the thinking of student teachers from the beginning to the end of a two-year postgraduate credential program (the Developmental Teacher Education Program), the model has now been tested and refined with teachers across a range of experience. As will be seen, this framework seems relevant to many of the dimensions of variation in teachers' thinking about service-learning already described, and it appears to bring some order to the mass of variation in teachers' goals and implementation strategies. The model is especially appropriate for application to service-learning utilized across the entire K-12 gradespan, because it emphasizes the coordination of understanding of child development, curriculum, and instructional practices.

The four strands of the model chart the emergence of qualitatively different ways of thinking about behavior, development, learning, and teaching, each of which is viewed not as wrong or right but as partially right. The model proposes that, given opportunities and support, teachers work their way from simpler, uni-dimensional, *behaviorist* ways of thinking to more complex, multidimensional, *constructivist* understandings of pedagogy. Each strand in the model is defined by a small set of core questions. As a teacher goes from one level to another within a strand, these questions are answered in different ways. For example, one question defining the *learning* strand focuses on different ideas about what is learned—information, the performance of a task, the correct understanding of a concept, a better understanding of a concept that is only gradually attained, and so forth. These different conceptions of what is to be learned clearly link to variations in teachers' goals for service-learning activities that were discussed earlier. Another question defining the learning strand focuses on what the learning process is like. Do students learn through exposure, through practicing and feedback, through independent discovery, through being helped to think in more complicated ways, or through guided reflection?

With regard to the question of how *teaching* is conceptualized, does teaching involve showing and telling students what they need to know, modeling and reinforcing behaviors, providing opportunities for hands-on exploration, guiding students' thinking in each domain, or guiding thinking across domains? Exhibit 3 contains a simplified outline of the model. In the interests of keeping this discussion brief, this version contains only the two strands of the model most essential to describing its application to service-learning, those dealing with learning and teaching.

EXHIBIT 3
Simplified Developmental Constructivist Model of Teachers'
Pedagogical Thinking (Paul Ammon)

| | Strands | |
Level	Learning	Teaching
1	Experiencing: Acquiring facts, rules, and attitudes through exposure	Showing and telling students what they need to know.
2	Acquiring skills and procedures through imitation, practice, and reinforcement.	Modeling and reinforcing correct behaviors.
3	Exploring: Acquiring correct under-standing from direct manipulation.	Providing active hands-on experience to induce understanding of content.
4	Sense-making: Attaining better under-standing of some content consistent with current developmental capacity.	Guiding thinking and reasoning within domains of content.
5	Problem Solving: Results from reasoning about reasoning.	Guiding thinking across domains and promoting general ways of understanding.

The rationale for using this model is that it emphasizes the importance of teachers' thinking about their practice rather than concentrating solely on the adequacy of implementation. It follows, then, from this model that a teacher's service-learning practices could not be evaluated simply by observing the activities but would require discussion with the teacher. What teachers know and think about teaching and learning can both be overestimated and underestimated by what they do in the classroom. On the one hand, they can follow a scripted curriculum which they do not fully understand; on the other hand, teachers can appreciate complexities of the teaching situation which they have not yet found a way to honor in their practice. Despite the fact that teachers' thinking also varies depend-ing on the particular context and teaching problem, the assumption is that there is considerable consistency in the thinking of teachers that affects what they try to do, and that there is regularity across time in the progres-sion of their thinking about their practice.

How might this framework be applied, in particular, to service-learning practices and thinking, and goal-setting? That is, what might progression in the development of pedagogical conceptions and implementation strat-egies for service-learning look like, using ideas from this framework?

A teacher whose predominant way of thinking about teaching and learning was at Level 1 might design a simple apprenticeship situation in which students watch adults in the community performing various civic roles that the students learn by simple exposure. In a buddy reading program, for example, students might be sent to a first grade classroom to learn how to be a tutor by observing the teacher work with her students.

Level 2 conceptions grow out of a teacher appreciating that there are many different aspects of a new to-be-learned behavior, that instruction should take into account what students already can do, and that students can benefit from practice and corrective feedback about their performance. Such thinking might lead a teacher to employ service-learning activities such as "coaching the performance" situations in which students are supposed to learn targeted civic or academic skills by having them modeled by the teacher or other adult and then are given the opportunity to practice and receive feedback and reinforcement for correct behaviors. Such a model might describe buddy reading programs where students primarily learn procedures to use with younger students (such as asking the younger students questions about details in the story or the meaning of "big words") but do not learn much about the reading process.

At Level 3, a teacher's thinking is influenced by the insight that students can learn different things from the same experience because they vary qualitatively in their ways of thinking. When students are allowed to pursue their own ideas, both their thinking and motivation can benefit. Since Level 3 is defined in terms of hands-on experience and exploration, it might be appropriate for describing the design of service-learning situations where students are supposed to independently develop service projects on their own, doing what they can to assess a community need, design an activity to address that need, and then write up what they learned. Though students would develop knowledge and skills by confronting tasks on their own, teachers might specify the types of projects to be undertaken based on their assessment of the capabilities of students. Evaluation of students' learning based on whether they achieved the "correct" understanding of the concepts involved would also be consistent with this stage of teacher thinking. A buddy reading project at this level might involve a student working independently with a younger child and developing his/her own activities and ways of assessing the child's reading improvement.

Level 4 pedagogical thinking involves viewing learning in particular domains in terms of students attaining better, but perhaps not yet complete, understandings. Teachers at this level also see the benefit of providing specific experiences (e.g., responding to provocative questions or alternative points of view) that will help individual students work through their ways of thinking rather than assuming they will learn simply from self-initiated experience. Level 4 thinking about service-learning would emphasize students coming to a better understanding of the subject matter area of their service activity and the need to provide appropriately challenging experiences and to actively facilitate students' attempts to understand concepts in the domain. Buddy reading programs that focus on what reading and writing involve and how young children learn to read might be consistent with this level of thinking about teaching and learning.

Level 5 describes pedagogical thinking that looks at issues and concepts at the "metalevel"; for example, coming to see that there are similarities in the processes of learning to read and learning about math. The example provided earlier of the teacher facilitating the application of the concept of an ecological perspective across domains might also be an indicator of thinking about service-learning implementation approaching this level. A buddy reading program where students were helped to use insights from earlier experiences tutoring science to inform their tutoring in reading would also fit into this level of teacher thinking.

These examples are just a first rudimentary attempt to apply the model to different service-learning goals and practices. Clearly more analysis and detail is needed to push the implications of the theory only briefly outlined in this paper. What is being proposed is that there is merit in considering a different, more functional way of differentiating levels of quality implementation in service-learning based on a developmental constructivist view of teachers' thinking and actions. What remains for the future is to examine the degree to which the framework can be widely applied to the practice of service-learning; whether teachers do progress through these ways of thinking about the implementation of service-learning with experience and appropriate professional development; and whether higher levels of notions about teaching, learning, development, and behavior are linked to better outcomes for students engaged in service-learning.

IMPLICATIONS

This examination of teachers' thinking about service-learning and of the ways teachers' goals and understandings may influence implementation and outcomes suggests a different, more theoretically-grounded way to view quality service-learning implementation. Not only might the described model provide a framework for unifying instances of service-learning that on the surface appear very dissimilar, but it has the potential for generating testable hypotheses about qualitative differences in service-learning implementation (such as hypotheses about the differential generalizability of tutoring skills learned by students in buddy reading programs characterized as Level 4 versus Level 2). Moreover, by integrating teachers' thinking and practices about service-learning into a more general model of teacher development, service-learning is transformed from a separate set of teaching practices into part and parcel of a teachers' entire pedagogical approach.

This discussion began with the assertion that it is a mistake to try to judge the quality of service-learning by looking exclusively at external features of activities or details of implementation (such as length of service, presence of direct interaction with a human recipient of service, or presence of some reflection activity) or by specifying a set of practices necessary for accomplishing particular service-learning goals. Observations of a service-learning activity may not be representative of a teacher's practice and may be ambiguous in terms of revealing the way any service-learning activity fits into the teacher's curriculum. In the process of making the point that it is useful to investigate teachers' thinking about service-learning, it was shown how indepth interviews are needed to clarify the nature of teachers' thinking about service-learning as well as other aspects of teaching and learning.

At the same time, the intention of this chapter has *not* been to suggest that attention should be shifted away from teaching practices and focused only on teachers' thinking. Although the development of teachers' thinking about teaching and learning in general and about service-learning in particular is central to definitions of good practice, what teachers say about their service-learning practices and their reasons for implementation decisions can lead to incomplete evaluations of their pedagogical development. Estimates of quality in service-learning implementation require information both about what teachers do and about how they think about and contextualize what they are doing.

Moreover, student (and community) perceptions about teachers' practices are important to consider, since the concern is not just with teacher development but also with student (and community) outcomes. The fact that student perceptions about teacher practices have been found to be more predictive of student outcomes than teacher reports of their practices is an important empirical finding (McCombs, 2002). Such research recalls the point made in the parable that the service-learning field needs to look at quality from multiple perspectives. Ultimately, this chapter suggests that clearer ideas about the ways teachers' thinking and practices develop with regard to service-learning may be useful both for professional development efforts and for future work aimed at studying the impacts of service-learning.

APPENDIX. THE BLIND MEN AND THE ELEPHANT
BY JOHN GODFREY SAXE

It was six men of Indostan
  To learning much inclined,
Who went to see the Elephant
  (Though all of them were blind),
That each by observation
  Might satisfy his mind

The First approached the Elephant
  And happening to fall
Against his broad and sturdy side,
  At once began to bawl:
"God bless me! but the Elephant
  Is very like a wall!"

The Second, feeling of the tusk,
  Cried, "Ho! what have we here
So very round and smooth and sharp?
  To me 'tis mighty clear
This wonder of an Elephant
  Is very like a spear!"

The Third approached the animal,
  And happening to take
The squirming trunk within his hands
  Thus boldly up and spake:
"I see," quoth he, "the Elephant
  Is very like a snake!"

The Fourth reached out an eager hand,
  And felt about the knee.
"What most this wondrous beast is like
  Is mighty plain," quoth he;
"'Tis clear enough the Elephant
  Is very like a tree!"

The Fith, who chanced to touch the ear,
  Said: "E'en the blindest man
Can tell what this resembles most;
  Deny the fact who can
This marvel of an Elephant
  Is very like a fan!?"

The Sixth no sooner had begun
  about the beast to grope,
Than, seizing on the swinging tail
  That fell within his scope,
"I see," quoth he, "the Elephant
  Is very like a rope!"

And so these men of Indostan
  Disputed loud and long,
Each in his own opinion
  Exceeding stiff and strong
Though each was partly in the right,
  And all were in the wrong!

NOTE

1. The differentiation of the three buddy reading programs in Exhibit 2 was only possible because detailed information about teachers' motivations, thinking, and implementation practices was obtained in the intensive study interviews. The surveys administered to the same teachers were not nearly as informative and were sometimes even misleading because of the brevity and ambiguity of some of the teachers' answers.

Acknowledgments: The author wishes to acknowledge the other members of the SLRDC research team—Bernadette Chi, Ellen Middaugh, and Andy Furco—for their collaboration in the collection, transcription, and analysis of the data for this study, and Barbara Weiss of the California Department of Education for her feedback on these efforts. In addition, she would like to express her appreciation to the teachers, students, administrators, and coordinators of the seven CalServe partnerships who volunteered their time and ideas to the "intensive" study of service-learning in their districts.

REFERENCES

Alliance for Service-Learning in Education Reform. (1995, March). Standards of quality for school-based and community-based service-learning. Alexandria, VA: Close Up Foundation.

Ammon, M. S., Furco, A., Chi, B., & Middaugh, E. (2002, March). *Service-learning in California: A profile of the CalServe service-learning partnerships 1997-2000* (Final Report to the California Department of Education). Berkeley, CA: The Service-Learning Research & Development Center.

Ammon, P., & Black, A. (1998). Developmental psychology as a guide for teaching and teacher preparation (pp.409-448). In N. M. Lambert & B. L. McCombs (Eds.), *How students learn: Reforming schools through learner-centered education.* Washington, DC: American Psychological Association.

Ammon, P., & Hutcheson, B. P. (1989). Promoting the development of teachers' pedagogical conceptions. *The Genetic Epistemologist, 17*(4), 23-30.

Honnet, E. P., & Poulsen, S. (Eds). (1989). *Wingspread Special Report: Principals of good practice for combining service and learning.* Racine, WI: The Johnson Foundation.

Kraft, R. (1996). Service-learning: An introduction to its theory, practice, and effects. *Education and Urban Society, 28*(2), 131-159.

Levin, B. B., & Ammon, P. (1996). A longitudinal study of the development of teachers' pedagogical conceptions: The case of Ron. *Teacher Education Quarterly, 23*(4), 5-26.

McCombs, B. L. (2002, April). How can we define teacher quality? The learner-centered framework. Paper presented at the annual meeting of the American Educational Research Association, New Orleans, LA.

Melchior, A. (1998). Final Report: National Evaluation of Learn and Serve America School and Community-Based Programs. Waltham, MA: Brandeis University, Center for Human Resources.

National Center for Education Statistics. (1999, September). Service-learning and community service in K-12 public schools (NCES 1999-043). Washington, DC: U.S. Department of Education, Office of Educational Research and Improvement.

Shumer, R., Berkas, T., & Murphy, N. (1992, July). *Describing service-learning: A Delphi Study.* Minneapolis: University of Minnesota, Department of Vocational and Technical Education.

Spillane, J. P., & Jennings, N. E. (1997). Aligned instructional policy and ambitious pedagogy: Exploring instructional reform from the classroom perspective. *Teachers College Record, 98*(3), 449-481.

Weiler, D., LaGoy, A., Crane, E., & Rovner, A. (1998). *An evaluation of service-learning in California: Phase II final report.* Emeryville, CA: Research Policy Practice International.

CHAPTER 4

THE SACRED AND PROFANE
Theorising Knowledge Reproduction Processes in a Service-Learning Curriculum

Janice McMillan

This chapter reflects an attempt to develop a theoretical framework to understand and analyse the relationship between academic and everyday knowledge in the context of undergraduate service learning curricula in higher education. One of the challenges of service learning is that in engagement with communities, students and the university come into contact and develop relationships with members of communities. These relationships between knowledge discourses have had little (if any) mention in the literature on research in the field. Drawing largely on studies in the sociology of education, the main focus of the chapter is the development of a conceptual framework which can point to ways in which such relationships can be explored.

INTRODUCTION

The title of this chapter is taken from a paper by Muller and Taylor (1994) who draw on the work of sociologist Emile Durkheim. Durkheim explores

Service-Learning Through a Multidisciplinary Lens
A Volume in: Advances in Service-Learning Research, pages 55–70.
Copyright © 2002 by Information Age Publishing, Inc.
All rights of reproduction in any form reserved.
ISBN: 1-931576-81-5 (cloth), 1-931576-80-7 (paper)

two orders of existence that relate thought and practice in two fundamentally different ways (Muller & Taylor, 1994). According to Muller and Taylor, Durkheim's hypothesis is that socially constructed knowledge depends on a hard distinction between every day, particular or profane knowledge, and esoteric, generalisable, sacred knowledge, examples of which include religions, sciences, and curricula. It is this relationship—between sacred and profane knowledge—that informs the main purpose of this chapter; namely, to develop a theoretical frame in order to understand the interaction between academic or discipline-based knowledge, and community or every day knowledge as might be played out in service-learning curricula.

The author has been involved in a research project on service-learning practice exploring higher education, community, and service sector partnerships (CHESP) at the University of Cape Town, South Africa. Through the research fieldwork, and through reflections on what was happening in the field, it became clear that looking at the interaction between these two forms of knowledge cannot be the starting point for such a research project. One needs instead to come to this understanding via another route. It is clear from reading the service-learning literature that understanding this form of educational practice often involves understanding a whole range of complex and challenging relationships, processes, and interactions that go beyond what we would understand as the formal curriculum in higher education (Cruz & Giles 2000; Stanton, Giles, & Cruz, 1999).

It could therefore be argued that much of service-learning work involves some form of boundary negotiation—of knowledge, language, roles, place, identity, and meaning, amongst other things. However, a theoretical frame to address service-learning as such seems missing from the literature, and in order to research this dimension of service-learning, such a frame seems important. In other words, developing a language and vocabulary for conceptualising and theorising the social and cognitive interactions, processes, and practices that service-learning entails, can assist researchers to come to an understanding of the relationship between forms of knowledge in a service-learning curriculum. In particular, it is hoped that this can lead to exploring service-learning as boundary work involving a wide range of brokers/agents, across a range of sites, engaged in a range of practices. It is through this lens that one can perhaps come to a better understanding, not only of service-learning curricula, but of the relationship between sacred and profane knowledge.

The chapter is as follows. Section One introduces the service-learning project and the South African context in order to provide some background for the reader unfamiliar with it. Section Two, the focus of the chapter, outlines the development of a conceptual framework that can assist one in making sense of service-learning as a form of social practice that can be deeply embedded in a range of contexts. It is hoped that this frame might challenge researchers to re-think service-learning as educational practice embedded in a range of complex relationships.

SECTION ONE: CONTEXT AND RESEARCH PROJECT

Community-Higher Education-Service Partnerships Project (CHESP)

From mid-1999 to the end of 2000, the University of Cape Town (UCT) was the recipient of a Joint Education Trust (JET)-Ford Foundation planning grant as part of a national project aimed at the potential of service-learning in the context of community/higher education/service partnerships (CHESP) across seven universities in South Africa. While the model developed in South Africa aims to address issues relevant to this context, the project has drawn much of its inspiration from the service-learning movement in the United States.

The aims of the CHESP project are, amongst others, to provide an opportunity for students to gain credit for academic learning while performing community service and to empower disadvantaged communities through the partnerships. In the local South African context, this translates into work towards "the reconstruction and development of South African civil society through the development of socially accountable models for higher education, research, community service and development" (CHESP project documents: April 1999:1). Central to these aims are the development of partnerships between historically disadvantaged communities, higher education institutions, and the service sector so as to meet the twin goals of:

- Addressing the needs of these communities; and
- Supporting the transformation of higher education institutions in relation to these priorities.

The emergence of the CHESP project must been seen against the backdrop of a South African context where the need for real change is crucial. In this section, the context of the community, service, and academic partners will be briefly discussed.

Service and Community Partners

Non-government organisations (NGOs) have had a turbulent yet vibrant history in South Africa working closely with communities, civics, trade unions, and destitute people in many areas of the country. Under the apartheid government, this often took the shape of welfare rather than development work given the poor and often non-existent services available to many communities. Development was clearly part of the agenda, yet for many, the path from welfare to development was not an easy one. Relationships between various stakeholders were often fraught with hostility or were even openly hostile and trust was difficult to establish. In the new context in South Africa, these alliances have shifted somewhat. According to Drabek (1987), the challenge to NGOs in the future will be to act as facilitators or catalysts of local development initiatives. Therefore, NGOs, once the source of both services and empowerment for communities, now need to forge new kinds of partnerships and relationships with government structures, and these are still in their early stages.

Higher Education Partner

In looking at the third partner in the CHESP model—the university—the picture becomes even more complex. In many countries, including South Africa, universities do not have a strong history of being in partnership with other organisations in civil society in order to make a direct impact on addressing development priorities. This is particularly the case with strong research-based universities, such as UCT. While it is clear that many universities might have a strong commitment to community service (Perold, 1998), this has not been the key business of the university sector. Their engagement in development has been indirect through research and publications and while there might be good intent behind the initiatives, these have not been directly assessed or evaluated in terms of broader reconstruction and development issues in the society as a whole. The South African Higher Education White Paper (1997) supports this argument by indicating that too many parts of the system carry out their teaching and learning practices in insular and tightly-bound disciplinary ways, which on the whole, mitigate against addressing "pressing local, regional and national needs of the South African society."

While higher education globally is confronting a series of challenges (Gibbons et al., 1994), the South Africa setting has provided a stark context for this. This is putting new pressures on higher education institutions to change as Cloete and Muller (1998, p. 525) indicate:

> South Africa...provides a particularly sharp example of a higher education system established within the European tradition, in terms of both its institutional and its academic culture, and a society in the process of radical change...[how to enable] South African higher education to be both for 'Western' (in terms of academic values and scientific standards) and also 'African' (in terms of its contribution to building the capacities of all people of South Africa). The tension between the university's claims to represent universal knowledge and the counter-claims that 'local' knowledge traditions should be accorded greater respect, therefore, is much starker than in Europe.

In taking up these challenges, national higher education policy has argued that there are a number of key responses facing institutions, which include:

- Increased participation in higher education by a diverse group of learners;
- Responsiveness to societal needs; and
- Cooperation and partnerships.

The second of these challenges in particular reflects much of the impetus behind the CHESP project, which, in addition to introducing service-learning into higher education, introduces the challenge of partnership development, one of the key goals underpinning the CHESP project.

The Research Project

In setting up this research project it became clear very early on that it is difficult to measure the relationship between kinds of knowledge as they play themselves out in service-learning curricula, particularly over the short two years of the project. Attempts were made to analyse two service-learning courses, one in urban geography and another in the health sciences. The courses both run in the second semester, and students complete a range of projects under the guidance of community and academic staff. These projects have been negotiated with the community partners prior to the course, and community members have been drawn in to work on the projects.

Interviews were conducted with students, community members, and academic staff in the hope of being able to discern any interesting issues in relation to knowledge and knowledge boundaries. Once immersed in the fieldwork data, it became apparent that there were a range of other issues to consider and that a theoretical frame was needed that could take account of service-learning as a social practice deeply shaped by relationships, power, and roles. In addition, it is a social practice located in the border terrain between the university and community where the students and academics involved engage the real world of community politics, identity, poverty, and knowledge discourses. Such a framework seemed absent from the service-learning literature, and so the first phase of the project became exactly that: to develop a frame that could support and help analyse what was emerging in the field.

In terms of a research paradigm, a qualitative frame is clearly advocated, given the issues being investigated. Shumer (2000) argues that the approach that is finally selected depends on what the research is intending to measure. He argues that if the intention is to assess or measure *degree of impact,* one can use a quantitative approach, but if you want to understand the *process,* then one needs to use a qualitative approach.

Whichever approach is selected, Shumer believes that "to insure validity, the approach one takes should adhere to the ontological, epistemological, and methodological constructs that make the paradigm logical and consistent" (p. 81). He argues that while quantitative approaches are ones mostly used in higher education, they are "not sufficient to support the dynamic, professional practitioner in the field of service-learning...other paradigms and approaches...are more philosophically consistent and more able to reveal the fine-grain texture of this work" (p. 81). This is supported by Stanton (2000) who argues that there is a need for more qualitative research that can begin to provide what he terms "rich portraits of practice."

The rest of this chapter attempts to outline this emergent frame. Key concepts informing the frame are social development, curriculum, and the relationship between curriculum and knowledge through understanding the importance of the concepts of boundaries and service-learning as a form of boundary work in higher education.

SECTION TWO: SERVICE-LEARNING AS BOUNDARY WORK: RELATIONSHIPS, POWER, AND KNOWLEDGE

The theoretical frame outlined here is one that attempts to understand service-learning as boundary work, and as a form of educational practice that involves understanding a range of factors that are often outside the frames used to understand and analyse more traditional higher education knowledge reproduction processes (teaching and learning practice). In addition, given the context of South African higher education within which this service-learning project arose, there are key features emanating from this context in particular. However, before one can understand and theorise service-learning in terms of boundaries and potential boundary brokers or agents, the processes, relationships, and sites that serve as signifiers of boundaries in this form of practice need to be unpacked. These include development processes and relationships, the relationship between forms of knowledge and institutional and pedagogic boundaries, and service-learning as a form of potentially transformatory pedagogic practice. While this framework is influenced by work in the South African setting, it has relevance across service-learning contexts more broadly.

Social Development and Partnerships: Understanding Relationships

The fact that South Africa is facing enormous development challenges implies that one needs to carefully consider any conceptions of development as part of the conceptual frame and as applied and understood in this context. In particular, the notion of development within the context of community/higher education/service partnerships needs to take cognisance of the fact that any conception of development needs to take into account the views of, and relationships between, a wide range of stakeholders—stakeholders that have not had the experience of strong relationships nor common goals given the history and legacy of apartheid in South Africa. In particular, legislation based on racial classifications meant that not only were South Africans forced to live in separate racially-demarcated neighbourhoods, but institutions, including universities, were racially segregated. This impacted not only on the levels of education in the country, but also on the budget allocations for services to different neighbourhoods or communities which resulted in the emergence of a sophisticated and well-developed urban core economy with a fairly good technological infrastructure from which the majority black population, who had previously been denied access to education, try to eke out a living (Bawden, 2000).

Therefore, in understanding development, it is important to focus on it as a set of relationships, between institutions and systems, and particularly between people engaged in the processes that development inevitably involves. Horton (1990), in discussing adult education and development, was quoted as saying that "we make the road by walking." This captures two important components of any attempt at arriving at a conception of a term as complex as development: the human *and* physical elements. Roads can be constructed but the process also requires human commitment and will to sustain them and make them useful and meaningful over the long term. In other words, it is clear that there is both a physical and human dimension to any concept of development and that the development process in itself is of importance.

This leads one to an understanding of change as social development—a process involving a complex set of relationships, connections, and interactions between various groups over a period of time. Implicit in the idea of relationships is the concept of power and various people's access to it in meaningful ways. Furthermore, it is important to understand social development as distinct from infrastructural and economic development: "It is through human development that individual, organisational, and community capacities are cultivated, and it is these that allow infrastructural and economic development to take hold and persist" (CDRA Annual Report, 2000/2001, p. 5). Social development is therefore about human development, and thus, when one seeks change in social development, one essentially seeks change in relationships. This is not however, in the realm of the purely internal, not in the field of individual self-development. Rather, it is:

> social relationship, that invisible but richly alive space between people that constitutes so much of what it means to be human at all. Development happens not between things, but between people...[T]his requires of us a simul-

taneous ability to understand each situation's unique circumstances in its own context and time; where things are coming from and where they are going to *in their own terms* (CDRA Annual Report, 2000/2001, p. 6, 8, emphasis in the original).

Understanding development as social development, as relationships and relationship-building, brings up the next important issue: the need to understand that embedded in relationships and relationship-building, the issues of boundaries and boundary work lay—boundaries between people, institutions, values, paradigms, and ways of knowing amongst others. Educational practice that strives build new forms of practice needs to heed this information and how these boundaries can both serve to facilitate but also to inhibit new ways of knowing, working, and doing. The next section begins to explore some of these issues as they play themselves out in curriculum theory and debates.

Curriculum, Boundaries, and Knowledge

According to Bernstein (1999), curricula reform emerges out of struggles between groups to make their preferences (and focus) state policy and practice. Curricula consist of different kinds of knowledge, selected and organised in particular ways depending on the context. Bernstein argues that there are two kinds of discourses, which in the educational field are sometimes referred to as school(ed) or official knowledge on the one hand, and every day common sense or local knowledge on the other. He also refers to them as vertical and horizontal discourses (2000). A vertical discourse is represented by the specialised symbolic structure of organised knowledge represented by formal, schooled knowledge, which aims at generality and abstraction. Thus, a specific context will control a whole range of things that need to be taught and will articulate a graded performance. The practice of a vertical knowledge discourse typically occurs in an official institution such as the school.

A horizontal discourse on the other hand, is the common sense knowledge of the everyday. Bernstein argues that it is common for three reasons:

- It is accessible to all;
- It is applicable/relevant to all; and
- It comes out of day-to-day practices.

Horizontal discourse includes a set of strategies that are local, context specific, and dependent. Linked to these characteristics, Bernstein argues that horizontal discourse is segmented; that is, it evolves or develops at particular points in time around certain activities that need to be learned. The knowledge and competencies in a horizontal discourse are contextually specific and context-dependent, embedded in ongoing practices and directed towards specific immediate goals that are highly relevant to the acquirer in the context of his/her life.

Bernstein's ideas have been used by others seeking to develop a new form of potentially transformatory pedagogy. Muller and Taylor (1994), for example, explore boundaries and boundary negotiation in the school curriculum. They are interested in the relationship between the "ordinary every day knowledge, and the codes, texts and canons the mastery of which is assessed and certified at school" (p. 2). Drawing on Bernstein, Pierre Bourdieu, and Emile Durkheim, Muller and Taylor interrogate the debate within which accounts of curriculum constitution and change are framed by the organising poles of insulation and hybridity. These two concepts are helpful in understanding curriculum knowledge in terms of boundaries. Insulation, represented by the traditional disciplines, emphasises the impermeability of cultural boundaries, of disciplinary autonomy, and the integral differences between systems of knowledge. Hybridity, in contrast, emphasises the continuity of forms and kinds of knowledge and the permeability of classificatory boundaries.

The paper by Muller and Taylor (1994) explores border crossing between knowledge domains and some of the perils or problems in doing this uncritically and unaware. The point Muller and Taylor end up making is not whether it is a good/bad thing to cross the boundary in curriculum terms between two forms of knowledge. Rather, they believe that one has to be mindful that these boundaries do exist and "to cross the line without knowing it is to be at the mercy of the power inscribed in the line" (p. 18). The key question they believe is "**how** to cross," and this they argue "means paying detailed attention to the politics of re-description, to the means required for a successful crossing" (p. 18). In other words, they argue that for a study of knowledge and curriculum, a useful starting point is to understand that a boundary, however problematic and seemingly exclusive, between forms of knowledge, does exist and that we need to be mindful of this.

In order to look at this in more concrete ways, it is useful to look at some of the work written on workplace and work-based learning studies. Solomon and McIntyre (2000) have looked at the issue of boundaries and reflect on the issue of interaction between modes of knowledge in their writings on work-based learning. Exploring these issues at both the level of learning arrangements or partnerships, as well as at the level of curriculum and knowledge, they argue that we need to understand that such learning arrangements are often based on a three-way partnership between the organisation, the learner(s), and the university. Such a partnership, they argue, "sets up additional layers of politics and power relations that are manifested in new discursive practices around the co-production of knowledge" (Solomon & McIntyre, 2000, p. 6).

The result of this is that various boundaries—between theory and practice, between one discipline and another, between working and learning—have become blurred. In addition, these boundaries have become "objects of contestation," and while they are being dismantled, new and different kinds of boundaries are emerging that provide the frame around work-based learning. In other words, the authors argue that the work-based learning curriculum is not unbounded or deregulated—rather it is "bounded and regulated in different ways...(and)...the knowledge that is involved is locally specific, more complex, more contested and more fluid" (Solomon & McIntyre, p. 7). As a consequence, academics and curriculum designers have to pay attention to boundaries and their roles as boundary workers or knowledge brokers.

These are important insights in understanding service-learning curricula. Such curricula are often negotiated across a range of stakeholders with different world views and knowledge bases. How these different viewpoints impact on curriculum, and how boundaries are negotiated, is important to understand. The next section looks at some of these concerns.

Service-Learning, Boundaries, and Knowledge

The concepts of boundaries and boundary brokering are important and useful in understanding service-learning practice as social practice.

While not discussing boundaries explicitly, Zlotkowski (1998) has looked at service-learning as a form of pedagogy that plays a potentially mediating role. The author argues that one of reasons why service-learning has increased in popularity and is increasingly evident on campuses across the U.S. for example, is that it is positioned at the point where two comprehensive sets of contemporary educational concerns intersect. On the one hand, it represents a pedagogy that extends our range of pedagogical resources by addressing directly those "problems of greatest human concern" that are "messy and confusing and incapable of technical solution" (Schon cited in Zlotkowski, p. 3). By linking the classroom to the world of praxis, it allows:

> induction to complement deduction, personal discovery to challenge received truths, immediate experience to balance generalisations and abstract theory. In and through service-learning, students learn to engage in problem definition and problem-solving in an authentic, powerful way (Zlotkowski, 1998, p. 3/4).

On the other hand, service-learning is positioned at a second, intersecting axis: "From knowledge as self-interest and private good, it creates a bridge to knowledge as civic responsibility and public good" (Zlotkowski, 1998, p. 4). Zlotkowski argues that it shows important qualities of flexibility and inclusion—just as knowledge as public work in no way denies the validity of knowledge as private good, knowledge as private good should also not exclude the former. Through service-learning activities, students can learn about the importance of attending to their needs as individuals and as members of a community. By bringing public work into the very heart of the educational system (i.e. the curriculum), service-learning helps students to avoid seeing private advancement disassociated from public standards and public need. This could be seen to be a form of boundary negotiation that students engage in through service-learning.

Bawden (2000), drawing on the work of Ernest Boyer and his notion of a 'scholarship of engagement,' has explored service-learning as the need for engagement in 'discourse as communities' and argues that universities need to work towards a 'universe of human discourse' in order to meet many of the challenges posed by globalisation. Engagement for Bawden does not, however, necessarily mean the dissolution of identity and thus of boundaries and the search for homogeneity. Rather, he believes it is about "the preservation and utilisation of difference as the sources of synergy" (p. 6). Following from this, he makes the point:

> It is this synergy, this emergence of surprising outcomes through interactions of difference that lies at the heart of the argument for engagement for communal discourse; for a communicative ethic that not only allows us to cross boundaries in our search for what might be termed 'inclusive well-being' (Prozesky, 1999 in Bawden, 2000) but impels us to do so (p. 6).

Chesler and Scalera (2000) look at service-learning as a form of pedagogy that allows one to better understand notions of difference through border crossing. The authors argue that various culturally-constructed differences, (e.g., race and gender), are more easily discussed and analysed through service-learning. In addition, given that these issues are relevant to all areas of higher education, Chester and Scalera argue that if service-learning is supported as an alternative educational experience, it needs to address, confront, and challenge sexism and racism in higher education. In other words, higher education needs to challenge cultural and political boundaries. Service-learning offers the opportunity of border crossing: through working with new and different groups of people outside of campus, service-learning can provide a real experience of linking theory with real life issues for both students and academics.

One study in South Africa has begun to look at these issues and is worth noting here. Muller & Subotzky (2001) have looked at the issue of modes of knowledge production in asking questions about the knowledge needed in the new millennium. Drawing on the work of Gibbons et al. (1994) and the thesis of new modes of knowledge production, Muller and Subotzky look at some of the pressing issues facing higher education in the context of globalisation. Through analysing community-based academic service-learning, they argue that service-learning is a way of giving substance to the notion of the 'engaged university.' As such, service-learning is claimed to be an effective means towards bridging the perceived widening gap between what they term the "knowing academy" and the "needy society." For the academy, this provides the opportunity:

> to break its myopic preoccupation with academic forms of knowledge... [F]urther, 'public intellectuals' are emerging who defy both the detachment of conventional academe...[T]his new faculty place strong emphasis on the social utility of research and are typically informed by particularist epistemologies in which truth should not be separated from personal experience (Muller and Subotzky, p. 10).

Muller and Subotzky go on to say that the combination of formal and informal knowledge production implies an expanded notion of socially-relevant scholarship that embraces and rewards not only more conventional discipline-based inquiry, but also Boyer's other three forms of scholarship; namely integration, outreach engagement, and teaching. Furthermore, such academics must therefore recognise the validity of:

> experiential, indigenous, tacit and pre-theoretical knowledge...(they) have to learn to bridge the gap between the meaning of research findings and the meaning(s) constructed by those affected by the results, and between academic and 'political' truth (Muller and Subotzky, p. 10).

Understanding Learning in Service-Learning

As can be seen from Solomon and McIntyre (2000), and Bernstein (1999), educational knowledge is generated in sites of tension and contestation. This could mean that a service-learning curriculum might not be as useful a unit of analysis unless one also begins to look at the question of learning—both within formal learning contexts as well as within community knowledge contexts. Therefore, not only how one thinks about knowledge, but also how we think about and define what counts as valid learning, is important to consider if we wish to find evidence for a shift in the power that more traditional discipline-based curricula have over what counts as knowledge.

What is not discussed however, is the impact of this on learning. This author believes it is an omission, and it is an important dimension to add to the framework. Given the attention to service-learning as a social practice, a starting point is understanding learning from the perspective of activity theory and situated learning—frames that focus explicitly on the varied *contexts* in which learning processes occur. This is a particularly useful lens to use to research learning processes situated, at least in part, in new learning contexts; namely, the context of relating to community priorities.

Situated learning theorists place high value on the relationship between *social and cultural processes* and view human knowledge and interaction as inseparable from the world. It contributes to a developing body of research in the human sciences that explores the situated character of human understanding and communication, and it takes as its focus, the relationship between learning and the social situations in which it occurs. This view of learning draws from the work of Vygotsky (1978) and his social development theory. His main argument is that learning happens first in relation to others and only later is it internalised individually. In other words, individual consciousness is built from the outside through social relations—it is social interaction that leads to cognitive development, not the other way around. Learning therefore becomes a social phenomenon, closely bound to context, inseparable from the world. In this frame, *intersubjectivity* (or agency) becomes important—learning happens through the understandings that develop between individuals/sub-communities as a result of interaction (Harris, 2000).

In this vein, the work of Lave and Wenger (1991) is important. They argue that the intersubjective aspects of learning are about positionings in the social world. Their concept of *legitimate peripheral participation in communities of practice* is particularly useful. The learning process, viewed in this way, becomes synonymous with identity change and transformation of the social practice—the practice of all the participants and the social practice as a whole is changed. Learning is therefore part of the generation of social practice, and the emphasis is on learning as a social practice rather than as pedagogic strategy.

In other words, Lave and Wenger (1991) argue that most accounts of learning have ignored its social character. They take an important step by proposing that learning is a process of participating in communities of practice. Rather than asking what kinds of cognitive processes and conceptual structures are involved in learning, they ask, "What kinds of social engagements provide the proper context for learning to take place" (Hanks, 1991, p. 14). The individual learner is therefore not gaining a discrete body of abstract knowledge which he/she will then transport and reapply in later contexts; he/she

> [A]cquires the skills to perform by actually engaging in the process, under the attenuated conditions of *legitimate peripheral participation* (Hanks, p. 14, emphasis in the original).

From this point of view, the activities of people and environment are seen as parts of a mutually constructed whole. There is a constant dialectic and mutual dependence between individual, mind, and culture—as a consequence, the learner acts *with* the environment rather than *on* it (Harris, 2000). As Lave (1991, p. 29) argues:

'Legitimate peripheral participation' provides a way to speak about the relationships between newcomers and old-timers, and about activities, identities, artifacts, and communities of knowledge and practice. It concerns the process by which newcomers become part of a community of practice. A person's intentions to learn are engaged and the meaning of learning is configured through the process of becoming a full participant in a sociocultural practice.

In terms of understanding service-learning as boundary work and as the relationship between kinds of knowledge, forms of practice, and ways of knowing, this is important insight. Situated learning allows one to understand that learning in service-learning is also about boundary work. It is about meaning-making and negotiation in context (McMillan, 1997) and involves understanding relationships and issues of power, identity, and context.

This has implications thinking about the roles and identities of academics. Johnston (1998) argues that in discussing this and the reconfigurations of boundaries, one of the key new roles for academics is that of the profession of knowledge-broker. She looks at the role of the university by considering it in relation to Boyer's four areas of scholarship (discovery, teaching, application, and integration), and argues that "this role is becoming ever more important in a rapidly changing world where values, standards, and quality are regarded as relative rather than absolute" (p. 267). In addition, such a role needs increasingly to mediate between various binaries: community or organisational learning/individual learning; informal/formal learning; development or performance outcomes/learning outcomes; doing/knowing; and community or working knowledge/disciplinary knowledge (Solomon & McIntyre, 2000). This will clearly pose challenges to the role of academics in higher education, including those involved in service-learning.

CONCLUSION

This chapter set out to explore the development of a theoretical framework for researching the practice of service-learning. In particular, it has argued for the usefulness of the concept of boundaries, boundary negotiation, and boundary brokers. This frame has emerged out of an immersion into practice and of a need to better understand service-learning as a complex and challenging form of educational practice. As argued earlier in the chapter, a frame such as the one presented here seemed absent from the literature on service-learning and made fieldwork data analysis difficult. It is this author's belief that drawing on this framework will allow one to understand service-learning as a form of boundary work in higher education. Many studies that one reads in the field (e.g., Chesler & Scalera, 2000) have alluded to the understanding of service-learning as a complex practice and for the need for more interpretive frames (e.g., Stanton, 2000). This chapter is an attempt to develop one that can begin to do justice to the rich and complex fields of both service-learning practice *and* research.

Researching educational practice is therefore often a difficult practice, particularly when one is trying to work with new frames and a different lens. However, it is often the most exciting kind of research, and for those service-learning researchers involved, it is demanding and challenging. It is hoped that new communities of researchers will come together to create rich "portraits of practice" and to explore service-learning as a field of practice and enquiry that challenges many of the boundaries that more traditional educational research implies. What is important is to identify key constructs, sites, and potential brokers or facilitating and/or inhibiting factors, as these can potentially provide a language for boundary-crossings and a way of describing and analysing a very complex practice, which, perhaps ultimately, can begin to address the relationship between sacred and profane knowledge as they play themselves out in service-learning curricula.

Acknowledgment: I would like to acknowledge the support of the National Research Foundation (NRF) of South Africa whose initial funding for the First Annual International K-H Service-Learning Research Conference in October 2001 resulted in the conference paper from which this chapter was born.

REFERENCES

Bawden, R. (2000). CHESP and the scholarship of engagement: Strategies towards a universe of human discourse. A report by Professor Richard Bawden on his visit to the eight CHESP pilot projects, South Africa.

Bernstein, B. (1999). Official knowledge and pedagogic identities. In F. Christie, *Pedagogy and the shaping of consciousness: Linguistic and social processes.* London: Continuum.

Bernstein, B. (2000). Vertical and horizontal discourse: An essay. In *Pedagogy, symbolic control, and identity: Revised edition.* Oxford, UK: Rowman and Littlefield.

Chesler, M., & Scalera, C. (2000, Fall). Race and gender issues related to service-learning research. *Michigan Journal of Community Service Learning,* (Special Issue 2000), 18-27.

Cloete, N. & Muller, J. (1998). South African higher education reform: What comes after post-colonialism? *European Review,* 6(4), 525-542.

Community Development Resource Association (CDRA). (2000/2001). Measuring development: Holding infinity. Annul Report published by CDRA, Cape Town, South Africa.

Cruz, N. & Giles, D. (2000, Fall). Where's the community in service-learning research? *Michigan Journal of Community Service Learning,* (Special Issue 2000), 28-34.

Department of Education. (1997). South African Higher Education White Paper. Pretoria: Government Printers.

Drabek, A. (1987). Development alternatives: The Challenge for NGOs—An overview of the issues. *World Development, 15,* Supplement, ix-xv.

Gibbons, M., Limoges, C., Nowotny, H., Schartzman, S., Scott, P., & Trow, M. (1994). *The new production of knowledge.* London: Sage.

Hanks, W. F. (1991). Foreword. In J. Lave & E. Wenger (Eds.), *Situated learning: Legitimate peripheral participation.* Cambridge, UK: Cambridge University Press.

Harris, J. (2000). Theories of learning and the Recognition of Prior Learning (RPL): Implications for South African Education and Training. Report prepared for the National Centre for Curriculum Research and Development (NCCRD), Department of Education, South Africa.

Horton, M. (1990). *The long haul.* New York: Doubleday.

Johnston, R. (1998). The university of the future: Boyer revisited. *Higher Education, 36,* 253-272.

Joint Education Trust (JET). (1999, April). Community-Higher Education-Service Partnerships (CHESP) project planning phase documents. Capte Town: Author.

Lave, J., & Wenger, E. (1991). *Situated learning: Legitimate peripheral participation.* Cambridge, UK: Cambridge University Press.

McMillan, J. (1997). Adult learners, access and higher education: Learning as meaning-making and negotiation in context. Unpublished M. Phil dissertation, Faculty of Education, University of the Western Cape.

Muller, J., & Taylor, N. (1994). Schooling and everyday life: Knowledges sacred and profane. Unpublished paper presented to School of Education seminar, University of Cape Town, South Africa.

Muller, J., & Subotzky, G. (2001). What knowledge is needed in the new millennium? *Organisation, 8*(2), 163-182.

Perold, H. (1998). Community service in higher education: Final report. Braamfontein, South Africa: JET.

Shumer, R. (2000, Fall). Science or storytelling: How should we conduct and report on service-learning research? *Michigan Journal of Community Service Learning,* (Special Issue 2000), 76-83.

Solomon, N., & McIntyre, J. (2000). Deschooling vocational knowledge: Work-based learning and the politics of curriculum. In C. Symes & J. McIntyre (Eds.), *Working knowledge: The new vocationalism and higher education.* Buckingham, UK: Open University Press.

Stanton, T. (2000, Fall). Bringing reciprocity to service-learning research and practice. *Michigan Journal of Community Service Learning,* (Special Issue 2000), 119-123.

Stanton, T., Giles, D., & Cruz, N. (1999). *Service learning: A movement's pioneers reflect on its origins, practice, and future.* San Francisco: Jossey-Bass.

University of Cape Town CHESP Strategic Plan. (2000). Centre for Higher Education Development (CHED), University of Cape Town.

Vygotsky, L. S. (1978). *Mind in society.* Cambridge, MA: Harvard University Press.

Zlotkowski, E. (Ed.). (1998). *Successful service-learning programs: New models for excellence in higher education.* Boston: Anker Publishing Company, Inc.

PART III

SERVICE-LEARNING AND THE DISCIPLINES

CHAPTER 5

AN INTERDISCIPLINARY STUDY OF SERVICE-LEARNING PREDICTORS AND OUTCOMES AMONG COLLEGE STUDENTS

Pamela Steinke, Peggy Fitch, Chris Johnson, and Fredric Waldstein

An interdisciplinary team of faculty and students from three institutions studied predictors of five outcomes of service-learning: cognitive learning, intellectual development, spiritual and ethical development, civic engagement, and community impact. By making clear distinctions among different types of service-learning outcomes, the results of the study provide support for best practices across different outcomes, suggest recommendations for best practices in the context of specific outcomes, and suggest directions for further investigations. Researchers and practitioners must be clear about the types of outcomes they wish to study or to affect in their students. This study provides a framework for distinguishing among different outcomes and data that support the need to clearly state outcome goals.

Service-Learning Through a Multidisciplinary Lens
A Volume in: Advances in Service-Learning Research, pages 73–102.
Copyright © 2002 by Information Age Publishing, Inc.
All rights of reproduction in any form reserved.
ISBN: 1-931576-81-5 (cloth), 1-931576-80-7 (paper)

Service-learning is recognized as a pedagogy that meets multiple, simultaneous goals. These goals include: student goals addressing cognitive or academic learning, intellectual development, spiritual and ethical development, and civic engagement as well as goals addressing community impact. Numerous studies in service-learning have looked at what predicts good outcomes of service-learning (e.g., Eyler & Giles, 1999; Mabry, 1998). Predictors or principles of best practice have been identified from theory and practice in service learning (Mintz & Hesser, 1996) and have included reflection, challenge or quality of placement, community engagement, cultural diversity of placement, and student control or voice. What is missing from the research literature is an understanding of how these principles or predictors differentially affect the identified goals or outcomes. Without this understanding, instructors are left not knowing which predictors are most relevant to their desired outcomes.

One type of outcome most important to faculty that has received research attention is cognitive learning or academic outcomes (e.g., Eyler & Giles, 1999; Mabry, 1998; Markus, Howard, & King, 1993). Cognitive learning has been measured by performance in the course on exams and other assignments, self-report of students such as whether they have a deeper and more complex understanding of material, and measurement of general academic skills such as critical thinking and writing skills (see Steinke & Buresh, 2002 for review). In general, self-report measures have produced consistently positive results. Students clearly *believe* that their service-learning experiences are enhancing their understanding of course material. Course grades have sometimes indicated more positive outcomes for service-learning students than for non-service-learning students (e.g., Markus et al.), but not always (e.g., Miller, 1994). Similarly, open-ended measures specific to course content have sometimes produced more positive results for service-learning students than for non-service-learning students (e.g., Kendrick, 1996) but not always (Osborne, Hammerich, & Hensley, 1998).

Other outcomes identified have captured student cognitive or intellectual development (e.g., Eyler & Giles, 1999; McEwen, 1996). These measures are based on Perry's (1968/1999) scheme of intellectual and ethical development describing how college students come to reason more complexly about knowledge, truth, learning, and commitment. The chapter on critical thinking in Eyler and Giles' report of two national studies of service-learning cogently explores how intellectual development is related to students' understanding of complex social problems. They used King and Kitchener's (1994) reflective judgment model, which is derived from Perry's scheme, to illustrate the evolutions in students' conceptions of causes of and solutions for various social problems such as homelessness and AIDS. Students in lower stages of the model saw social problems as having essentially clear definitions and right answers, if only they could be found. By contrast, students in the upper stages of the model understood that social problems were inherently "messy" and ill-defined, having multiple causes, and that appropriate solutions depended on how one defined the problem. They recognized the importance of seeking new information and alternative perspectives and of making a tentative commitment to a solution, but also appreciated that the solution could change with new information about the problem.

The relationship between service-learning and the spiritual, ethical, and moral development of students has been examined separately (e.g., Boss, 1994; Delve, Mintz, & Stewart, 1990; Gorman, 1994). Researchers and theorists have asked whether qualities of moral character such as altruism, perceptiveness, compassion, and honesty can be cultivated and nurtured through the practice of service. From this perspective, to live a good life and to live it well requires the development of certain cognitive, emotional, and behavioral skills, habits, and dispositions. Qualities of moral character can be cultivated and nurtured (or conversely, stunted and killed) over time in the course of living with others in various contexts (Cates, 1987; Jones, 1995). Many have argued that a person can be helped to grow in her or his religious faith or spiritual life through the cultivation of specific habits and practices such as prayer, contemplation, forgiveness, and service (e.g., Bonhoeffer, 1954). The question being asked by service-learning researchers and practitioners is how service-learning as a form of experiential learning that immerses students in what we might call "practicing the craft of Life," may contribute to students' spiritual/religious and ethical development.

Civic engagement has also been examined as an outcome of service-learning among college students (e.g., Vogelgesang & Astin, 2000; Guarasci, Cornwell, & Erlandson, 1997). A sustainable democracy depends upon the active engagement of an enlightened citizenry in the conduct of public affairs and service-learning may provide a particularly effective way of transmitting the sense of responsibility for civic engagement from one generation to the next. All social institutions including the family, the church, the school, and the immediate residential community are expected to play a role in the education of the young to prepare them for lives of responsible citizenship when they come of age.

John Dewey (1916) was one of the original strong exponents of the role educational institutions could and should play in the civic development of the young. In short, the perception of service-learning advocates is that normative values associated with civic engagement and democracy, learning, and meeting specific community needs converge and are mutually reinforced in the service-learning pedagogy (Guarasci et al., 1997). Based on the results from a comprehensive study of the effects of service-learning and community service on the cognitive and affective development of college undergraduates, Vogelgesang and Astin (2000) reported that neither growth in leadership ability nor involvement in leadership activities, such as student government or leadership training, were predicted more by involvement in service-learning than in generic service activities. Thus, the results of this study are not consistent for those items that pertain to personal attributes most closely associated with civic engagement. The authors offer two explanations for these findings: course-integrated service-learning focuses more on cognitive outcomes, and co-curricular leadership development programs are student-run and thereby offer students many leadership opportunities.

Finally, a set of outcomes that is too often overlooked consists of those that assess the impact of service-learning not on the student but on the community (Cruz & Giles, 2000). Service-learning is a response not only to the recognition that student education is in need of reform but also that many communities are in dire need of service, and that nonprofit agencies responsible for delivering many community services are often underfunded and understaffed. Students at all levels who are involved in service-learning often believe they are impacting the community in positive ways (Waterman, 1997). Students' beliefs about the positive impact they are making must be corroborated with other measures of impact; however, there is a lack of evidence documenting the effects of these programs on the community (Kraft, 1996).

The little research that has been done on community impact suggests that service-learning projects can be valuable to both the students and the community members because they learn from each other (Greene, 1998). Ferrari and Worrall (2000) found that the student supervisors of community-based organizations unanimously rated students as helpful and rated them positively on a number of service and work skills. When students get involved, potential benefits to the community are not only social but also economic (Driscoll, Holland, Gelmon, & Kerrigan, 1996). Further research on community impact needs to go beyond documenting that a positive impact has been made to understanding when service-learning will be most beneficial to the community (Kraft, 1996). Gelmon, Holland, Steifer, Shinnamon, and Connors (1998) examined the effects of service-learning on the community and concluded that the key to success in a service-learning program is that community partners need to be involved equally in the program.

While in aggregate, service-learning courses have the potential to enhance all of the outcomes discussed above, any given course will be focused on some of these outcomes more than others. As instructors plan the goals and objectives of their service-learning courses, they are either implicitly or explicitly asking themselves which of the above outcomes they are most interested in affecting. In addition, their choices about course structure and type of service-learning projects are often unwittingly focusing students on particular outcomes. Given that students do seem to experience a variety of outcomes from participating in service-learning activities even when they are not explicit goals of the course or its service-learning component, it seems likely that student growth in these areas could be deepened by more purposeful attention to the outcomes on the part of the faculty.

It is simplistic to believe that following general principles of good practice in service-learning will affect all outcomes equally. In reality, some of the practices that best enhance one outcome may do very little for another. Principles of good practice in service-learning that have been identified include the need for ongoing reflection in order to place the experiences into a broader context, a quality placement that engages students in responsible and challenging action, community engagement characterized by action that is in response to and meets the needs of the community, working with diverse populations that challenge students to take a more multicultural understanding of human differences, and student voice in the form of control and choice in their own learning (Mintz & Hesser, 1996).

Research in service-learning has tested many of the good practices identified to see whether they predict better outcomes (Eyler & Giles, 1999; Mabry, 1998). One of the predictors that has received attention is amount of reflection. Mabry found that written reflection and discussion predicted better self-reported academic outcomes among service-learning students. Eyler and Giles found that both reflection through discussion and reflection through writing predicted a number of self-reported cognitive and social/personal outcomes. Application as defined by Eyler and Giles is the active process of integrating classroom material with service experiences and can be viewed as another measure of reflection and processing. Eyler and Giles found application to be the strongest positive predictor of cognitive outcomes.

Quality of placement has also been researched as a predictor of better outcomes. Characteristics of high quality placement are that students are involved in responsible, productive work and that they are working in conjunction with practitioners in the field on challenging issues (Eyler & Giles, 1999). Eyler and Giles found that placement quality predicted higher levels of a variety of student cognitive as well as social/personal outcomes including that students learned more and grew spiritually.

The importance of community engagement has also been suggested by a number of research findings. One aspect of community engagement is the amount and quality of contact with community members. Mabry (1998) found that the number of service hours and amount of contact with beneficiaries predicted better academic outcomes among service-learning students. Another aspect of community engagement is community voice defined as whether the service project meets needs identified by representatives from the community (Eyler & Giles, 1999). Eyler and Giles found that community voice predicted some positive cognitive and social/personal outcomes, but also negatively predicted the cognitive outcome of students feeling intellectually challenged in service-learning.

There has been much recent interest in the relationship between the cultural diversity of service-learning placement and student outcomes related to community engagement. Cultural diversity has been defined by whether students work with people from diverse ethnic groups during their service-learning project, although clearly other kinds of diversity including religious and economic are also of interest to researchers (Eyler & Giles, 1999). Eyler and Giles' findings on cultural diversity showed some similarity to their findings on community engagement with cultural diversity predicting both positive and negative cognitive outcomes and positive personal/social outcomes. Specifically, cultural diversity was a negative predictor of student reports that they were intellectually challenged in service-learning, and that they understood and could apply the material. Cultural diversity predicted more positive social/personal outcomes including students' reports that they came to know themselves better and grew spiritually. Another issue regarding cultural diversity that is in need of further research is how the cultural background of the students impacts student outcomes (Chesler & Scalera, 2000).

Finally, another predictor that has generated attention recently is student voice. Student voice can be defined as student choice and control over service-learning placements or assignments and how the students carry out these assignments on site. Werner and McVaugh (2000) argue that these characteristics of student voice are crucial for engendering students' immediate commitment to service-learning and their long-term commitment to service in general. Although student control was one of the first principles generated by early service-learning leaders (Minz & Hesser, 1996), there is a lack of research on whether student voice predicts student outcomes. This research gap is particularly notable given the strong interest in mandatory service (e.g., Barber, 1994).

The present study was done to explore the relationships between each of the five predictors discussed above (reflection, placement quality, community engagement, diversity, and student voice) and each of the five outcomes discussed previously (cognitive learning, intellectual development, civic engagement, spiritual values, and community impact). Data from 12 service-learning courses each taught at a different private college in Iowa were used in the study. Quantitative analyses including regression analyses as well as qualitative analyses of narratives were used to understand these relationships.

METHOD

Twelve service-learning classes were assessed, each representing a different private, four-year, liberal arts institution. All courses were nominated by someone other than the instructor as being good candidates for the study, and all had to explicitly integrate service-learning experiences with course content to be a part of the study. Exhibit 1 shows a summary of the relevant characteristics of each course and service learning project. Service-learning projects included those in which students worked directly with the people being served (e.g., tutoring) to those in which students provided support to agencies serving the community (e.g., public relations, fundraising). Comparison courses that did not involve service-learning but were at the same level and in the same discipline as the service-learning courses were included in the original study, but this chapter will focus on predictors and outcomes of the service-learning students only.

EXHIBIT 1
Characteristics of Service-Learning Courses by College

College/ Discipline	n	Course in major? (mode)	Required course? (mode)	Number of SL weeks (range)	Hours of SL/week (range)	Notes
Buena Vista/Philosophy & Religion	14	No	No	3 to 4	>14	January Interim
Central/English	3	Yes	No	13 to >14	1 to 2	
Clarke/Social Work	5	Yes	No	7 to 14	3 to 12	
Coe/Elementary Education	16	Yes	Yes	7 to 8	3 to 4	
Cornell/Women's Studies	22	No	No	3 to 4	3 to 4	Block Course
Dordt/Physical Education	23	Yes	No	9 to 12	<1 to 2	
Grinnell/Sociology	6	Yes	No	13 to 14	13 to >14	Practicum
Loras/Honors	8	No	No	7 to 12	3 to 8	
Luther/Social Work	14	Yes	Yes	3 to 14	3 to 8	
Mt. Mercy/SL & Social Justice	7	No	No	1 to 2	>14	SL Done in Mexico
St. Ambrose/ Philosophy, Business, Psychology, Sociology, Communication	22	No	No	1 to 10	1 to 6	Modules
Wartburg/Communication	13	Yes	Yes	7 to 14	1 to 8	

Student data were collected via pre-test and post-test surveys. The pre-test assessed demographic information and self-report measures on most of the outcome variables. The post-test consisted of two parts. Part one assessed outcomes using closed-ended scales designed for this study; Part two assessed predictors using closed-ended scales that included items adapted from previous studies (Eyler & Giles, 1999; Steinke & Harrington, in press). All of the predictor measures and all of the outcome measures for the regression analyses, except intellectual development (described below), were created by identifying the items intended to assess each predictor and outcome, then comparing all of these potential items with one another to assure that they were positively correlated. The items that comprised each scale were all significantly positively correlated at the .01 level with the majority of the other items in the scale. The average of these items was used to create each measure. Exhibits 2 and 3 list the items that comprised the predictor and outcome measures in the order in which they were presented to the students. The predictor items were intermingled when presented whereas the outcome items were presented in separate blocks.

The second part of the post-test asked for students' open-ended responses to assess intellectual development and spiritual and ethical development outcomes. A qualitative narrative- and character-ethics approach was used to analyze the data on spiritual and ethical values as supported by the rich philosophical and theological literature on the interrelationships of narrative, moral agency, personhood, and community (e.g., Flanagan, 1991; MacIntyre, 1984; Taylor, 1989). Students were asked to discuss the important ways being involved in service-learning affected their spiritual and/or ethical development. [1] Their responses were examined for common themes.

Intellectual development was measured by Knefelkamp and Widick's *Measure of Intellectual Development* (MID) (as cited in Moore, n.d.), an open-ended essay-type instrument coded by trained raters based on Perry's scheme. The MID was administered at the end of the semester/block. The particular version of the MID used here asked students to write about their ideal learning environment. MID essays were scored independently by two trained raters who used a manual of prototypical statements or cues that reflected each Perry position and the transitions between positions. Essays were given a three-digit score that represented the rater's judgment of the dominant position and, if applicable, a transition between positions. For example, an essay that received a score of 223 indicated that the writer was reasoning primarily from position 2 (Dualism), but was in transition to position 3 (Early Multiplicity). An essay rated 233 indicated primarily position 3 with traces of position 2 reasoning. Each digit represented one-third of a stage. Thus, the two ratings in this example were in agreement within one-third of a stage. Inter-rater reliability was 76 percent for agreement within one-third of a stage, a figure which is somewhat lower than the 90% percent recommended in the instrument manual for the MID (Moore, n.d.). Exhibit 4 displays sample responses at each position from the present study.

EXHIBIT 2
Items in Each Predictor Scale

Reflection Items

Rated on 4-point scale (1 = very infrequently or never, 4 = very frequently)*

- Met with other students to discuss our projects.
- Discussed my project with faculty.
- Completed writing assignments about my project.
- Gave speeches or presentations about my project.
- Wrote about my project.
- Applied current course material to my project.
- Had direct contact with faculty while working on my project.
- Engaged in faculty-led class discussions about my project.
- Applied previous things I learned in college to my project.
- Faculty responded to my writing about the project.

Quality of Placement Items

Rated on 5-point scale (1 = strongly disagree, 5 = strongly agree)

- I had important responsibilities as part of this service-learning project.
- The tasks I did were challenging.
- I made important decisions as part of my project.
- I worked on a variety of tasks.
- Worked with professionals in the field to complete my project.*

Community Engagement Items

Rated on 5-point scale (1 = strongly disagree, 5 = strongly agree)

- I feel I made a real contribution.
- The project met needs identified by members of the community.
- I did not make a positive impact on the community. (reverse coded)
- Interacted with people in the community about my project.*

Diversity Items

Rated on 5-point scale (1 = strongly disagree, 5 = strongly agree)

- The people I served are like me. (reverse coded)
- I worked with people from diverse ethnic backgrounds.
- By the end of this project, I felt comfortable working with this community.
- Interacted with diverse people as part of my project.*

Student Voice Items

Rated on 5-point scale (1 = strongly disagree, 5 = strongly agree)

- I was forced into doing the project. (reverse coded)
- I was not free to develop or use my own ideas. (reverse coded)
- I had a great deal of choice about my project.
- I was very interested in doing this project.
- I wish I had been given more options about my service-learning project. (reverse coded)
- I felt uncomfortable working with faculty on this project. (reverse coded)

EXHIBIT 3
Items in Each Student Outcome Scale

Cognitive Learning Items
Rated on 5-point scale (1 = strongly
disagree, 5 = strongly agree)
In this course, course requirements that
went beyond participation in class and
assigned readings:

- helped me to make connections between the ideas and questions I encounter in different classes and/or fields of study.
- did not teach me how to apply things I learned in class to real problems. (reverse coded)
- did not greatly enhance my learning in the course beyond what I gain from reading the text and attending class. (reverse coded)
- helped me to spontaneously generate my own examples of principles and concepts I am learning about in class.
- helped me to see the complexity of real life problems and their solutions.
- did not provide me with a greater understanding of the social and ethical issues in that field.(reverse coded)
- did not enhance my understanding of the logic behind various perspectives about controversies in that field. (reverse coded)
- allowed me to gain a much deeper appreciation of the importance of things I am learning about in class.

Spiritual and Ethical Development Items
Rated on 5-point scale (1 = strongly
disagree, 5 = strongly agree)
- I am very involved in religious activities.
- It is more important to me personally to provide service than it is to be the recipient of service.
- I do not consider myself to be a spiritual person. (reverse coded)

- Religious faith is a private matter, and should not be expressed publicly. (reverse coded)
- Spiritual and ethical development have little to do with getting a college education. (reverse coded)
- My religious/spiritual faith and moral values are important to me as I make career planning decisions.
- College is about helping students to become leaders, and leaders are people who serve.
- Strengthening students' commitment to service should not be an educational goal of the college. (reverse coded)
- Service to others is an important expression of spirituality and religious faith.
- I will want the company or organization I work for someday to exhibit values like compassion and giving back to the community.
- Values of tolerance, compassion and forgiveness do not need to be promoted in the classroom.(reverse coded)
- One of the most important qualities of an effective leader is a commitment to serve others.
- My coursework has strengthened my commitment to service.
- It is not that important to me personally to volunteer my time to help people in need. (reverse coded)

Civic Engagement Items
Rated on 5-point scale (1 = strongly
disagree, 5 = strongly agree)
- Being actively involved in campus community issues or activities is important to me.
- What happens on campus generally is of no concern to me as an individual. (reverse coded)

(continued)

EXHIBIT 3
Continued

Civic Engagement Items
Rated on 5-point scale (1 = strongly disagree, 5 = strongly agree)

- If you were to ask my friends, they would say I was concerned about my community.
- I rarely spend time thinking and discussing with others what might be done to make our campus better for everyone. (reverse coded)
- If our community had a natural disaster I would prefer not to be involved in the clean-up. (reverse coded)
- Working with others to define a common goal and achieve it is important.
- I don't spend much time with people outside my immediate circle of friends. (reverse coded)
- Involvement in campus or community activities is time that could be better spent meeting my personal goals and objectives. (reverse coded)
- I came here to study and any other demands on my time are not well spent. (reverse coded)
- Helping others without being paid is important.
- I enjoy learning about the political issues and debates in Washington.
- The prospect of serving in student government on my campus does not interest me. (reverse coded)
- I plan to vote in the presidential election next fall.
- I would like the experience of working in a political campaign.
- I don't really care to get involved in the governance of a campus organization. (reverse coded)
- My friends and I frequently discuss campus, local, or national political issues.

Community impact was assessed by a separate survey of community agency representatives involved in the project. Questions assessed: the days and times the participants received student help and the days and times the organizations needed the most student help; student characteristics such as reliability, friendliness, professionalism, creativity, and approachability; and the community impact of the service-learning project. The six five-point Likert scale items that measured community impact were as follows: met a community need, was helpful to community, had a negative impact on the community (reverse scored), was a success, was ineffective (reverse scored), and benefits are ongoing. All six of these items were positively correlated, the majority at the .01 level, so they were combined into one community impact score. Open-ended questions about the positive and negative effects of student service projects on the community were also included.

EXHIBIT 4
Sample Essays To Illustrate Intellectual Development
Positions Measured by the MID

Instructions: Please answer the questions below about your ideal learning environment. Again, there are no right and wrong answers. What is important is the way you think about learning. Please be as specific and complete in your answer as possible. Feel free to use the back of the page if needed.

If you were to design a course that would embody the best learning environment for you, what would it look like? What types of assignments would be given? How would your performance be evaluated? What types of demands would the course include? What would the professors be like? What would the class "atmosphere" be like? What would be your role as a student in the course?

(© Knefelkamp & Widick; available from Moore (n.d.) at CSID)

Reconciled ratings are given in ( ) after each essay.

Dualism & Transition 2/3
- "I like a structured learning environment for most things related to my major, with lectures, objective tests and assignments, etc. I like to be taught what I need to know and learn it on my own by reinforcement through assignments. Demands do not include papers or long-term projects. The professors would stick to the information that needs to be learned and then allow students to ask other questions as needed." (223)
- "I need a course which provides me with a lecture-type situation. After gaining all facts from the teacher, I would like to be given an assignment with which I can apply the information to my own life/understanding. Peer interaction and other resources should be allowed to be used. Performance should still be evaluated on test and project quality—If a student truly understands what they've learned, applying to test should not be difficult. Professors would demand respect but be open to suggestions. Classroom would be orderly, but friendly for interaction b/w teacher and students. As a student, I would learn from the authority, while being allowed to ask questions and gaining ideas." (233)

Early Multiplicity (Position 3)
- "A course that would be the best learning environment for me would be one that has a lot of discussion as well as application. We wouldn't sit and take notes, but instead be active in our learning. Assignments would be based on what we've discussed and practice, and wouldn't be 'busy work' but authentic, practical things we'd need to do in a real life career. Performance would be evaluated on our participation, effort and how we did on our assignments. The professors would have tons of experience and be able to share stories that would help us be better at our chosen careers. The class atmosphere would be supportive and comfortable. My role as a student would be to participate and get involved." (333)

(continued)

EXHIBIT 4
Continued

Transition 3/4
- "The ideal learning environment would include readings, lectures, videos, and open discussion. There would be structure in what topics were covered, but not how the conversation progresses. Assignments could include worksheets, thought paper responses, short presentations, and one research paper of the student's choosing. Performance could be evaluated by tests, participation, and other assignments. I wouldn't want any group projects though, because work is never done equally. The professor would be concerned about student learning and progress, but also demanding and very informative. Although they should provide the base knowledge and information, they should also leave some learning and info searching to the students. My role as a student would be to show up, participate, and learn outside of the direct contact in class." (334)
- "There would be little group work -- I'm an independent learner. There would be times, however, for lecture/discussion. I find I learn a lot about the ideas of my peers. The independence would come mostly in projects. I like to have control over my work. I would like reading and discussion assignments, assigning each student to a topic to discuss for the day. Occasionally there would be projects to show application of classroom ideas. I would prefer project assessments over tests. Professor would be open to explaining the students' ideas. All ideas would be accepted by peers yet challenged. Critical thinking would be encouraged." (344)

Late Multiplicity (Position 4)
- "Learning environments should work both ways, with both teacher and students asking questions. Being fed information only works for so long. Actively engaging your mind by being asked to think a problem through on your own, or other methods of teaching accomplish more for the student and make learning more interesting. Assignments could be anything. Papers work nice for working ideas through and showing a grasp of the material, as well as presentations. Reading assignments to get the actual info. Performance would be evaluated by effort, which is a little tricky though. Effort is relative to how much a person is capable of giving, although we're usually capable of giving more than we do. I think some indication of grasp of knowledge is an important evaluation. The atmosphere would be one where ideas can be exchanged freely, with lots of discussion. Although grades matter, trying to get students to not worry about them and focus on learning would probably (hopefully) relieve some of the grade anxiety and make students more interested in the ideas." (444, glimpse 5)

Contextual Relativism & Transition 4/5
- Assignments: Independent, investigative study into the fields of service that you are interested in. Pros and cons of different areas of service. Keep a journal, include news articles or any pertinent research on subject being studied. Evaluation: Did the study inspire the student to broaden their focus? Does journal contain pertinent information about the subject being investigated? Demands: The student should be creative and innovative in their assignments. Presentation of completed assignments. Professors: They would be available to help guide the student, give constructive criticism and offer suggestions, and share their expertise on the subject being studied. Class Atmosphere: Enthusiastic, sharing, and lots of questions. Role as Student: To complete tasks assigned and never stop being curious and wanting to learn more." (455)

RESULTS

Regression Analyses

Multiple regression analyses were computed to explain how changes in the cognitive learning, intellectual development, spiritual and ethical development, and civic engagement outcomes could be explained by the following characteristics of the service-learning projects: reflection, quality of placement, community engagement, diversity, and student voice. All characteristics were entered simultaneously allowing these authors to assess the expected change in each of the outcomes as predicted by each of the characteristics controlling for all the other characteristics. The overall regression equations were significant in predicting cognitive learning [R Square $= .28$, $F(5,99) = 7.68$, $p < .001$], spiritual and ethical development [R Square $= .22$, $F(5,96) = 5.27$, $p < .001$], and civic engagement [R Square $= .13$, $F(5,91) = 2.70$, $p < .03$], but not intellectual development [R Square $= .09$, $F(5,89) = 1.65$, $p = .16$].

Reflection ($b = .19$, $t = 1.96$, $p = .05$) and student voice ($b = .26$, $t = 2.48$, $p = .02$) were both positive predictors of cognitive outcomes. Community engagement was a near significant positive predictor ($b = .26$, $t = 1.88$, $p = .06$) of intellectual development. Reflection was a near significant positive predictor ($b = .20$, $t = 1.93$, $p = .06$) and diversity was a significant negative predictor ($b = -.44$, $t = -4.69$, $p < .001$) of spiritual and ethical development. Diversity was a significant negative predictor ($b = -24$, $t = -2.33$, $p = .02$) and student voice was a significant positive predictor ($b = .28$, $t = 2.32$, $p = .02$) of civic engagement.

Correlations

Correlations were computed between the items in each of the predictor scales and the outcome scores to get a better idea of the relationship between different aspects of each main predictor and each outcome. The patterns of individual correlations shed light on which aspects of each predictor are contributing to each outcome. Exhibit 5 presents a complete listing of these correlation coefficients.

As suggested by the regression analyses, the correlations between items on the reflection scale and student outcomes were strongest for cognitive learning outcomes followed by spiritual and ethical development outcomes. Although the overall reflection scale was not a significant predictor of either civic engagement or intellectual development, individual items were positively correlated with these two outcome measures. Application of course material, both past and present, showed the strongest correlations across outcomes. The correlations between items on the quality of placement scale and student outcomes revealed that the only significant correlations were with the cognitive learning measure. The correlations between individual items on the community engagement scale and student outcomes revealed that the only outcome not correlated with at least one community engagement item was spiritual and ethical development. Interacting with people in the community about the project showed the strongest relationships across outcomes. The correlations between individual items on the diversity scale and student outcomes revealed that three items were significantly negatively correlated with spiritual and ethical development. The only item that did not show this relationship was the item assessing how comfortable students felt with the community by the end of the project which was positively correlated with both cognitive learning and intellectual development. The correlations between individual items on the student voice scale and student outcomes revealed that five items were significantly positively correlated with cognitive learning and two were significantly positively correlated with civic engagement. No significant correlations were found between student voice and intellectual development or spiritual and ethical development.

EXHIBIT 5
Correlations Between Items on Predictor Scales and Student
Outcome Measure

Predictor Scales	Cognitive Learning *r(110)*	Intellectual Development *r(100)*	Spiritual/ Ethical Development *r(107)*	Civic Development *r(101)*
Reflection				
Met with other students	.34**	.02	-.02	.07
Discussed project with faculty	.29**	.08	.15	.17
Completed writing assignments	.19*	.16	.08	-.02
Gave speeches or presentations	.19	.26**	.08	.19
Wrote about project	.18	.06	.01	-.02
Applied current course material	.28**	-.02	.20*	.07
Had direct contact with faculty	.16	.04	.11	.05
Had faculty-led class discussions	.14	.10	.22*	.09
Applied previous things	.26**	.01	.22*	.23*
Faculty responded to writing	.17	.24*	-.01	-.01

(continued)

EXHIBIT 5
Continued

Predictor Scales	Cognitive Learning r(110)	Intellectual Development r(100)	Spiritual/ Ethical Development r(107)	Civic Development r(101)
Quality of Placement				
Had important responsibilities	.26**	-.02	.11	-.04
Tasks were challenging	.33**	.06	.07	.11
Made important decisions	.23*	.02	-.14	-.16
Variety of tasks	.19	-.02	-.10	.04
Worked with professionals	.35**	.05	-.02	.18
Community Engagement				
Made a real contribution	.25**	.03	-.01	.07
Project met community needs	.22*	.22*	.15	.05
Did not make a positive impact[a]	.23*	-.01	.04	.11
Interacted with people in community	.28**	.27**	.15	.26*
Cultural Diversity				
People were like me[a]	-.04	.12	-.24*	-.14
People ethnically diverse	.01	.10	-.34**	-.15
By end felt comfortable	.28**	.30**	.02	-.03
Interacted with diverse people	.13	.06	-.33**	-.03
Student Voice				
Forced into doing the project[a]	.27**	.09	-.01	.22*
Not free to develop my own ideas[a]	.23*	-.00	.05	.15
Had a great deal of choice	.23*	-.05	-.03	-.00
Very interested in doing this project	.42**	.08	.17	.19
Wish I had been given more options[a]	.31**	.02	.07	.20*
Felt uncomfortable with faculty[a]	.13	.01	.04	.14

[a] reverse coded   * p < .05   ** p < .01

Narratives: Spiritual and Ethical Development

A number of themes emerged in student responses to the open-ended post-test question, "Please discuss the important ways in which being involved in service learning this semester has affected your spiritual and/or ethical development." Below is a brief summary of the five themes identified that are most relevant to the other analyses in this paper.

No Effect

Several respondents noted that their prior spiritual and ethical attitudes and beliefs remained unchanged by the experience. "Being involved with service-learning this semester has made almost zero impact on my spiritual and ethical development," wrote one student. Some elaborated on their claim that there was no spiritual or ethical effect by describing themselves as people for whom there could be none because of the kind of persons they take themselves to be, as in this case: "I do not consider myself a very religious person, and therefore this project did not influence my spirituality."

Enhanced Connectedness With the Community

Several respondents gave voice to an understanding of human beings as fundamentally connected to one another in the tapestry or web of community and social relations. Such an understanding of what it means to be human is itself a dimension of moral character and thus is often shaped by one's spirituality or religious faith (e.g., Gustafson, 1975). "We all have a much higher responsibility to serve our community," wrote one student, "I always thought individual works were the most important, however every individual is a part of the community. Not only do we have the ethical responsibility to clients and disadvantaged groups, but also to the community."

Affirmation of the Importance of Diversity

Many students reported being exposed to people with whom they had never before had contact, and coming to see them as valuable and deserving of the same respect and love as all God's children. "I have realized again how important each person in the world is. Each of us is loved by God." Another wrote: "The principle that was really made more obvious to me is that we cannot judge others—our job is to love unconditionally. I already knew that, but this project really supported that idea."

Awareness of One's Own Privileged Position

There was a sense in the reflections of several students surveyed that the helping response evoked by the needs of others often flows from a position of relative abundance and privilege, and from a sense of gratitude. Service-learning can help students to recognize, appreciate, and act on the gifts they have (and may otherwise take for granted), including the opportunity to be in college in the first place and the chance to contribute to the common good because they "have the resources to help or understand those around [them]." Echoing this, another respondent said: "Reaching out and helping people is important. It makes you realize the things you have. You feel more respect for yourself and others. This has improved my spiritual development. I felt like I was making a contribution to the world."

Deeper Understanding of the Intrinsic Reward of Service

This sense of service as an empowering and uplifting experience, for others and for oneself, was reflected in the several responses that spoke of the intrinsically gratifying feelings that service generates, feelings that often translated into a desire or commitment to continue to engage in service after the course's end. "Being involved made me feel good about what I was doing," wrote one respondent. "It was nice to be doing something for someone rather than for money or a company. Now that I know about the service-leadership aspect, I plan to use it in the future."

Community Impact Analyses

The five-point Likert scale items that measured community impact were all rated positively. The means and standard deviations of each of the items were as follows: met a community need ($M = 4.31$, $SD = .79$), was helpful to community ($M = 4.35$, $SD = .80$), had a negative impact on the community (reverse scored, $M = 4.62$, $SD = .74$), was a success ($M = 4.12$, $SD = .96$), was ineffective (reverse scored $M = 4.22$, $SD = .95$), and benefits are ongoing ($M = 3.89$, $SD = .90$).

Exhibit 6 presents the Pearson correlation results of the student characteristics and the combined community impact score. The student characteristic showing the highest correlation with community impact was student creativity, followed by efficiency, helpfulness, and enthusiasm. The only student characteristic that did not correlate significantly with community impact was friendliness. Likert items measuring quality of communication and project organization did not significantly correlate with community impact. Community impact was significantly positively correlated with hours desired by agency, $r(55) = .35$, $p < .01$, hours students worked, $r(54) = .39$, $p < .01$; with days desired by agency, $r(54) = .32$, $p = .02$, and near significantly correlated with days students worked, $r(50) = .27$, $p = .06$.

EXHIBIT 6
Correlations Between Student Characteristics
and Community Impact Score

Characteristics	r (50)	p
Creativity	.62	< .001
Efficiency	.58	< .001
Helpfulness	.57	< .001
Enthusiasm	.54	< .001
Approachability	.50	< .001
Reliability	.48	< .001
Knowledge	.46	< .001
Professionalism	.44	< .001
Interest in project	.42	< .01
Organization	.35	< .01
Friendliness	.16	= .22

DISCUSSION

Reflection

The regression analysis on cognitive learning suggests that instructor focus on reflection, application, and feedback activities can help students to better appropriate and process information and concepts. This is consistent with previous findings (Eyler & Giles, 1999; Mabry, 1998), yet leaves open the question of what specific reflection techniques will best enhance cognitive outcomes (Eyler, 2000). An examination of the pattern of correlations shows that meeting with other students and with faculty to discuss the project was most strongly related to cognitive outcomes followed by application of current and previous course material, writing, and giving speeches about the project. The strength of the correlations with application and discussion are consistent with the recommendations of cognitive scientists about how to improve learning. Application involves comparing the new cases generated by the service-learning experience with old cases learned in other contexts, and discussion allows for students to get feedback as they work to differentiate the cases (Schank & Joseph, 1998; Schwartz & Bransford, 1998). Application can also be viewed as the ability to transfer knowledge to new contexts which is a key component of expertise (Bransford, Brown, Cocking, Donovan, & Pellegrino, 2000) that has particular relevance as a cognitive outcome of service-learning (Steinke & Buresh, 2002).

The regression analyses did not support the claim that reflection activities are related to greater intellectual development. However, the individual correlations suggest that reflection activities that encourage students to take on multiple perspectives are related to greater intellectual development. Both giving speeches and faculty responding to writing were positively correlated with intellectual development. Giving speeches entails preparing for an audience, and faculty responding to writing often provides students with an alternative, valid interpretation of students' experiences. Intellectual development is encouraged by more openness to alternative perspectives and more complex ways of reasoning about course content, social issues, and beliefs.

The positive role of reflection in students' spiritual and ethical development was supported by regression analyses. Moreover, the impact of service-learning on students' religious and ethical development was more readily acknowledged and better articulated by those who were encouraged to do so as part of the critical reflection process. The prompt of the open-ended question seemed to encourage reflection and help students identify a variety of ways in which their service-learning experiences applied to their spiritual and ethical development, some of which were not represented in any of the closed-ended measures (e.g., awareness of privileged position, understanding of the intrinsic reward of service). An examination of the correlations supports previous findings on the importance of application to positive social/personal outcomes (Eyler & Giles, 1999). In addition, the positive relationship between faculty-led discussions about the project and spiritual and ethical development highlights the importance of faculty guidance in the reflection process.

Evidence that reflection aided in civic engagement was less clear. The regression analysis did not indicate that reflection was a significant predictor, and the only positive correlation was with application of previous things in college. One explanation for this is that the type of civic engagement measured here was primarily political involvement so may not have adequately assessed other aspects of civic engagement such as concern about community issues. In support of this explanation, some of the outcomes identified in students' reflective answers to the spiritual and ethical development question were representative of a broader definition of civic engagement (e.g., responsibility to serve the community, desire to continue to engage in community service).

The community impact findings suggest mixed results on the importance of reflection to the success of the project. The two highest correlations between student characteristics and community impact were creativity and efficiency. The importance of creativity suggests that the ability to reflect upon current situations or problems and be able to place them in new contexts or perspectives was perceived by community agency representatives as beneficial. However, the importance of efficiency suggests too much time spent on reflection activities was not perceived as beneficial.

Quality of Placement

In contrast to previous research (Eyler & Giles, 1999), the overall regression analyses revealed that quality of placement (i.e., level of challenge and responsibility) did not predict better outcomes. One interpretation of this finding is that because all courses were academic service-learning courses in which the coursework was fully integrated with the service-learning experience, as long as the instructor knew that the experience was one that was very much related to the course goals, what the students were doing during that experience was less important than the instructor's ability to help students process that experience in line with desired outcomes.

The correlations did reveal significant positive relationships between the individual items that made up the quality of placement scale and cognitive learning. These findings are more consistent with past service-learning research (e.g., Eyler & Giles, 1999) and with recent work in the cognitive sciences. According to Schank, Berman, and Macpherson (1999) student expectations must fail in order for learning to take place. In a challenging service-learning assignment with a lot of responsibility, students will be constantly asked to generate expectations for the outcomes of their actions and these expectations will necessarily fail on occasion. The importance of challenge along with the feedback provided by the course instructor suggests service-learning can provide an ideal learning environment for students.

Although the quantitative analyses did not support a relationship between quality of placement and spiritual and ethical development, the narratives did suggest that the service needed to be meaningful and substantive for the students. One possible reason for the discrepancy between the narratives and the quantitative analyses is that a number of students reported that they did not feel that their service-learning experiences impacted their spiritual and ethical development. Therefore, the other themes that emerged were necessary only from the subset of students who did feel impacted.

The positive correlations between student knowledge and professionalism and community impact suggest that student placement in responsible positions was perceived by community representatives as contributing to the success of the project.

Community Engagement

Results from regression analyses revealed that intellectual development was predicted by active engagement with members of the community in ways that met community needs. Because service-learning can allow students to gain a new understanding and sense of connection with the perspective of a broader community, outcome goals related to equipping students to be more critical thinkers in understanding pressing social needs will be enhanced by increased community engagement. Civic engagement and spiritual and ethical development were not predicted by community engagement perhaps in part because these outcomes will only be affected to the degree that these goals are consistent with connecting students to the broader community.

Although the regression did not find community engagement to be a significant predictor of cognitive learning, the positive correlations between items on the community engagement scale and cognitive learning highlight the importance of meaningful goals to the learning process. Meaningful learning goals that students care about and that are connected to real life are crucial for student learning (Bransford et al., 2000; Schank & Joseph, 1998). These goals can be provided by interesting and engaging service-learning projects.

The two positive correlations with intellectual development were: the project met needs that were identified by members of the community, and students interacted with people in the community about the project. Both of these items are related to students encountering multiple, alternative perspectives about their project, a key characteristic of intellectual development. The feeling that students made a contribution or positive impact is not as relevant to the perspective taking that characterizes intellectual development.

The one positive correlation found with civic engagement was interacting with people in the community about the project suggesting the importance of first-hand interactions or experiences to civic engagement. Knowing second-hand about the needs of and impact on the community does not necessarily lead students to the belief that they should be more involved.

Although the quantitative analyses did not support a relationship between community engagement and spiritual and ethical development, an analysis of the narratives did identify an enhanced sense of connectedness with the larger community as a clear theme. These responses suggest that students were at least becoming aware that having a positive impact on the community and meeting the needs of the community could in some circumstances enhance their spiritual and ethical development.

Consistent with Kraft's (1996) claims, amount of time spent working with community agencies measured in hours and days showed positive relationships with community impact. Interestingly, amount of time desired by agencies as measured in hours and days also showed positive relationships with community impact. Perhaps community agencies that need more help are able to see more community benefits from any amount of help they receive.

Diversity

In contrast to previous research (e.g., Eyler & Giles, 1999), the regression analyses revealed diversity was a negative predictor of civic engagement and spiritual/ethical values and was not a predictor of cognitive learning or intellectual development. One problem with the measure used here was that it was not varied enough to get at all aspects of diversity of placement.

The correlations showed that the one item of feeling comfortable with the community by the end of the project was positively correlated with cognitive learning and intellectual development suggesting that the cognitive and affective processes involved in students working through their initial discomfort and confronting previously unchallenged expectations can enhance academic learning and critical thinking. Just being introduced to diversity without working through these initial feelings and assumptions, however, seems, at best, to have no effect as in the case of cognitive learning and intellectual development, or at worst, be harmful as in the case of spiritual and ethical development and civic engagement. Indeed, as Stukas, Clary, and Snyder (1999) cogently describe in their literature review, "multicultural" service-learning experiences may actually reinforce stereotypes if students are not prepared adequately for working with a community and if community members are not empowered in the process. This is clearly a potential problem with the current sample as only one-third of the projects explicitly focused on diversity.

Boyle-Baise and Efiom (2000) also acknowledge the critique of using service-learning as a pedagogical tool in multicultural education, noting the possibility that "service starts in privilege and ends in patronage" (p. 209). They note that there is limited research on the effects of service-learning on multicultural education, but what exists suggests that it has the potential to positively impact awareness and acceptance of cultural diversity and the examination of prejudicial and stereotypical beliefs. Their report of a qualitative study of 24 preservice teachers reveals the complexity of helping students process and learn from experiences with service-learning in multicultural settings. Much depended upon the students' readiness to learn. While many white preservice teachers' reflections evidenced deficit views of children and families in these communities, others' reflections demonstrated greater self-awareness of privilege and explicitly dealt with issues of equality. The authors emphasized the critical role of instructor-guided reflection and class activities, which is consistent with the present findings and recommendations.

In contrast to the quantitative findings, strong support for the importance of encountering cultural diversity in service-learning experiences was found in students' narratives about how service-learning had affected their spiritual and ethical development. Students reported that working with diverse others led them to a new understanding of unconditional love and respect for all God's people. Perhaps the students who were able to reflect upon the impact of cultural diversity were those students who had worked through their initial feelings of discomfort, which is why the comfort item was not negatively correlated with spiritual and ethical development.

None of the student characteristics that were studied in the community impact survey addressed cultural diversity which suggests an area for future research.

Student Voice

Regression analyses revealed that students' perceptions of choice predicted more positive cognitive and civic engagement outcomes. Giving students a voice in their service-learning assignments can increase students' perceptions that they had a choice, which can increase motivation for the service-learning project.

The strongest correlations between the individual items of student voice and outcome measures were with cognitive learning, and the strongest relationship was between cognitive learning and student interest in the project. These findings are consistent with a goal-based approach that focuses on students' desire to pursue intrinsically meaningful goals as a crucial element of the learning process (Schank, 1994) and with current research on how people learn (Bransford et al., 2000).

The pattern of correlations with civic engagement showed positive relationships with items assessing students' perception of control over initial choices given by faculty about engaging in the service-learning project but not with items assessing students' perception of control over choices given by site supervisors about how the project was done once the student was involved. Perhaps due to the importance of individual values and beliefs to civic engagement, service-learning students must feel that the type of engagement they are involved in is one that they do value and have chosen freely.

Consistent with quantitative analyses, no connection between student voice and spiritual and ethical development was identified by students in the narratives.

In the area of community impact, student creativity, efficiency, helpfulness, and enthusiasm correlated most strongly with community impact suggesting that instructors' efforts to match student strengths and interests with the needs of the community can positively affect community outcomes.

CONCLUSION

Through its interdisciplinary approach, this research project sought to link work grounded in theoretical, conceptual, and empirical research on service-learning (e.g., Eyler & Giles, 1999; Mabry, 1998; Mintz & Hesser, 1996; Vogelgesang & Astin, 2000), while relying on discipline specific literature in understanding the outcomes. For example, work in cognitive science (e.g., Bransford et al., 1999; Schank, 1994) was used to interpret the cognitive learning findings; the section on intellectual development was grounded in Perry's (1968/1999) scheme of intellectual and ethical development in college students; and the section on spiritual and ethical values cited Dietrich Bonhoffer's (1954) Life Together as an important example of the intersection between classic spiritual disciplines and the life of active, socially engaged faith.

The results of this interdisciplinary approach revealed that the best practices for service-learning cannot be universally applied to all outcomes. While some predictors such as reflection were positively related to all outcomes, even in this case the specific type of reflection activities recommended by these findings varied by outcome. Furthermore, the results suggested that some predictors such as quality or challenge of placement may enhance some outcomes such as cognitive learning while doing nothing for other outcomes. Finally, some predictors such as cultural diversity can in some circumstances negatively impact outcomes such as spiritual and ethical development. Specific desired outcomes will necessarily suggest different best practices. Researchers need to be clear about the types of outcomes their research addresses and practitioners need to be clear about the outcome goals they have for their students when planning their service-learning courses. Interestingly, the one consistently positive predictor across outcomes was interacting with people in the community, which highlights the importance of getting students out of the classroom in order to meet the varied goals of educational institutions.

The results also provide support for the importance of researchers distinguishing between different types of related but not identical outcomes. For example, cognitive learning and intellectual development outcomes are both concerned with students' cognitive skills but assess different cognitive processes. Similarly, intellectual development and spiritual and ethical development are both related to moral development but are not identical. Distinguishing types of outcomes is also of interest to teaching faculty. For those faculty who feel their student learning goals need not go beyond academic or cognitive learning outcomes, the results are particularly encouraging because cognitive outcomes showed the most positive relationships with all types of predictors, suggesting that instructors who increase the quality of their service-learning efforts will most impact student learning.

This interdisciplinary approach also has implications for methodology. For the most part, quantitative methods were used, but in the case of spiritual and ethical development, it seemed impossible to capture the important data without also relying on narratives. In some cases the differences between the quantitative and qualitative results for this outcome suggested ways in which these two data sources might inform each other and provide a more complex understanding of how service-learning affects outcomes. Rather than supporting either a strictly quantitative (Bringle & Hatcher, 2000) or a strictly qualitative (Shumer, 2000) approach as a model for service-learning methodology, the current project supports a combined approach. Unfortunately, the data did not allow qualitative analyses for each outcome but the results from spiritual and ethical development suggest that this dual approach would be recommended for future studies. Better efforts at integrating quantitative and qualitative methods will also help to ensure the contextual validity of the quantitative findings. A truly interdisciplinary approach needs to go beyond the use of interdisciplinary methods and interpretations of outcomes to how the particular qualitative context of each course discipline studied is brought to bear on the quantitative findings. Another area where an understanding of context is crucial is in the area of cultural diversity and community impact, an area lacking in research.

A number of directions for future research identified by previous researchers as contemporary topics for service-learning research are encouraged by the findings presented here. The findings from the present study add to each of these areas but also support the claim that there is a need for more research. Clearly student voice is an area that needs to be given more research attention in relationship to all types of outcomes (Werner & McVaugh, 2000). In addition, the relationship between cultural diversity and different outcomes needs further attention (Chesler & Scalera, 2000). Identifying the types of reflection that encourage positive outcomes is another important research objective (Eyler, 2000). More attention also needs to be given to how the predictors used here are directly related to community impact (Cruz & Giles, 2000).

Finally, this project suggests some more specific recommendations about how to improve research on service-learning outcomes. The predictor and outcome scales used here were in large part designed for this study. Further work is needed to test and refine scales for measuring different types of predictors and outcomes of interest to service-learning researchers so that the same measures can be compared across studies. Additional predictor measures needed that were not part of the current study include scales assessing prior commitment to service and initial motivation for the course (Steinke & Harrington, in press). In regards to the open-ended measures, further work is needed to develop useful protocols and coding schemes for each type of outcome of interest to researchers. Ideally, each outcome should be assessed by both closed-ended and open-ended measures. For example, Steinke and Harrington found a closed-ended self-report measure of cognitive learning to be highly correlated with amount of knowledge shared with instructor, a cognitive learning measure based on student responses to an open-ended problem-solving protocol. Stronger measures will help in furthering the validity and reliability of findings on the relationship between service-learning predictors and outcomes within and across disciplines.

NOTE

1. The definition of "spiritual" or "ethical" was left up to the individual student.

Acknowledgments: We thank Central College Students Abby McCrae and Andrea Williams for their invaluable assistance with the community impact piece of this research project. The research presented in this paper was supported by a Faculty Development and Enrichment grant from the Iowa College Foundation and Carver Trust Fund.

REFERENCES

Barber, B. R. (1994). A proposal for mandatory citizen education and community service. *Michigan Journal of Community Service Learning, 1,* 86-93.

Bonhoeffer, D. (1954). *Life together.* New York: Harper & Row.

Boss, J. (1994). The effect of community service work on the moral development of college ethics students. *Journal of Moral Education, 23*(2), 183-198.

Boyle-Baise, M., & Efiom, P. (2000). The construction of meaning: Learning from service learning. In C. R. O'Grady (Ed.), *Integrating service learning and multicultural education in colleges and universities.* Mahwah, NJ: Lawrence Erlbaum.

Bransford, J. D., Brown, A. L., Cocking, R. R., Donovan, M. S., Pellegrino, J. W. (Eds.). (2000). *How people learn: Brain, mind, experience, and school.* (Expanded ed.). Washington, DC: National Academy Press.

Bringle, R. G., & Hatcher, J. A. (2000). Meaningful measurement of theory-based service-learning outcomes: Making the case with quantitative research. *Michigan Journal of Community Service Learning*, (Special Issue 2000), 68-75.

Cates, D. F. (1987). *Choosing to feel: Virtue, friendship, and compassion for friends.* South Bend, IN: University of Notre Dame Press.

Chesler, M., & Scalera, C. V. (2000). Race and gender issues related to service-learning research. *Michigan Journal of Community Service Learning*, (Special Issue 2000), 18-27.

Cruz, N. I., & Giles, D. E., Jr. (2000). Where's the community in service-learning research? *Michigan Journal of Community Service Learning*, (Special Issue 2000), 28-34.

Delve, C. I., Mintz, S. D., & Stewart, G. M. (Eds.). (1990). *New directions for student services: Vol. 50. Community service as values education.* San Francisco: Jossey-Bass.

Dewey, J. (1916). Democracy and education. New York: MacMillan.

Driscoll, A., Holland, B., Gelmon, S., & Kerrigan, S. (1996). An assessment model for service-learning: Comprehensive case studies of impact on faculty, students, community, and institution. *Michigan Journal of Community Service Learning, 3,* 66-71.

Eyler, J. S. (2000). What do we most need to know about the impact of service-learning on student learning? *Michigan Journal of Community Service Learning*, (Special Issue 2000), 11-17.

Eyler, J., & Giles, D. (1999). *Where's the learning in service-learning?* San Francisco: Jossey-Bass.

Ferrari, J. R., & Worrall, L. (2000). Assessments by community agencies: How "the other side" sees service-learning. *Michigan Journal of Community Service Learning, 7,* 35-40.

Flanagan, O. (1991). *Varieties of moral personality: Ethics and psychological realism.* Cambridge, MA: Harvard University Press.

Gelmon, S. B., Holland, B. A., Seifer, S. D., Shinnamon, A., & Connors, K. (1998). Community-university partnerships for mutual learning. *Michigan Journal of Community Service Learning, 5,* 97-107.

Gorman, M. and Others. (1994). Service experience and the moral development of college students. *Religious Education, 89*(3), 422-31.

Greene, D. (1998). Reciprocity in two conditions of service-learning. *Educational Gerontology, 24,* 411-424.

Guarasci, R., Cornwell, G., & Erlandson, G. (1997). Democratic education in an age of difference: Redefining citizenship in higher education. San Francisco: Jossey-Bass.

Gustafson, J. M. (1975). *Can ethics be Christian?* Chicago: University of Chicago Press.

Jones, L. G. (1995). *Embodying forgiveness: A theological analysis.* Grand Rapids, MI: William B. Eerdmanns.

Kendrick, J. (1996). Outcomes of service-learning in an introduction to sociology course. *Michigan Journal of Community Service Learning, 3,* 72-81.

King, P. M., & Kitchener, K. S. (1994). Developing reflective judgment: Understanding and promoting intellectual growth and critical thinking in adolescents and adults. San Francisco: Jossey-Bass.

Kraft, R. (1996). Service learning: An introduction to its theory, practice, and effects. *Education and Urban Society, 28,* 131-160.

Mabry, J. B. (1998). Pedagogical variations in service-learning and student out-comes. How time contact, and reflection matter. *Michigan Journal of Community Service Learning, 5,* 32-47.

MacIntyre, A. (1984). *After virtue.* (2nd ed.). South Bend, IN: University of Notre Dame Press.

Markus, G., Howard, J., & King, D. (1993). Integrating community service and classroom instruction enhances learning: Results from an experiment. *Educational Evaluation and Policy Analysis, 15*(4), 410-419.

McEwen, M. K. (1996). Enhancing student learning and development through service-learning. In B. Jacoby & Associates (Eds.), *Service-learning in higher education* (pp. 53-91). San Francisco: Jossey-Bass.

Miller, J. (1994). Linking traditional and service-learning courses: Outcome evaluations utilizing two pedagogically distinct models. *Michigan Journal of Community Service Learning, 1,* 29-36.

Mintz, S. D. & Hesser, G. W. (1996). Principles of good practice in service-learning. In B. Jacoby & Associates (Eds.), *Service-learning in higher education: Concepts and practices.* San Francisco: Jossey-Bass.

Moore, W. S. (n.d.). *The measure of intellectual development: An instrument manual.* Olympia, WA: Center for the Study of Intellectual Development. Available from the author at CSID, 1505 Farwell Ct. NW, Olympia, WA 98502 (wsmoore51@attbi.com)

Osborne, R. E., Hammerich, S., & Hensley, C. (1998). Student effects of service-learning: Tracking change across a semester. *Michigan Journal of Community Service Learning, 5,* 5-13.

Perry, W. G. (1999). *Forms of intellectual and ethical development in the college years: A scheme.* San Francisco: Jossey-Bass. (Original work published in 1968).

Schank, R. C. (1994). Goal-based scenarios. In R. C. Schank & E. Langer (Eds.), *Beliefs, reasoning, and decision making: Psycho-logic in honor of Bob Abelson* (pp. 1-32). Hillsdale, N.J.: Lawrence Erlbaum.

Schank, R. C., Berman, T. R., & Macpherson, K. A. (1999). Learning by doing. In C.M. Reigeluth (Ed.), *Instructional-design theories and models* (Vol. 2., pp. 161-181). Mahwah, NJ: Lawrence Erlbaum.

Schank, R. C., & Joseph, D. M. (1998). Intelligent schooling. In R. J. Sterberg & W. M. Williams (Eds.), *Intelligence, instruction and assessment,* (pp. 43-65). Mahwah, NJ: Lawrence Erlbaum.

Shumer, R. (2000). Science or storytelling: How should we conduct and report service-learning research? *Michigan Journal of Community Service Learning,* (Special Issue 2000), 76-83.

Schwartz, D. L., & Bransford, J. D. (1998). A time for telling. *Cognition and instruction, 16*(4), 475-522.

Steinke, P., & Buresh, S. (2002). Cognitive outcomes of service-learning: Reviewing the past and glimpsing the future. *Michigan Journal of Community Service Learning, 8*(2), 5-14.

Steinke, P., & Harrington, A. (in press). Implementing service-learning in the natural sciences. *N.S.E.E. Quarterly.*

Stukas, A. A., Jr., Clary, E. G., & Snyder, M. (1999). Service learning: Who benefits and why. *Social Policy Report, 13*(4).

Taylor, C. (1991). Sources of the self: *The making of modern identity.* Cambridge, MA: Harvard University Press.

Vogelgesang, L. J., & Astin, A. W. (2000). Comparing the effects of community service and service-learning. *Michigan Journal of Community Service Learning, 7,* 25-34.

Waterman, A. (1997). *Service-learning: Applications from the research.* Hillsdale, NJ: Lawrence Erlbaum Associates.

Werner, C. M., & McVaugh, N. (2000). Service-learning "rules" that encourage or discourage long-term service: Implications for practice and research. *Michigan Journal of Community Service Learning, 7,* 117-125.

CHAPTER 6

SERVICE-LEARNING AND STUDENT WRITING
An Investigation of Effects

Adrian J. Wurr

This paper reports on a recent study investigating the impact of service-learning on the writing performance of first-year college composition students. Linguistic and rhetorical features commonly identified as affecting judgments of writing quality are compared to holistic essay ratings to describe the impact of different teaching and learning contexts on writing performance. The implications of the study will be of interest to composition instructors interested in learning more about service-learning and writing assessment, and more generally to service-learning researchers interested in empirical approaches to service-learning research.

INTRODUCTION

As a discipline, composition has remained one of the more active fields in the service-learning movement. Several writing conferences [1] have been devoted to the subject, many job descriptions now specify expertise in ser-

Service-Learning Through a Multidisciplinary Lens
A Volume in: Advances in Service-Learning Research, pages 103–121.
Copyright © 2002 by Information Age Publishing, Inc.
All rights of reproduction in any form reserved.
ISBN: 1-931576-81-5 (cloth), 1-931576-80-7 (paper)

vice-learning[2], and a growing number of books (e.g., Deans, 2000; Ford & Schave, 2001; Ross & Thomas, 2002; Trimbur, 2000) and journal articles [3] continue to explore what is broadly referred to as "community-based writing" from a variety of perspectives. A new journal, *Reflections on Community-Based Writing Instruction,* was also launched in 1999.

One of the first books in a planned series of 18 volumes on service-learning in the disciplines published by the American Association for Higher Education was devoted to composition. *Writing the Community: Concepts and Models for Service-Learning in Composition* (Adler-Kassner, Crooks, & Watters, 1997) presents many thoughtful chapters on composition courses using service-learning. The editors and Arca (1997) discuss the beneficial impact service-learning can have on post-secondary basic writers, while Herzberg (1994, 1997) presents a good discussion of the consciousness raising students at a small liberal arts college experienced as a result of a year-long service-learning course cluster that coupled sociology and first-year composition with volunteer work in an inner-city, halfway house as adult literacy tutors.

The two chapters by Arca and Herzberg focus on the use of service-learning in composition classrooms and contexts most similar to those in the present study. Both describe service-learning writing projects in which students write *about* their service experiences, as opposed to other models in which students write *for* or *with* community partners. As Deans (1999) notes in an article explicating these different approaches to service-learning in composition, writing-about-the-community courses generally emphasize, in varying degrees, personal reflection, social analysis, and/or cultural critique (p. 24). The audience usually remains an academic one, but the writer's arguments should have broader social implications.

Arca (1997), an instructor at Foothill Community College in California, discusses the benefits of using community service as both content and pedagogy with post-secondary basic writers. She describes her course as "community service writing," a course in which community service is the focus of class discussions and writing assignments, but in which students are not required to actually volunteer in the community, though many choose to do so. The course curriculum is organized, as many basic writing programs are, to move students from the personal to the social or from known to researched topics. The course, as Arca describes it, encourages students:

> to explore an ever-expanding circle of responsibility relationships—the family and community, self and community, society and community, and ending with a rather philosophical discussion centered around the systems thinking elaborated on in the movie Mindwalk (p. 135).

To promote reflection and critical thinking on these topics, students are required to interview a community service volunteer, then write about their experiences as concerned observers of or volunteers in the community agency. Noting that such assignments help her students gain a better sense of themselves and their connection to the community, Arca provides many excerpts from her students' writing to support her claims that their writing has become more complex and thoughtful, with "a rich mix of sources—student observations, recalled experiences, interviews, texts—and a wide range of interesting and locally-focused topics" (p. 140). She concludes that the students' engagement with the issues, as demonstrated in their writing and class discussions, results from the increased sense of authority, power, and responsibility they gained from community service writing.

Herzberg's (1994, 1997) description of the service-learning course he teaches at a small, private East Coast college is perhaps the most well-known account[4] of writing about the community. He focuses class discussions and writing assignments on topics related to literacy and schooling in America.

> We do not set out to study teaching methods or composition pedagogy. The students learn some of the teaching methods they will need in tutor-training sessions that take place largely outside of class time. But in the class itself, our goal is to examine the ways that literacy is gained or not gained in the United States, and only in that context do we examine teaching theories and practices (Herzberg, 1997, p. 60).

The writing assignments progress from personal reflections on literacy to an analysis of systemic discrimination in education to a final research essay on the social forces shaping illiteracy in America.

Drawing on a critical pedagogy rationale to justify the focus on democracy and social justice in his composition curriculum, Herzberg (1997) attempts to invoke "an understanding of the way social institutions affect our lives, and a sense that our responsibility for social justice includes but also carries beyond personal acts of charity" (p. 66). This, he notes, is difficult to accomplish with business students from privileged backgrounds. But he offers excerpts of students' writing to show how their thoughts develop over the year, as well as self-reported data from students demonstrating an increased sense of personal agency and social awareness (p. 58).

Useful and encouraging as these reports are, they can be faulted for a lack of scientific rigor, a point Adler-Kassner et al. (1997) draw attention to in their summary of the research findings to date on service-learning and composition:

> Though the evidence is largely anecdotal, it points to a source in the sense that service-learning makes communication—the heart of composition—matter, in all its manifestations. Whether teaching, learning, planning and executing assignments, exploring the writing process, or even grading

papers, students and instructors feel a greater sense of purpose and meaning in the belief that their work will have tangible results in the lives of others (p. 2).

Establishing a relationship between improved learning of traditional school subjects as a result of service-learning participation has proven difficult for researchers because of pedagogical differences in how the service component is structured in different courses and institutions. Mabry (1998) notes that sometimes service-learners fare better academically than other students and sometimes their academic outcomes are no different from other students (p. 33). Supporting Mabry's claim are two recent large-scale studies that report conflicting results regarding the academic gains of service-learning. Astin, Vogelsang, Ikeda, & Yee (2000, p. 19) found "connecting service with academic course material does indeed enhance the development of cognitive skills" (see also Vogelgesang & Astin, 2000, p. 25); while Gray, Ondaatje, Fricker, & Geschwind (2000, p. 34) found no difference between service-learning and comparison groups on academic measures.

The Astin et al. (2000) study is of particular interest since it is one of the first empirical studies to show gains in writing performance as a result of service-learning participation. The researchers analyzed self-reported data from over 22,000 undergraduate students to determine that service-learning had a significant effect on improved writing skills over generic volunteer experiences (Beta = .02; $p < .01$) and traditional writing courses without any community-based writing component (Beta = .04; $p < .001$). However, these results are somewhat compromised by the fact that the researchers never actually looked at any student writing samples; rather they relied solely on students' self-reported sense that their writing had improved as a result of service-learning. While such self-assessments are an important data source, the results are less than conclusive without corroborating the findings with textual analyses of actual student writing. The present study addresses this gap in our understanding of exactly how service-learning impacts student writing performance by assessing samples of student writing in several ways and then triangulating this with self-reported data.

RESEARCH DESIGN

This study examines the impact of a required service-learning component in an introductory-level first-year college composition course on student writing performance, motivation, and social orientation. The specific research question focused on in this paper is "Does service-learning contribute to improved student writing? If so, in what ways?"

Participants consisted of a select group of native (NS) and non-native English speaking (NNS) students enrolled in separate sections of English 101 and 107, respectively. These first-year composition courses are designed to introduce students to academic writing and research practices and conventions, especially those relating to analytical, persuasive, and personal-reflective writing. Students write in and outside of class to develop a repertoire of writing skills and to prepare for different writing situations in university and public life. One student described the service-learning coursework in the following way.

> ...most of the techniques that I learned in class, I was able to apply in helping Fort Lowell. This helped me learn exactly what works and why. Fort Lowell became a practical application of the techniques I learned in class. I learned in class to research for our rhetorical analysis and persuasive essay, but for Fort Lowell I did not have the luxury of a teacher pointing me in the right direction every step of the way. I had to do all of the research alone. [...] Overall, the work that I did for Fort Lowell Elementary School really helped me to connect the techniques I learned in class to the real world.

As shown in Exhibit 1, each class section had a total enrollment of between 17 and 20 students[5] and one graduate student or adjunct faculty instructor. There were a total of 19 NS participants in the service-learning section of English 101 (G1), 16 NNS in the service-learning section of English 107 (G2), 19 NS in the comparison section of English 101 (G3), and a combined total of 19 NNS students from two different comparison sections[6] of English 107 (G4). Male and female participants were roughly equal in numbers and age. Over half the participants in the service-learning courses stated some religious affiliation in a demographic survey. The majority of these students identified themselves as Muslim, Christian, or Catholic; other religious groups identified included Jewish, Hindu, Greek Orthodox, and Lutheran affiliations. Though a sample of convenience, the participants in this study are representative of the diverse student populations typically found on large, urban college campuses in America today.

Participating students in selected service-learning and comparison sections wrote a rhetorical analysis, persuasive, and reflective essay, as outlined in Exhibit 2.

EXHIBIT 1
Groups by Participants' Language Background and Curricula Offered

	NS (English 101)	*NNS (English 107)*
Service-Learning	G1 (N = 19)	G2 (N = 16)
Comparison	G3 (N = 19)	G4 (N = 19)

EXHIBIT 2
Essay Assignment Descriptors for Service-Learning and Comparison
Groups

Service-Learning Sections	Comparison Sections
1. Rhetorical Analysis essay (5 to 7 pages): Students research a local environmental or social problem from various viewpoints.	1. Rhetorical Analysis essay (5 to 7 pages): Students closely examine one or more texts to better understand the rhetorical strategies used by the authors.
2. Persuasive Essay (4 to 6 pages): Students suggest ways to solve or reduce the impact of the environmental or social problem they researched.	2. Persuasive Essay (4 to 6 pages): Students research a controversial issue and attempt to persuade readers to their view of the issue. In the NS group (G3), this essay took the form of an ideological analysis of a place in the university with which the writer was familiar. In the NNS group (G4), students wrote a letter to the editor.
3. Reflective Essay (4 to 6 pages): Serves as a preface to a portfolio on their accomplishments over the semester: Students explain why they chose the texts they did, for whom they are intended, and what purpose the texts or portfolio is meant to serve.	3. Reflective Essay (4 to 6 pages): Students reflect upon their semester-long inquiry of an issue or discipline.

Traditional library research and background knowledge on the topic formed the knowledge-base for the writing students produced in the comparison groups. Students in the service-learning groups also drew upon first-hand observations gleaned from volunteering at nonprofit, community agencies with service projects related to the course theme of the land and people of the Southwest for 15 hours or more over a one-to-two-month period. None of the participants knew of the possible service-learning component before enrolling in the course, although those in service-learning sections were informed of this and other assignments in the first week of the semester, so it is unlikely that certain personalities or types of students would have selected their course section based on prior knowledge of the service-learning component. Persuasive essays from both service-learning and comparison groups were analyzed in order to highlight the impact of each teaching and learning context on writing performance.

Procedures

To answer the question: Does service-learning contribute to improved student writing, and if so, in what ways, the writing performance of students was assessed through a combination of direct measures, including holistic and primary trait analyses [7] of persuasive essays and other formal and informal texts written by participants, and indirect measures such as course evaluations, surveys, and interviews.

With regard to direct-assessment measures, persuasive essays written by students in the service-learning and comparison sections of first-year composition were compared in two distinct ways. First, all essays were rated holistically and analytically by teams of trained independent readers. Holistic and primary trait scores for use of rhetorical appeals, reasoning, coherence, and mechanics were established by averaging any inter-rater discrepancies in scores for each essay. Inter-rater reliability rates were .83, .94, .89, and .93 for holistic, rhetorical appeals, reasoning, and coherence, respectively[8]. Next, all essays were analyzed using a computer-mediated multi-feature/multi-dimensional (MF/MD) method developed by Douglas Biber (1988). Factor analysis, which correlates multiple variables individually and in groups, was used to find linguistic features that had high co-occurrence rates. These features describe different dimensions, roughly akin to genres, of written texts. The holistic writing assessments helped determine if service-learning contributed to improved student writing or not. The factor analysis identified specific linguistic features of the writing produced in service-learning and traditional first-year composition courses that differed significantly.

Based on previous research (Biber, 1985; Connor, 1990), two underlying dimensions of linguistic features were identified as potentially important characteristics distinguishing the writing produced by both groups: the "Interactive versus Edited textual dimension" and "Abstract versus Situated Content textual dimension." The "Interactive versus Edited textual dimension" demonstrates the writer's level of personal involvement and interaction with the topic. The "Abstract versus Situated Content textual dimension" contains features marking a highly abstract and formal style. The features comprising each dimension are listed in Exhibit 5; a complete description of each linguistic feature and its computer algorithm can be found in Biber (1985, p. 221-245).

Factor analysis was then used to determine which of these potentially revealing features were evident in the students' writing. The number of features in each text and group was counted and then normalized to a text length of 1000 words (i.e., a ratio of the number of items per 1000 words was generated), to prevent varying text length affecting the factor scores. Because of differences between the scales used and scores generated, the numbers were then standardized to ensure that all features included in the factor score were weighted equally. Factor scores were computed by summing the salient features of each factor for each essay. To complete the first writing assessment procedure, these factor scores were analyzed along with other primary traits to determine their contribution to holistic assessments of writing quality. To complete the second writing assessment procedure, the MF/MD analysis, the mean factor scores for each group were compared to determine if there was a significant difference in the clustering of linguistic features between and among both groups' writing.

Results

The results from the holistic and analytic assessments of the students' writing show a significant difference between the writing produced in service-learning and traditional writing sections. As shown in Exhibit 3, these results indicate that independent raters judged the essays produced by students in service-learning sections of first-year composition to be superior to those produced in comparison sections in a variety of ways. This between-group difference in mean scores on logic and coherence had less than .1 percent likelihood of occurring by chance (i.e., p < .001); and the between-group difference on use of rhetorical appeals and the holistic scores had less than .2 percent (p < .002) and 2.5 percent (p < .025) likelihood of occurring by chance. The between-group difference on mechanics was calculated by counting the number of errors per word in order to account for differences in sentence length (p < .04).

EXHIBIT 3
Between Group Comparison of Writing Assessment Scores

	Group	N	Mean*	Std. Deviation	Significance (2-tailed)	T value
Holistic	SL	36	3.4722	.7923	p < .025	2.287
	Control	39	3.0385	.8459		
Appeals	SL	36	2.1750	.3544	p < .002	3.255
	Control	39	1.8810	.4214		
Logic	SL	36	2.2417	.3948	p < .0001	3.255
	Control	39	1.8810	.4214		
Coherence	SL	36	3.1436	.5508	p < .001	3.673
	Control	39	2.6410	.6277		
Mechanics	SL	36	3.16E-03	2.4025E-03	p < .04	-3.767
	Control	39	4.67E-03	3.6471E-03		

*Note: The range of possible scores for each variable above was 1-5 for holistic scores, 0-3 for appeals, 1-3 for logic, and 1-4 for coherence. Mechanics had an unlimited range from zero up.

Although these results provide some indication that service-learning does improve student writing in various ways, the results so far are only based on a single writing sample and may not indicate long-term effects on writing performance. One would hope to see changes in participants' attitudes and behavior concerning writing, as well as in the actual writing produced before concluding that a particular course or methodology had an impact on student writing performance. For insights on this aspect of writing performance, we turn now to the students' own self-assessment of their writing development as a result of the course, as indicated by responses to the end-of-the-semester Teacher/Course Evaluations (TCE) and interview data. These direct and indirect quantitative measures were compared with qualitative assessments of the students' informal journal writing to gain a more complete picture of the impact of service-learning on student writing performance. Such triangulation of the data analysis provides some insight of the impact of service-learning on both text-based measures of writing performance and the students' attitudes, motivation, and self-assessment of their own writing.

As shown in Exhibit 4, self-assessment scores in response to the question, "After taking this course, I think my writing is: 5 = very much improved; 4 = much improved; 3 = somewhat improved; 2 = not much improved; 1 = not at all improved" indicate that more service-learning students thought their writing had improved as a result of the course than in the comparison sections (p < .001). The figures shown in the graph represent the percent of the total number of students in each group. The service-learning group had a mean score of 3.6 compared to 3.2 for the control. Comments from students in the service-learning sections provide some indication of how their attitude and motivation in the composing process changed over time. For example, prior to beginning her service-learning project, one interview participant commented, "I have my [writing] style that I've had since high school, and I don't see how [work-

EXHIBIT 4
Service-Learning vs. Control Groups' Self-Assessments of
Writing Development

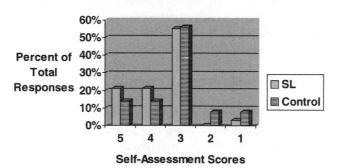

ing with] kids can change that for me right now." Later in the semester, however, she wrote:

> In doing service learning, you can directly interact with people who are different from the students on campus. The subtle feeling about people makes your writing more vivid and specific. I think personal experience about the life of other people is the most vital and rich raw materials for literature.

NNS students in particular spoke enthusiastically about the ways in which their interactions in the community shaped their thinking and writing. Here are some excerpts from their final reflective essay on the semester's work.

- Thanks to English composition class, I have become able to dig into myself so that I can find out what I really want to do in the future and why I do so by applying these concepts from composition to my real-life situation. . . . This volunteering experience turned out one of my biggest confidence builders and actually turned my attention to the "real-world" American community.
- When I had daily conversations with supervisors from service-learning site, I learned how to describe my situation [...] and how to respond to their words. When I attended the class, I learned how people have different opinions and how they present them. I learned how to express myself even from what a child said.
- The more I worked at the Shalom House the more I began to experience totally different environment that I had been ever exposed to. [...] The more one can understand others' concerns, the better he can communicate with them and help to solve their problems.

These comments show the service-learning participants' increased awareness of the cultural dimensions of language and learning. Through their work in the community, these students came to appreciate the richness and complexity of the people and issues involved in their writing topics. The service-learning students' higher mean scores on the holistic and primary trait assessments of their writing (e.g., reasoning, coherence, and use of rhetorical appeals) may provide some measure of this enriched understanding, while the reduced number of mechanical errors may also reflect spending additional time and attention on their writing since the topics were more meaningful to them.

Macroscopic Textual Analysis

To further understand how the writing produced in service-learning courses might differ from that produced in traditional comparison sections of first-year composition, macroscopic textual analyses were conducted on the persuasive essays written by participants in the study in order to identify specific linguistic and rhetorical features used by writers in each group. Following the method of macroscopic textual analysis pioneered by Biber (1988), factor analysis was conducted on 19 linguistic features in the essays identified by Biber as co-occurring in texts along two dimensions – Dimension 1: Interactional versus Edited Text Dimension and/or Dimension 2: The Abstract versus Situated Dimension. These features and the dimension to which they are associated are outlined in Exhibit 5. The 75 essays from the comparison and service-learning groups comprised the corpus, or data set. Any differences in writing styles or language use between groups would be revealed by variations in each group's factor score for each dimension.

EXHIBIT 5
Selected Syntactic Variations

Factor 1: Interactional vs. Edited		Factor 2: Abstract vs. Situated	
Interactional	*Edited/Informational*	*Abstract*	*Situated*
'I'/ 'you'	word length	nominalizations	place and time
questions	type-token ratio	prepositions	adverbs
pro-verb 'do'		passives	contractions
general hedges		'it' clefts	general conjuncts
general emphatics		precise conjuncts	
'it'		split auxiliaries	
final prepositions		word length	
'that' clauses		infinitives	
other subordinators			
(contractions)			

Using the principal component extraction method, the initial factor analysis revealed seven components (aka: 'factors' or 'dimensions') with Eigenvalues of 1.0 or greater, cumulatively accounting for 64 percent of the variance. Three factors accounted for nearly half of this variance, so a second factor analysis was conducted to extract only three factors. In other words, distributing the 21 features into seven different groups of related items accounted for 64 percent of the difference between groups, but since three groups accounted for almost half of the variance, a second distribution was performed to sort the 21 features into just three groups[9]. The resulting three groups and the relative strength of each linguistic feature in the group, as expressed by the item's correlational coefficient, are shown in Exhibit 6.

Most of the features related to personal involvement and interaction that were hypothesized to comprise factor 1 loaded most strongly on that factor. This dimension comes closest to Biber's Dimension 1, the Interactional Versus Edited Text dimension. Features that mark an informal writing style with a high level of interaction are: final prepositions, it, first and second person pronouns, and *that* relative clauses (in both the subject and object positions). Features indicative of more formal, high-density texts with an informational focus occurred infrequently, as indicated by the negative values for nominalizations, type/token ratio, and word length additionally support this interpretation as high frequencies of these.

EXHIBIT 6
Three-Component Factor Analysis Results

Feature	Component 1	2	3
Nominals	**-.641**	.118	7.422E-02
Agentless passives	-.214	**.554**	.186
'by' passives	-3.51E-02	1.880E-02	**.725**
'it' clefts	5.468E-02	**.713**	-.125
Conjunctions	-.204	(-.391)	**-.434**
Split Auxiliary	-.278	-5.13E-02	-.179
Place Adverb	9.734E-02	**-.417**	-.8.23E-02
Time Adverb	.115	7.178E-02	**-.420**
Contractions	.258	**.581**	5.017E-03
Final Preposition	.350	7.078E-02	-.247
1st and 2nd person	**.696**	.255	.133
PNs	-3.71E-02	-4.46E-02	**.401**
Interrogatives	.197	-7.21E03E	**.625**
Hedges	-7.35E-02	**-.422**	(.336)
Emphatics	**.319**	.299	.202
It	**.329**	2.458E-02	5.620E-02
That	(.424)	**.462**	-.187
Wh-clauses	**-.352**	3.390E-02	-2.38E-02
Type/token	**-.855**	.123	3.661E-02
Word length			

Note: SPSS Principal Component Analysis was used for extraction method and Promax with Kaiser Normalization was used for the rotation method. Features with absolute values of .3 or greater are significant indicators of the underlying factor and thus bolded. Those in parentheses had greater loadings on a different factor.

Factor 2 is characterized by features associated with Biber's Dimension 2: Abstract Versus Situated Texts. Factor 2 is the least well-defined dimension in this corpus. Only four features—two with positive and two with negative loadings—loaded most heavily on it, although three other features also appear to be active on the dimension, as indicated by an absolute correlational coefficient score of .30 or greater. Agentless passives, 'it' clefts, and WH-clauses (subordinate and interrogative) all co-occur in high frequency on this dimension, indicating an abstract, formal writing style. Features that are embedded more in the context, (e.g., 'situated' features such as conjunctions, place adverbs, contractions, and emphatics) occur less frequently in such formal prose, and thus appear with a negative value on this factor.

Though not predicted, a third dimension also appeared to help characterize the writing produced by participants in the study. Factor 3 contains a mixture of features Biber (1988) claims more frequently mark Dimensions 1 and 2. For example, Biber (1988) places hedges in Dimension 1 because of their interactional function, and 'by' passives on Dimension 2 because of the abstract writing style they help characterize. The low frequency occurrence of conjunctions, time adverbs, and questions on factor 3, combined with a high frequency of 'by' passives, hedges, and emphatics, suggests an underlying narrative versus non-narrative dimension. Biber identifies such a dimension as common in English texts and has labeled this "Dimension 3: Reported Versus Immediate Style."

Using the Scheffé test, a more careful analysis of differences between all four groups' use of the individual features comprising factors 1 and 3 revealed that a significant difference existed between groups on 9 of the 12 salient linguistic features comprising factors 1 and 3. These between-group differences, summarized in Exhibits 7, 8 and 9, indicate that the writing topic each class focused on had a greater effect on the style and form of the students' writing than did each pedagogical context.

EXHIBIT 7
Between Group Comparison of Factor Scores

	Groups	*N*	*Mean*	*Std. Deviation*	*Std. Error Mean*
FACTOR1	cntl	39	1.5073	3.7397	.5988
	SL	36	-1.6329	3.0462	.5077
FACTOR2	cntl	39	-2.99E-02	3.4473	.5520
	SL	36	3.242E-02	3.2056	.5343
FACTOR3	cntl	39	1.0559	2.7904	.4468
	SL	36	-1.1439	2.4675	.4113

Between-group differences on factor 1 suggest that the essays in the comparison sections displayed more interactive features than in the service-learning groups. The specific factor 1 features showing a significant between-group difference were nominalizations, first and second person pronouns, 'it,' and type/token ratio. Nominalizations and the type/token ratio both load negatively on factor 1, meaning that these features occur infrequently in interactive texts. The Scheffé test results show that the NS service-learning section ("G1") used significantly more nominalizations and had a significantly higher type/token ratio than the comparison NS section ("G3"). Since the essay assignment in the comparison NS section asked students to ideologically analyze some aspect of their experience at the university, the less formal writing style these students employed, as indicated by the low frequency of nominalizations in their writing, is more understandable. The lower type/token ratio found in the NS comparison essays likewise suggests an informal, narrative structure. Thus the writing assignment in the comparison NS section led the students in that section to include more narrative elements in their essay, whereas the students in the service-learning section discussed issues in the community in a more formal, planned style.

EXHIBIT 8
Summary of Significant Between-Group Differences on Factor 1
Features Using the Scheffé Test

Dependent Variable	(A) Group	(B) Group	Mean Difference (A-B)
NOMINALS	G3	G1	-.9749413*
	G1	G3	.9749413*
I/YOU	G4	G1	.9073138*
	G1	G4	-.9073138*
TYPE/TOKEN	G3	G1	-1.1026968*
	G1	G3	1.1026968*

*Note: The mean difference is significant at the .05 level.

EXHIBIT 9
Summary of Significant Between-Group Differences on Factor 3
Features Using the Scheffé test

Dependent Variable	(A) Group	(B) Group	Mean Difference (A-B)
'BY' PASSIVES	G3	G1	1.0244232*
	G1	G3	-1.0244232*
HEDGES	G4	G1	.9001457*
	G1	G4	-.9001457*

*Note: The mean difference is significant at the .05 level.

A between-group difference in the use of first and second person pronouns also occurred between the NNS comparison ("G4") and NS service-learning ("G1") sections. First and second person pronoun use loads positively on factor 1, indicating that they are used frequently in interactive texts. NNS students in the comparison section ("G4") used first and second person pronouns more frequently than did service-learning students, though this only reached a statistically significant level with the NS service-learning students. The assignment in the comparison NNS section ("G4") asked students to write a letter-to-the-editor of a magazine or newspaper. In Biber's 1088 study, letters were found to have a higher mean factor 1 score than academic texts, so the duplication of those results in the main study should not be too surprising (p. 128).

The between-group differences on factor 3 add further support to this interpretation. The mean comparison section scores on factor 3 were significantly higher than the service-learning groups' scores. This indicates that the comparison section students displayed a more distant writing style than did the service-learning students. The specific factor 3 features that showed a significant between-group difference were 'by' passives, time adverbials, questions, and hedges.

The results of the Scheffé test revealed that NS students in the comparison section ("G3") used more 'by' passives and time adverbials in their essays than did NS service-learning students ("G1"). There is no easy explanation for this result, however, since the two features are inversely correlated on factor 3. On the one hand, the more frequent use of 'by' passives by the comparison section NS students suggests they are more distant from their subject, or at least the agent of the proposition is more distant from the subject at hand as Biber (1988) suggests, than the NS service-learning students were to theirs. On the other hand, the NS comparison section students' more frequent use of time adverbials suggests they were more involved with their subject (Chafe & Danielewicz, 1987) than were NS service-learning students. Given the essay assignment in the NS comparison section, it is plausible that the students used 'by' passives to describe actions performed by university authorities that alienated or distanced them as writers, as in the following example: "Students are deprived from their education *by* being forced to attend lecture hall classes." The students may have needed to use time adverbials more frequently to describe the sequence of events surrounding this action, however, juxtaposing involvement in alienating actions.

NS students in the comparison section of English 101 also included more questions in their essays than did service-learning students, particularly the NNS service-learning students. Use of interrogatives can indicate a concern for interpersonal functions (Biber, 1988, p. 227), and this concern would be understandable for first-year students asked to critique the university by an authoritative figure employed by that same university.

The same would be true of using hedges, which students in both comparison sections used more frequently than service-learning students. Since service-learning students used fewer hedges than students in the comparison sections did on average, it could be argued that the service-learning students' personal involvement with their writing topic made them feel more confident about their opinions on the topic. When personal involvement is coupled with previous experience with, or background knowledge on, the topic at hand, an even sharper difference

appears, as seen in the significantly different number of hedges comparison NNS students and NS service-learning students used. Most NNS students do not have a lifetime of personal experience with American society
like most readers of American magazines and newspapers would likely
have had. Yet this is the audience NNS students in the comparison sections
were asked to target in their essays. Examples such as the following hedge
were common in the letters-to-the editor written by comparison ESL students: "Now, I have lived in the United States as a college student for *almost*
a year. As a foreigner, or a resident of the United States, I...." NS service-learning students, on the other hand, were more familiar with subjects
relating to American society, and their combination of primary and secondary research on a specific aspect of that society may have led them to
feel more expert on the subject than their target audience, which in most
cases was their instructor, as seen in the following example from an NS student in the service-learning group: "The lawyer tried to gain any *kind* of
sympathy they [sic] could for their defendant."

From this analysis, it becomes apparent that the writer's rhetorical situation influences the writing style, and genre students opt to use more than
the pedagogical context of the classroom in their writing. The relationship
between the writer, target audience, and topic, as well as format or genre
constraints posed in the writing assignment, all influence the decisions any
writer makes in producing a text. These rhetorical considerations appear
to supersede how the writer was introduced to the assignment. Apparently,
the writer's sensitivity to his or her rhetorical situation influences writing
style and form to a strong degree.

SUMMARY

The present study investigated the impact of service-learning on student
writing by comparing the analytic and holistic measures of the writing quality of essays produced by service-learning and comparison groups of students in a variety of ways.

- By comparing the self-assessments students in service-learning and
  comparison groups made of their writing development for the semester;
- By assessing the attitudes and beliefs service-learning students held in
  regard to writing as a result of their semester's work in first-year composition; and finally,
- By comparing salient linguistic and rhetorical dimensions and features in the writing produced by each group.

The results indicate that service-learning had a positive impact on student writing both in terms of their written product and their attitude
towards, and understanding of, the writing process. In terms of writing

quality, the essays written by service-learning students were judged by independent raters to be better than the comparison essays on every measure (see Exhibit 3). Holistic assessment scores for service-learning essays were .43 points or 8 percent higher than comparison essay scores on a five-point scale (p < .025). Converting points to letter grades, in other words, reveals that service-learning essays were judged to be better than comparison essays by about half a letter grade. Analytic assessments of each group's effective use of rhetorical appeals, logic, coherence, and mechanics show service-learning essays to be superior to comparison essays by an average of 13 percent (p < .002 for appeals, logic and coherence; p < .04 for mechanics). Students in the service-learning sections also rated their own writing as improving more as a result of the course than students in comparison sections (p < .001).

When reflecting on their work, service-learning students demonstrated greater appreciation for the complexity of the issues and people they were writing and researching about, which led to greater understanding not only of community issues, but also writing and research strategies and processes, compared to their initial comments made at the beginning of the semester. In sum, these results provide empirical support for including service-learning in college composition curricula. While other studies have demonstrated the positive impact service-learning can have on the community (e.g., Gelmon, Holland, Seifer, Shinnamon, & Connors, 1998; Gray et al., 2000), this study has shown that incorporating service-learning in college composition improves student writing, improves understanding of the course content, and improves student satisfaction with the course.

Finally, macroscopic textual analyses of the students' writing revealed that essays written by students in non-service-learning comparison sections exhibited significantly more interactional features (factor 1) and less distance from the topic (factor 3) than service-learning essays. Linguistic and rhetorical differences between and among the writing produced in the comparison and service-learning sections suggests that the rhetorical situation between reader, writer, and topic, as well as any formal constraints placed in the writing assignment, have a greater influence on the writing style students employ than the pedagogy used by the instructor.

These findings are significant in that few previous service-learning studies have provided empirical evidence for gains in student learning of course content; and this is perhaps the only study to have done so in first-year college composition through the assessment of actual student writing samples.

NOTES

1. For example, the Writing Program Administration (WPA) summer conference in 1998 was entitled, "Service-Learning in the Writing Program."

2.   The 1999 and 2000 Modern Language Association's Job Information Lists contained about a dozen listings each, equivalent to approximately 1% of the total, for jobs specifically requesting expertise in service-learning (Laurence & Welles, 2000).

3.   See, for example: the *Michigan Journal of Community Service-Learning* (http://www.umich.edu/~mjcsl/) and *Reflections on Community-Based Writing Instruction* (http://www.ncte.org/service/reflections.html)

4.   The chapter is reprinted from an earlier article that appeared in *College Composition and Communication*. Herzberg's course has also been the subject of at least one subsequent study by Deans (1999) that appeared in the *Michigan Journal of Community Service Learning*.

5.   One student in G2 and G4 declined to participate in the study, hence the difference in the number of enrolled students and study participants.

6.   Because of a low participation rate in the comparison section of English 107, an additional, group of ESL participants was added from a combined English 101/107 class, bringing the total number of comparison ESL participants to 19.

7.   Holistic writing assessments look at the text as a whole rather than at discreet parts of the text. Primary trait analysis focuses on a single writing skill such as organization or mechanics.

8.   A 1-point difference in raters' scores was allowed for in determining inter-rater reliability. See Wurr (2002) for a more complete description of the instruments and procedures used in direct measures of writing quality.

9.   To confirm that a 3-factor extraction was most appropriate, analyses were also conducted with 4 and 2 components extracted. These were rejected as too few features loaded on each factor in the 4-component extraction, and the correlation between factors in the 2 and 3 component extractions suggested that factor 3 was significantly distinct from factors 1 and 2 to justify retaining 3 distinct factors. See Biber (1988, pp. 79-99) for a more complete discussion of determining how many factors to extract.

REFERENCES

Adler-Kassner, L., Crooks, R., & Watters, A. (Eds.). (1997). *Writing the community: Concepts and models for service-learning in composition*. Washington, DC: American Association for Higher Education.

Arca, R. (1997). Systems thinking, symbiosis, and service: The road to authority for basic writers. In L. Adler-Kassner, R. Crooks, & A. Watters (Eds.), *Writing the community: Concepts and models for service-learning in composition* (pp. 133-142). Washington, DC: American Association for Higher Education.

Astin, A. W., Vogelgesang, L. J., Ikeda, E. K., & Yee, J. A. (2000). *How service-learning affects students*. Los Angeles: Higher Education Research Institute.

Biber, D. (1985). Investigating macroscopic textual variation through multi-feature/multi-dimensional analyses. *Linguistics, 23*, 337-360.

Biber, D. (1988). *Variation across speech and writing*. Cambridge, U.K.: Cambridge UP.

Chafe, W. L., & Danielewicz, J. (1987). Properties of spoken and written language. In R. Horowitz & S. J. Samuels (Eds.), *Comprehending oral and written language* (pp. 37-51). New York: Academic Press.

Connor, U. (1990). Linguistic/Rhetorical measures for international persuasive student writing. *Research in the Teaching of English, 24*(1), 67-87.

Deans, T (1999). Service-learning in two keys: Paulo Friere's critical pedagogy in relation to John Dewey's pragmatism. *Michigan Journal of Community Service Learning, 6,* 15-29.

Deans, T. (2000). *Writing partnerships: Service-learning in composition.* Urbana, IL: National Council of Teachers of English.

Ford, E., & Schave, E. (2001). *Community matters.* New York: Addison-Wesley/Longman.

Gelmon, S. B., Holland, B. A., Seifer, S. D., Shinnamon, A., & Connors, K. (1998). Community-university partnerships for mutual learning. *Michigan Journal of Community Service Learning, 5,* 97-107.

Gray, M. J., Ondaatje, E. H., Fricker, R. D., Jr., & Geschwind, S. A. (2000, March/April). Assessing service-learning: Results from a survey of "Learn and Serve America, Higher Education." *Change,* 30-39.

Herzberg, B. (1994). Community service and critical teaching. *College Composition and Communication, 45,* 307-319.

Herzberg, B. (1997). Community service and critical teaching. In L. Adler-Kassner, R. Crooks, & A. Watters (Eds.), *Writing the community: Concepts and models for service-learning in composition* (pp. 57-70). Washington, DC: American Association for Higher Education.

Laurence, D., & Welles, E. B. (2000). Job market remains competitive. *MLA Newsletter, 32*(1), 6-7.

Mabry, J. B. (1998). Pedagogical variations in service-learning and student outcomes: How time, contact, and reflection matter. *Michigan Journal of Community Service Learning, 5,* 32-47.

Ross, C., & Thomas, T. (2002). *Writing for real: A handbook for writers in community service.* New York: Longman.

Trimbur, J. (1998). *The call to write.* New York: Addison-Wesley.

Vogelgesang, L., & Astin, A. W. (2000). Comparing the effects of service-learning and community service. *Michigan Journal of Community Service Learning, 7,* 25-34.

Wurr, A. J. (2002). Text-based measures of service-learning writing quality. *Reflections: A Journal of Writing, Service-Learning, and Community Literacy, 2*(2). 40-55.

CHAPTER 7

IMPACT OF SERVICE-LEARNING ON OCCUPATIONAL THERAPY STUDENTS' AWARENESS AND SENSE OF RESPONSIBILITY TOWARD COMMUNITY

Rhonda Waskiewicz

This dual design study looked at the value and impact of using service-learning as pedagogy to improve occupational therapy students' awareness, commitment, and sense of responsibility toward community. Sixty-nine students were divided into experimental and comparison groups. All participants completed a demographic survey and a pre-test/post-test consisting of a semantic differential (SD) and the Community Service Involvement Preference Inventory (CSIPI). The experimental group was required to keep a journal.

Analysis of variance (ANOVA) of the concepts and factors of the SD showed minimal change; however, descriptive analysis of the adjective pairs did indicate a change in attitude occurred. ANOVA of the CSIPI indicated no

Service-Learning Through a Multidisciplinary Lens
A Volume in: Advances in Service-Learning Research, pages 123–150.
ISBN: 1-931576-81-5 (cloth), 1-931576-80-7 (paper)

movement through phases for both the experimental and comparison groups. But, qualitative analysis of the journal entries, using the Service-Learning Model, indicated developmental differences between experimental groups existed. The data suggest that design and implementation of service-learning programs should consider using developmental learning models to clarify expectations and maximize positive outcomes.

INTRODUCTION

One type of volunteerism that was emphasized in the National and Community Service Trust Act of 1990 and the National and Community Service Trust Act of 1993 targeted the relationship between college students and their institution's respective communities. It was called service-learning because it was thought that student involvement in the community surrounding a college or university emphasized and enhanced learning. According to Eyler and Giles (1999), the popularity of service-learning in higher education has rapidly increased over the last decade. Students, faculty, and administrators of colleges and universities across the country share this interest. A 1998 Campus Compact survey, as reported in Eyler and Giles, estimated 10,800 faculty members were involved in teaching 11,800 courses with a service-learning component. In addition, there was a 35 percent increase in some form of support for faculty to implement service-learning courses between 1994 and 1998. Support in the form of federal grants came from the Corporation for National Service's Learn and Serve Higher Education (LASHE). The 458 colleges and universities that participated in the three-year grants developed and implemented approximately 3000 new service-learning courses (Eyler & Giles).

The popularity of service-learning is grounded, in part, in the belief that it "is an idea whose time has come. As our economy becomes more complex, natural resources more limited, and social problems more acute, the importance of educating our youth to a life of responsible citizenship cannot be ignored" (Leder & McGuinness, 1996, p. 47). Service-learning links the classroom to the community by providing an organized service activity that meets real community needs. Students are asked to reflect on the service activity to gain further understanding of course content, a broader appreciation of the discipline, and an enhanced sense of civic responsibility (Bringle & Hatcher, 1996). The belief is that service-learning fosters thought about where one fits into the bigger picture, what skills and abilities one already has, and what skills and abilities one needs to acquire. As a result, moral reasoning is turned into moral action, theory into application, and the abstract into the practical. Through reflection, in collaboration with core values, individuals create ideas about what their role is in bringing about change (Grace, 1996).

The potential of service-learning as pedagogy, to better prepare occupational therapy students for the changes in health care service delivery, bears consideration. The trend of service delivery away from in-patient rehabilitation and medical facilities, and toward a community-based delivery system, offers new challenges for occupational therapy practitioners and educators. Traditional health care has been, and is, most often delivered in hospitals and rehabilitation centers. Payment for services has been retrospective, and there is an expectation that patients will accept the advice and directives given by medical and allied health professionals. Prospective payment systems for health care, or health maintenance organizations (HMO's), however, have begun to permeate our society and change the way we look at health care. First, HMO's have helped us to move from a tertiary to a more preventive perspective of health and wellness. Health care maintenance is occurring in fitness centers and gymnasiums and in city parks and senior citizen centers, to name a few. As a result, prevention of illness occurs less in hospitals and rehabilitation centers, and more in the community. Second, individuals are being called on to take more responsibility for managing their own health care needs. Rather than relinquishing control to the professional, clients are encouraged to become knowledgeable, to collaborate with health care providers to prevent illness where possible, and to manage chronic disease to maintain optimum function and independence within the community.

This shift in emphasis has created a need for occupational therapists and occupational therapy students to focus on the community as an additional place to provide their services. In an accredited occupational therapy program, students are heavily exposed to course work in psychosocial and physical disability practice, and with clinical experiences that focus on assessment and treatment intervention that takes place primarily in a clinical setting. Treatment protocols that are designed for the clinical setting, however, may not, and often do not, meet the needs of the general client population within the community. For example, there may be conflict between how the occupational therapist and the client define illness or health, how they decide on goals to achieve optimum function, and what constitutes a safe living environment. The environment itself is less sterile, less standardized, and less amenable to manipulation by the occupational therapist. Training in home health service delivery (a community-based treatment setting) is frequently considered a specialty practice and is often limited to a certain segment of the population, the elderly. Although occupational therapy students receive academic exposure to this practice area, they rarely receive experiential exposure. Given the shift toward community-based practice that encompasses prevention and wellness, as well as treatment and assessment of secondary and tertiary needs, it is important for occupational therapy educators to consider ways to help occupational therapy students become more familiar, comfortable, and skilled with community practice possibilities.

Occupational therapy was founded on the principle that health and well-being are intricately linked with the meaning and satisfaction one places on one's occupation. As the profession evolved, other principles were added. They included the ideas that through engagement in occupation, people can influence their state of health (Reilly, 1962), that humans are resourceful in finding productive ways to interact with their environments (Engelhardt, 1977; Reilly, 1962; Rogers, 1983), and that culture is the mode through which people attach meaning to their occupations (Yerxa et al., 1990). The profession identifies occupation as permeating all areas of life including daily living tasks, work and productivity, and play or leisure. Yet the practice of occupational therapy, for the last four decades, has been limited in its scope. A medical model of service delivery, in response to illness and disability, has dominated how and in what settings occupational therapists practice. The move toward community-based practice is actually a move away from this present model and toward the founding paradigm.

Within the profession, researchers have been calling for changes in service delivery and academic preparation for practice (Fazio, 2000; Kielhofner, 1992; Kniepmann, 1997; Wilcock, 1998). These changes will bring heightened demands and pressures on practitioners such as autonomous decision making, advocacy, community awareness, and sensitivity to cultures within the community environment (as opposed to a medical facility). The 1998 Pew Health Professions Commission report offered five recommendations for all health professional groups to prepare for the demands of the changing health care system. Of those, three recommendations are directed, in part or total, toward health care educators. The first states, "In spite of the dramatic changes affecting every aspect of health care, most of the nation's educational programs remain oriented to prepare individuals for yesterday's health care system" (p. iii). The second recommendation is that education should move out of more traditional training settings (hospitals) and into more ambulatory care settings (community-based). Finally, the Commission encourages all health professionals to become involved with public service.

The 1998 educational standards put forth by the Accreditation Council for Occupational Therapy Education (American Occupational Therapy Association [AOTA], 1998) reflect the concerns of the Pew Health Commission. The standards require that occupational therapy curricula provide students with an understanding of trends, models, roles, and responsibilities of policy development, service provision, and service delivery, related to, but not limited to, community. Occupational therapy chairpersons, program directors, and faculty are therefore challenged to develop and implement curriculum and instruction that supports these directives and to look at developing strong community ties that relate to potential service delivery opportunities.

Researchers have suggested that institutions of higher education have spent the last few decades encouraging individualism and competitive ideologies at the expense of altruism and collaboration for social purposes. As a result, students in the '90s lack some of the sense of responsibility toward others that previous generations have enjoyed (Couto, 1994; Giles & Eyler, 1994; Kalata, 1996). Knowledge of, or interest in, community is not considered a priority with much of today's youth. The 1999 Higher Education Research Institute (HERI) report on national norms for college freshmen (Sax, Astin, Korn, & Mahoney, 1999) indicates that although percentages of students who desire to participate in community action programs, influence social values, and become community leaders are still higher than their lowest percentage point in the '70s, overall student commitment to social activism is on the decline. Measurements of commitment to cleaning up the environment and helping people who are in difficulty fell to their lowest percentage points in over a decade and commitment to helping promote racial understanding dropped for the third consecutive year. The report also states that today's college freshmen are frequently bored in class, come late or miss class more, spend less time studying, and report high level of academic self-confidence. This suggests that students are entering colleges and universities with attitudes of reduced commitment to social issues already in place.

When considering ways to design and implement curricula to better prepare occupational therapy students for community-based practice, it may first be necessary for occupational therapy educators to begin with exploring basic methods of developing awareness of, positive attitudes towards, and responsibility or commitment to community. One of the tools that educators have used extensively for these purposes, as well as for improving academic performance, is service-learning. Through participation in service-learning, some educators have found that students frequently gain knowledge of community needs, develop community relationships, achieve some level of personal insight and growth, and make stronger connections to course work. A longitudinal study begun in 1995 at UCLA evaluated the Corporation for National Service's Learn and Serve America Higher Education (LSAHE) (Astin & Sax, 1998; Astin, Sax, & Avalos, 1999; Sax & Astin, 1997). The study looked at over 100 service-learning programs at colleges and universities nationwide and evaluated the impact of service-learning on three areas of student development: civic responsibility, academic development, and life skills. The findings concerning academic outcomes included improved knowledge and grades, and an increase in the amount of time devoted to academic endeavors for those students who participated in rigorous service (more than 20 hours).

Their results also suggested that participation was positively associated with improved life skills and civic responsibility outcomes. The literature generally refers to these types of outcomes as affective benefits indicating concepts such as awareness of and involvement in community, self-awareness, personal and professional growth, and civic responsibility (Batchelder & Root, 1994; Chambliss, Rinde, & Miller, 1996; Cohen & Kinsey, 1994; Corbett & Kendall, 1999; Driscoll et al., 1998; Driscoll, Holland, Gelmon, & Kerrigan, 1996; Markus, Howard, & King, 1993; Nnakwe, 1999; Paulins, 1999; Sax & Astin, 1997). The life skills outcomes, related to awareness and involvement in the community, included understanding of community problems, knowledge and understanding of different races and cultures, and interpersonal skills. During their college years, service-learning participants reported higher levels of satisfaction than non-participants in leadership opportunities, relevance of coursework to everyday life, and career preparation. Outcomes related to civic responsibility indicated that more than twice as many senior student participants as non-participants reported a stronger or much stronger commitment to community than when they were freshmen. More than four times as many student participants as non-participants reported they planned to continue their service commitment. In fact, the study reported that the strongest effect of participation in service-learning was on students' lifelong commitment to volunteerism and community activism.

A follow up to the UCLA longitudinal study endeavored to determine if any of these outcomes lasted beyond undergraduate school (Astin et al., 1999). Of the four categories of dependent variables, two categories, behavior outcomes and values, related most closely to affective outcomes. Behavioral outcomes included frequency of socializing with persons from other racial or ethnic groups and number of hours per week spent in service. Values included helping those in difficulty, degree of commitment to community action programs, participation in cleaning up the environment, promoting racial understanding, and developing a meaningful philosophy of life. The researchers found that the positive effects of participation in service-learning persisted beyond college and were greater for those who had a history of frequent community service in high school and college.

The Corporation for National Service (CNS) contracted with RAND for a three-year evaluation of the effects of service-learning programs on students, communities, and institutions. Data were collected from 1995 through 1997 from institutions that received grants from Learn and Serve America, Higher Education (LSAHE) (Gray, Ondaatje, Fricker, & Geschwind, 2000). The evaluation surveyed over: 1300 students from 28 institutions, 400 community organizations, and 260 program directors, and conducted over 30 visits to LSAHE sites. Part of the evaluation was devoted to a survey comparing self-reported attitudes, experiences, and outcomes of students participating in a course with a service-learning component to students participating in a similar course without a service-learning component. The results suggested that participation in course-based service did not necessarily translate to improved professional skills (i.e., confidence in major and career choice, career preparation, and graduation expectations). However participation was statistically significant for civic participation and life skills. In addition, the study found that students who served more than 20 hours per week were better able to regularly apply course concepts to their service experience, discuss their experiences in class, and exhibit higher academic and affective (civic and life) skills than those who served less than 20 hours per week. Other factors influencing positive outcomes were age (students over 25) and the ability to self-select the service site. These findings agree with Eyler and Giles' (1999) findings that certain service-learning program characteristics (i.e., placement quality, application, and reflection) are strong predictors of positive student outcomes. It may be concluded that it is not the simple presence of service-learning, but how service-learning is implemented and integrated into a course that relates to positive student outcomes.

Beginning in 1994 a group of researchers at Portland State University, funded by CNS and the Portland State University's Center for Academic Excellence, began to look at methods of measuring outcomes from participation in service-learning (Driscoll et al., 1996). One piece of that process included identifying and defining student outcomes linked to both academic and affective benefits. The study resulted in a workbook of strategies and methods for assessing service-learning. It provided, among other things, a refined table of variables (academic and affective), indicators

EXHIBIT 1
Variables and Indicators of Affective Outcomes from the Literature [1]

Awareness of Community	Information about community issues, needs, strengths, problems, and resources.
Involvement with Community	Quantity and quality of interactions, attitudes toward involvement, feedback from community, and reciprocity between community and students.
Commitment to Service	Positive and negative feelings and thoughts toward current service experience, plans for and barriers to future service, and reactions to demands and challenges of the service experience.
Self-Awareness	Understanding of strengths, limitations, goals, and fears and identified change in preconceived understandings.
Sensitivity to Diversity	Attitude, understanding of diversity, knowledge of new communities, self-confidence, and comfort with cultures different from one's own. This includes diversity issues and communities related to race, gender, age, disability, and economic and educational status.
Sense of Ownership	Autonomy and independence for supervisors/teachers, responsibility for community project, and sense of own role in the partnership.

[1] Adapted from Driscoll et al., 1998, p. 11

(definitions), and measurements of student outcomes (Driscoll et al., 1998). The variables and indicators most closely aligned with how the literature has defined affective outcomes are outlined in Exhibit 1.

Service-learning has been used by education, nursing, and the social sciences in higher education to enhance academic and affective outcomes or to improve student understanding of course material while developing a sense of community awareness, an attitude toward community service, and civic and social responsibility. However, there is a scarcity of literature in occupational therapy, and allied health care in general, concerning its use. Since the need for community-based occupational therapy services is growing, the need to prepare occupational therapy students for this practice area is also growing. Using the literature as a basis for analysis of affective outcomes, this study attempted to determine what impact participation in a service-learning experience, within occupational therapy practice courses, might have on occupational therapy students' awareness of and attitudes toward community and sense of civic and social responsibility.

RESEARCH QUESTION

This study was designed to determine the extent to which occupational therapy students who participated in service-learning were different, after the experience, in their awareness of community, attitude toward community, and/or their sense of responsibility for or commitment to community from occupational therapy students who did not participate in a service-learning experience.

METHODOLOGY

This study used a quasi-experimental design because experimental and comparison groups were used and, even though there was simple random selection without replacement of the groups, subjects were not randomly assigned to groups. The experimental groups participated in a single treatment or intervention (a service-learning experience for one semester) and the comparison groups had no treatment or intervention. The service-learning intervention was designed to connect to course work; meet a real and identified community need; be of sufficient quality to challenge attitude, awareness, and commitment; and provide opportunities for reflection. It differed from a typical internship in that it used students' community service to enhance learning, and vice versa, rather than applying students' learned skills to client or group needs and then evaluating those skills.

Because this study investigated the potential for service-learning to prepare occupational therapy students better for community-based practice,
the two courses chosen were directly related to the practice of occupational therapy. The 200-level course was concerned with laying the foundation for practice by exposing the student to theoretical frames of reference
used in occupational therapy practice, uniform terminology, and basic
clinical reasoning. This course was the first of two courses that presented
the material in a sequential manner over the life span. This course dealt
primarily with children and adolescents. The 400-level course provided
training and practice in evaluation, assessment, and treatment techniques
applied to various functional and physical disabilities primarily related to
adults. Both courses were offered in the fall semester. These types of
courses are required in all occupational therapy curricula because they
address the development of core skills and abilities necessary for therapeu-
tic practice and because they help occupational therapy curricula to meet
accreditation standards.

There were four groups, an experimental and comparison group for
each course. All groups were given a pre-test and post-test consisting of a
series of semantic differentials (SD) and the Community Service Involvement Preference Inventory (CSIPI). Only the experimental groups participated in a service-learning experience. In the data analysis, there were
times when the groups were treated as four groups and there were other
times when the groups were collapsed into two groups (all experimental
and all comparison).

This study also had a qualitative component in the form of journals and
responses to open-ended questions on a demographic survey. All groups
responded to the open-ended questions on the demographic survey at the
beginning of the semester and prior to initiating the service-learning experience. Only the experimental groups did written reflection on the service-learning experience in the form of journals.

Definitions

In this study, community is generally defined as the community of adults
with disabilities and children in the Scranton area. There are, however, facets or characteristics of community that will be specific to each participant
based on their service site. For example, the community of children may
include adults that have relationships with the children such as teachers,
day care supervisors, parents, and the participants in the study. Similarly,
the locality (school versus day care), cultural dimension (Jewish versus
Irish), or social dimension (Bingo versus girls' club) may differ from one
participant's service experience to another.

Attitude toward community is defined as a reflection (verbal, written, or behavioral) of the level of recognition (awareness or attentiveness) and understanding of races, cultures (including age, gender, disability, economic status, educational status, and the like) and community goals and needs and, the values that are assigned to them (Driscoll et al, 1998). Therefore it follows that in order to place a value on something, it is necessary to first be aware of it. Awareness that something exists requires a level of attentiveness and an accumulation of information about that something. In this study, awareness of community refers to demonstrating an accumulation of information about topics such as demographics and resources as well as showing a level of understanding about community issues and problems. The first three elements of Eyler and Giles' (1999, p.157) Five Elements of Citizenship contain the essence of awareness of community. The presence of Values (I ought to do), Knowledge (I know what I ought to do and why), and Skills (I know how to do) is a precursor to active and meaningful participation.

Commitment to community is characterized first by how involved an individual is in community service activities and second by an ongoing or future commitment to serving community needs (Driscoll et al., 1998). Future or ongoing commitment is linked to the belief that an individual participating in community service can make a difference. The last two of the Five Elements of Citizenship (Eyler & Giles, 1999) are Efficacy (I can do, and it makes a difference) and Commitment (I must and will do).

The literature also implies that individuals with a strong sense of citizenship, as defined by Eyler and Giles (1999), have all the elements of social responsibility. In this study, social responsibility implies a long-term, proactive, and self-motivated commitment to community and societal needs that is often connected to personal or career goals (Driscoll et al., 1998). Efficacy, or the belief that one can make a difference, is important to this concept. Putnam (1996) defines this type of belief in a responsibility toward society as civic engagement or the connectedness with community life brought about by individuals wanting to come together for a common purpose. Conversely, civic disengagement occurs because individuals see themselves as outsiders when it comes to social or civic concerns. They either do not believe they can make a difference or believe that experts or government agencies are better at bringing about social change (Boyte & Kari, 1996).

Sample Selection

The sample was purposive and convenient. The criteria for inclusion in the study were:

- Being enrolled full time in the occupational therapy curriculum;
- Willingness to participate in the study; and
- Enrollment in the particular OT course chosen for the study.

The 200-level course has a one-hour lecture and three lab sections. The 400-level course has a two-hour lecture and three lab sections. Labs were chosen by simple random selection.

Instruments

A Demographic Profile provided basic information about the participants that helped to better describe the sample population. The information included age, gender, grade level, and so forth, that bound or defined, the groups more clearly. The profile also provided information about participants' past service experiences, their feelings about those experiences, and what types of service experiences they would like to have if given a choice.

The semantic differential (SD) used in this study is similar to the one designed and used by Conrad and Hedin (1981) as an assessment of attitudes towards different objects or concepts in service-learning experiences. In general, the SD is "a method of observing and measuring the psychological meaning of concepts" (Kerlinger, 1973, p. 566). It is considered a useful and flexible approach to obtaining measures of attitudes, values, and affective sentiments (Grabhorn, 1998; Lawson, 1989; Nunnally, 1978). Originally developed by Charles Osgood in the 1950's, it has come to mean any "collection of rating scales anchored by bipolar adjectives" (Nunnally, p. 608). In addition, researchers state that it is useful for determining an individual's understanding of concepts and changes in attitudes (Kerlinger; Osgood, Suci, & Tannenbaum, 1971)). Concepts are rated by means of adjective pairs that fall into a particular factor of meaning (usually evaluation, potency, and activity). Evaluative factors are those that provide an assessment of value such as good-bad or clean-dirty. Potency refers to levels of strength such as strong-weak or aggressive-timid. Activity denotes movement or action such as fast-slow or active-passive. Reliability for test and retest were correlated across the 100 subjects and the 40 items, producing an N of 4000. The resulting coefficient was .85 (Osgood et al., 1971). It has also been tested across cultures with similar results.

The Community Service Involvement Preference Inventory (CSIPI, Payne, 1992) uses a Likert scale to measure levels of agreement or disagreement with statements related to community service and journal entries. The CSIPI was designed to measure service-learning implementation, impact on the development of civic values and responsibilities, and levels of involvement in community service. Concurrent validity of the CSIPI was determined by analyzing the relationship between responses on the four phases of the CSIPI and Kolb's Learning-Style Inventory (LSI, Kolb & Fry, 1975).

> Phase 3 of the [CSIPI] had a significant and positive correlation with Phase 1 of the LSI (r = .2308, $p < .01$) and a negative and significant correlation with Phase 2 of the LSI ($r = -.1526$, $p < .05$). Phase 4 of the [CSIPI] had a positive and significant correlation with Phase 1 of the LSI ($r = .2020$, $p < .01$) and a negative and significant correlation with Phase 2 of the LSI ($r = -.1502$, $p < .05$). None of the other correlations were significant (Payne, 1992, p. 125).

Payne attempted to explain this weak showing of concurrent validity by pointing out that the LSI identifies differences in learning styles, rather than the development of learning, and, as a result, the LSI may not reflect the developmental nature of understanding what it is to be a responsible citizen, purported by the Service-Learning Model, and attempted by the CSIPI. Internal reliability for each phase of the CSIPI ranged from $r = 0.5266$ (Phase 1—Exploration) to $r = 0.7582$ (Phase 3—Experimentation). Although this is not indicative of a very high level of internal consistency, there is a clear consistency of responses to test items across the phases, and Payne believed the coefficients were in the right direction and showed considerable promise. Subsequent studies on the reliability have produced better results (Payne & Bennett, 1999, Payne under review). Internal reliability for Phase 1—Exploration, and Phase 2—Affiliation, increased to ($r = 0.6383$) and ($r = 0.7001$) respectively. Phase 3—Experimentation and Phase 4—Assimilation coefficients were slightly decreased at ($r = 0.7414$) and ($r = 0.7062$), respectively.

The journals were the final measurement tool and were in part analyzed using the Service-Learning Model (Delve, Mintz, & Stewart, 1990). The research seems to indicate that commitment to service increases as participation in quality service experiences increases. The long-range affective effects of participation positively impacts on life skills and civic skills or civic responsibility. This suggests that growth in life and civic skills is, in part, a developmental process. The instruments used in this study attempted to address this developmental component. The SLM was an attempt to conceptualize the process that students go through as they participate in service-learning experiences. The authors developed a theoretical framework that identified and explained a series of five phases that participants pass through culminating in a state of internalization of a life-long commitment to community service. Stewart (1990), one of the authors of the SLM, believed that Kolb's (1984) Experiential Learning Theory was an appropriate foundation for deciding how to structure a service-learning experience to best accommodate different learning styles. For example, individuals who tend to focus more on people or activity may prefer a direct hands-on approach to service, whereas people who tend to be more reflective may be better planners. Each phase of the Service-Learning Model is identified by the quality of the intervention, the level of commitment to the service activity, the participant's behavior, and the amount of balance achieved between the challenges of the experience and the support systems needed. The authors believe that in order for students to progress, there needs to be sufficient balance between challenges and overload to prevent retreat from participation and to promote the ability to move on.

The phases of the SLM are Exploration, Clarification, Realization, Activation, and Internalization. Four variables (intervention, commitment, behavior, and balance) apply to each phase, and each variable is further subdivided into two descriptive classifications. The goal for transition through the phases is to cycle from charity to justice and from individual exploration to internalization of issues relating to society.

The theoretical framework of the SLM led Payne (1992) to develop the CSIPI. He advocated that service-learning participants pass through four phases as they advance toward an integrated relationship with the community and a stronger sense of civic responsibility and citizenship. As explained above, Payne also used Kolb's Experiential Theory Model to determine how a service-learning experience may be designed and understood differently by different types of learners.

RESULTS

A total of 69 students from two different level occupational therapy practice courses participated in the study. One hundred percent (n = 29) of the 200-level course students, and 93 percent (n = 40) of the 400-level course students participated. There were 44 students in the experimental group and 25 in the comparison group.

Because this study investigated the potential for service-learning to better prepare occupational therapy students for community-based practice, the courses chosen were directly related to the practice of occupational therapy. The 200-level course was concerned with laying the foundation for practice by exposing the student to theoretical frames of reference used in occupational therapy practice, uniform terminology, and basic clinical reasoning and dealt primarily with children and adolescents. The 400-level course provided training and practice in evaluation, assessment, and treatment techniques applied to various functional and physical disabilities primarily related to adults. Both courses were offered in the fall semester.

Overall the data from the Demographic Profile appear to indicate little difference between experimental and comparison groups for each level and, to some extent, across the course levels. Age ranges for the 200-level group were from 18 to 20 and for the 400-level group from 20 to 22. The average age was 20. All students had service experience prior to participating in this study. It is clear that participants tended to respond in a similar fashion to most experience types and preferences for service experiences.

Semantic Differential

Concepts for this study included the population served (e.g., children, adolescents, adults, and people with disabilities), community, and community service. Students participating in the 200-level course completed a semantic differential for the concepts of Children, Adolescents, Community, and Community Service. Students participating in the 400-level course completed a semantic differential for the concepts of Adults, People with Disabilities, Community, and Community Service.

EXHIBIT 2

ANOVA for the Factors of Semantic Differential for 200 Experimental and Comparison Groups for the Concepts Children and Adolescents: Differences Between Pre-test and Post-test Means

Concept/Factor	Mean Square	df	F	Sig.
Children				
Evaluative				
Pre/post ('e' & 'c')*	.106	1	.464	.502
Potency				
Pre/post ('e' & 'c')	1.529	1	4.862	.036
Activity				
Pre/post ('e' & 'c')	.473	1	1.369	.253
Adolescents				
Evaluative				
Pre/post ('e' & 'c')	.101	1	1.007	.322
Potency				
Pre/post ('e' & 'c')	.123	1	1.289	.263
Activity				
Pre/post ('e' & 'c')	.024	1	.107	.745

* 'e' = experimental, 'c' = comparison

The analysis of the changes in distance and direction on the semantic scale (between adjective pairs) for pre-test to post-test means indicate that there were no global changes but rather very selective ones. Three observations can be made. First, the experimental groups overwhelmingly showed more moderate and maximal changes than did the comparison groups. Second, of the changes that occurred, 87 percent (20) of the experimental groups' changes were moves toward a semantic pole whereas only 31 percent (5) of the comparison groups' changes were movements toward a pole. This suggests that the participants in the experimental groups showed a tendency to become more certain about a concept while participants in the comparison groups tended to become less certain. Third, the changes in attitude were greatest within the experimental groups, and these changes occurred more in the 200-level experimental group (Children, Adolescents, and Community) than the 400-level experimental group (Community). This may suggest that overall the 200-level experimental group was the group most influenced by participation in service-learning. It may also suggest that the 400-level experimental group was less amenable to change because they were older and had had more experience with service-learning. However, since the 400-level experimental and comparison groups had participated equally in service-learning since enrolling at the university, except for this semester, it would be expected that the difference between the groups' responses to the concept community should not be so notable.

EXHIBIT 3

ANOVA for the Factors of Semantic Differential for 400 Experimental and Comparison Groups for the Concepts Adults and People with Disabilities: Differences Between Pre-test and Post-test Means

Concept/Factor	Mean Square	df	F	Sig.
Adults				
Evaluative				
Pre/post ('e' & 'c')*	1.708	1	4.793	.038
Potency				
Pre/post ('e' & 'c')	.422	1	1.168	.290
Activity				
Pre/post ('e' & 'c')	1.143	1	1.938	.176
People with Disabilities				
Evaluative				
Pre/post ('e' & 'c')	.009	1	.092	.764
Potency				
Pre/post ('e' & 'c')	.017	1	.085	.772
Activity				
Pre/post ('e' & 'c')	.027	1	.133	.717

* 'e' = experimental, 'c' = comparison

The analyses of variance for the concepts of the semantic differential show that there was only one significant pre-test to post-test change in attitude (as measured by factor) for the 200-level group (see Exhibit 2), and one for the 400-level group (see Exhibit 3). The *potency* factor for the concept Children had an F value of 4.862 at a .036 significance level. The *eval-*

uative factor for the concept Adults had an F value of 4.793 at a .038 significance level. There were no significant differences between experimental and comparison groups or between course levels for the concepts that combined 200 and 400-level groups (see Exhibit 4).

EXHIBIT 4

ANOVA for the Factors of Semantic Differential for Combined 200 and 400 Experimental and Comparison Groups for the Concepts Community Service and Community: Differences Between Pre-test and Post-test Means

Concept/Factor	Mean Square	df	F	Sig.
Community Service				
Evaluative				
Pre/post ('e' & 'c')*	.452	1	2.627	.110
Pre/post (course)	.039	1	.227	.636
Potency				
Pre/post ('e' & 'c')	.007	1	.027	.871
Pre/post (course)	.039	1	.158	.692
Activity				
Pre/post ('e' & 'c')	2.180	1	2.704	.105
Pre/post (course)	.003	1	.003	.956
Community				
Evaluative				
Pre/post ('e' & 'c')	.377	1	1.198	.278
Pre/post (course)	.005	1	.175	.677
Potency				
Pre/post ('e' & 'c')	.480	1	2.264	.137
Pre/post (course)	.001	1	.005	.941
Activity				
Pre/post ('e' & 'c')	.655	1	2.687	.106
Pre/post (course)	.064	1	.264	.609

* 'e' = experimental, 'c' = comparison

CSIPI

The CSIPI is divided into four phases. The phases of the CSIPI (exploration, affiliation, experimentation, and assimilation) were designed to correspond with the first four phases of the SLM (exploration, clarification, realization, and activation). Phase three (realization) of the SLM marks the beginning of community awareness whereas Phase four (activation) marks the beginning of civic responsibility.

Each of the four phases has an affective, behavioral, and cognitive dimension. The affective dimension identifies characteristics that are evaluative. The behavioral dimension defines the action or activity level. And the cognitive dimension concerns those processes that underlie the level of understanding.

ANOVA, calculated as a difference score of the pre-test and post-test mean, indicated there were no statistically significant pre-test to post-test changes for any of the phases of the CSIPI when accounting for course-level or comparison and experimental groups. ANOVA were also calculated to account for the effect of course-level and comparison and experimental groups on the pre-test to post-test differences for the factors of the CSIPI (affective, behavioral, and cognitive) for each phase. Again, there was no statistically significant pre-test to post-test changes for any of the factors in any of the phases (Exhibits 5 and 6).

EXHIBIT 5

ANOVA for the Phases of the CSIPI: Pre/Post Interaction Accounting for Differences Between Experimental and Comparison Groups and Courses

Phases	Mean Square	df	F	Sig.
PHASE 1				
Pre/post ('e' & 'c')*	2.585	1	.157	.693
Pre/post (course)	3.347	1	.204	.653
PHASE 2				
Pre/post ('e' & 'c')	7.512	1	.270	.605
Pre/post (course)	8.132	1	.292	.591
PHASE 3				
Pre/post ('e' & 'c')	.987	1	.051	.822
Pre/post (course)	15.331	1	.797	.376
PHASE 4				
Pre/post ('e' & 'c')	.608	1	.030	.864
Pre/post (course)	16.697	1	.816	.370

* 'e' = experimental, 'c' = comparison

EXHIBIT 6
ANOVA for the Factors of the CSIPI by Phase: Pre/Post Interaction
Accounting for Differences Between Experimental and Comparison
Groups and Courses

Factors/Phases	Mean Square	df	F	Sig.
PHASE 1				
Affective				
Pre/post ('e' & 'c')*	2.628	1	.577	.450
Pre/post (course)	1.886	1	.414	.522
Behavioral				
Pre/post ('e' & 'c')	5.384	1	1.823	.182
Pre/post (course)	.298	1	.101	.752
Cognitive				
Pre/post ('e' & 'c')	5.446	1	1.069	.305
Pre/post (course)	7.059	1	1.386	.244
PHASE 2				
Affective				
Pre/post ('e' & 'c')	8.685	1	1.492	.227
Pre/post (course)	.296	1	.051	.822
Behavioral				
Pre/post ('e' & 'c')	1.014	1	.168	.683
Pre/post (course)	3.950	1	.656	.421
Cognitive				
Pre/post ('e' & 'c')	.641	1	.108	.744
Pre/post (course)	.102	1	.017	.896
PHASE 3				
Affective				
Pre/post ('e' & 'c')	.074	1	.024	.879
Pre/post (course)	1.669	1	.533	.468
Behavioral				
Pre/post ('e' & 'c')	1.444	1	.284	.596
Pre/post (course)	1.444	1	.284	.596
Cognitive				
Pre/post ('e' & 'c')	.010	1	.004	.952
Pre/post (course)	2.557	1	.896	.348
PHASE 4				
Affective				
Pre/post ('e' & 'c')	.898	1	.263	.610
Pre/post (course)	.176	1	.052	.821
Behavioral				
Pre/post ('e' & 'c')	2.952	1	.576	.451
Pre/post (course)	1.422	1	.278	.600
Cognitive				
Pre/post ('e' & 'c')	.0024	1	.001	.982
Pre/post (course)	6.443	1	1.374	.246

* 'e' = experimental, 'c' = comparison

Journal

There was an 82 percent return rate on journals. Descriptive analysis of the entries was accomplished by looking for evidence of the concepts of awareness of community, attitude toward community, commitment toward community, and civic responsibility.

There was an awareness of community noted for both 200- and 400-level participants. This awareness was noted when participants commented on the populations served, resources, or the lack of resources, and basic identification of issues affecting the organization or those served.

Those participants who displayed attitudes toward the community that were negative or attitudes about the experience that were directed toward self, tended to indicate a frustration or lack of commitment to community service that was connected to course requirements. One-half of the 200-level participants, and nearly half (45%) of the 400-level participants, displayed either a strong dislike for the experience or a lack of interest in continuing the experience beyond the course requirements. Some of this discontentment was due to a dislike of the population ("I really do not like children," and "I would not choose to volunteer with the elderly"), but some was also a response to *having* to perform service ("It takes the beauty out of it and strips it of its meaning and value"). Conversely, where attitudes toward community were positive, there was a tendency toward a positive commitment to community as well ("I feel very strongly about serving others because I feel as though in doing so we gain a better appreciation for people, life, and ourselves"). This commitment was indicated by faithful attendance to the service site and/or a decision to continue the service experience beyond the semester or course requirement.

Civic responsibility necessitates that one be aware, committed and have a reflective attitude toward community. It frequently includes individuals making personal or career choices that will help them to respond more effectively to community needs. This last component is evident in 18.75 percent of the 200-level and 15 percent of the 400-level participants.

The descriptive analysis of journal entries also identified four recurrent themes other than those described above. First, most participants tended to react to situations rather than initiate solutions. Thirteen 200-level (81.25%) and twelve 400-level (60%) participants described situations requiring some type of intervention, not necessarily skilled. Often these situations, as described, were within the scope of the participant's knowledge and ability to intervene (e.g., seeking information, initiating activities or a plan to act, suggesting simple solutions). Participants reacted in writing but never progressed, cognitively or actively, to initiating a response to a situation. Second, participants asked many questions about their experiences, but gave no indication in subsequent journal entries that answers to their questions had either been found or sought. Third, those who questioned authority early in their service experience were more inclined, and better able, to achieve some positive change. One 200-level participant (6.25%) and five 400-level participants (25%) openly questioned authorities at their service sites within the first few visits to the site. Although this is not a large showing, each one was able to produce some change in how a certain client or situation was handled at least when the participant was present. The fourth theme is related to longevity of service. Participants who voluntarily spent more hours participating in a service-learning activity than required or who expressed a personal commitment to community service, were more effective in their reflection. In fact, it may not actually be considered a theme because none of the 200-level participants and only two (10%) of the 400-level participants shared this level of reflection. These individuals clearly spent time considering their service experience. Issues of social justice, fairness, hypocrisy, culture, and lack of resources were common sources of unrest for these participants. Rather than causing them to retreat, these issues appeared to increase their commitment to providing community service, not because it made them feel good, but because their lives were being changed.

Journal entries were also coded using the Service-Learning Model (SLM, Delve, Mintz, & Stewart, 1990) as a rubric to identify developmental levels of participation in the service experience as reported by participants in their journals. The data from the rubric were coded by phases and developmental variables and were reported using frequencies (percentages). The intent was to acquire a sense of any developmental progress that the participants may have gone through. For example, did a participant grow from Phase 2 of the SLM to Phase 3? According to the authors, although a participant can enter the rubric at any point (Phase 1 through Phase 5), relative to their learning style and past experiences with community service, their developmental level for each variable should remain consistent within that Phase. For example, those functioning at a Phase 1 level prefer structured, group service activities that are short-term and non-threatening. For a complete grid of the SLM, see Exhibit 7.

The 200-level participants tended overall to fall within either Phase 1 or Phase 2 (see Exhibit 8). Phase 1 participants expressed a desire for the experience to be short-term, did not initiate involvement, and frequently wrote about their need to feel good about the experience as a measure of a successful experience. Phase 2 participants performed their service with classmates and had a combination of direct and indirect contact with the populations being served. They were unclear about what was expected of them and required frequent clarification and structured activities in which to be involved.

Exhibit 8 shows that journal entries for 400-level participants tended to fall in either Phase 2 (Clarification) or Phase 3 (Realization). Phase 2 participants worked and developed relationships based on groups. It was through group process that they chose, or were assigned, the activities in

EXHIBIT 7

Rubric Adapted from the Service-Learning Model[2]

Developmental Variables	Phase 1 Exploration	Phase 2 Clarification	Phase 3 Realization	Phase 4 Activation	Phase 5 Internalization
Intervention					
Mode	Group	Group	Group	Group	Individual
Setting	Non-Direct Contact Indirect Contact	Non-Direct Contact Indirect Contact Direct Contact	Indirect Contact Direct Contact	Indirect Contact Direct Contact	Indirect Contact Direct Contact
Commitment					
Frequency	One Time	Several Activities or Sites	Consistently at One Site	Consistently at One Site	Consistently at One Site
Duration	Short-Term	Long-Term Commitment to Group	Long-Term Commitment to Activity, Site, or Issue (Beginnings of Community Awareness)	Lifelong Commitment to Issue (Beginnings of Civic Responsibility)	Lifelong Commitment to Social Justice

(continued)

EXHIBIT 7
Continued

Developmental Variables	Phase 1 Exploration	Phase 2 Clarification Group Non-Direct Contact Indirect Contact Direct Contact	Phase 3 Realization Group Non-Direct Contact Indirect Contact Direct Contact	Phase 4 Activation Group Non-Direct Contact Indirect Contact Direct Contact	Phase 5 Internalization
Behavior					
Needs	Participate in Incentive Activities	Identify with Group Camaraderie	Commit to Activity, Site, or Issue	Advocate for Issue(s)	Promote Values
Outcomes	Feeling Good	Belonging to a Group	Understanding Activity, Site, or Issue	Changing Lifestyle	Living One's Values
Balance					
Challenges	Becoming Involved	Choosing from Multiple Opportunities/Group Process	Confronting Diversity and Breaking from Group	Questioning Authority/Adjusting to Peer Pressure	Living Consistently with Values
Supports	Activities are Non-Threatening and Structured	Group Setting, Identification and Activities are Structured	Supervisors, Coordinators, Faculty, and Other Volunteers	Partners, Clients, and Other Volunteers	Community—Have Achieved a Considerable Inner Support System

[2]Adapted from Delve, Mintz, & Stewart, 1990

which they would participate, and it was to the group they retreated when needing support. Journal entries for 400-level participants that corresponded highly to Phase 3 indicated they had considerable direct contact with populations served and were consistently at the same service site. Their reflections were more extrinsic in nature. They were also beginning to show deeper levels of understanding related to what they were doing, the service site itself, or a particular issue that was broader than either of their activities or the site.

EXHIBIT 8
Results of Journal Entries Using the Service-Learning Model

	Phase 1 Exploration		Phase 2 Clarification		Phase 3 Realization		Phase 4 Activation		Phase 5 Internalization	
200: n = 16 400: n = 20	200%	400%	200%	400%	200%	400%	200%	400%	200%	400%
Mode	12.5		62.5	45.0	6.3	20.0		5.0	12.5	25.0
Setting	18.8		62.5	35.0	18.8	60.0				
Frequency	6.3		37.5	15.0	56.3	85.0				
Duration	81.3	85.0	6.3	5.0	12.5	10.0				
Needs	37.5		37.5	55.0	25.0	45.0				
Outcomes	68.8	30.0	6.3	15.0	12.5	55.0	12.5	5.0		
Challenges	75.0	5.0	6.3	55.0	12.5	15.0	6.3	25.0		
Supports	37.5		43.8	50.0	12.5	45.0				

Phase 3 marks the beginning of community awareness. Phase 4 marks the beginning of civic responsibility. Based on journal entries alone, an average of 20 percent of 200-level participants and 40 percent of 400-level participants were at Phase 3 and could therefore be considered to have the beginnings of community awareness. Similarly an average of about 2 percent of 200-level participants and 4 percent of 400-level participants exhibited the beginnings of civic responsibility.

DISCUSSION AND CONCLUSIONS

Inferential analyses of results from instruments used to measure awareness of community suggest that no change occurred between experimental and comparison groups as a result of participation in service-learning. However, the descriptive data suggests that differences did occur. It may be that different methods of measuring awareness of community, or longer or more frequent service experiences, are needed in order to determine if participation has any effect. The data suggest though that even minimal participation can provide a meaningful experience.

Similarly, the inferential analyses indicate no differences in attitude toward community occurred as a result of participation in a service-learning experience. However, the descriptive analyses and the qualitative data analyses indicate that not only did both the experimental and comparison groups have more definitive attitudes toward community at the end of the study, but the 200-level experimental group showed the most change.

Finally, the 200-level group did not achieve a level of civic responsibility but was more interested in commitment to and responsibility toward community than the 400-level group. The 400-level group, however, was higher functioning. Based on the Semantic Differential, the 200-level experimental group showed more movement in distance and direction than any of the other groups for attitudes toward concepts, but there were no statistical differences between groups for the factors of the SD. The CSIPI also showed no statistical differences for the phases. And finally, the journal entries, overall, indicated that the 200-level experimental group was functioning within the introductory and awareness phases whereas the 400-level experimental group was functioning within the awareness and commitment phases. It may be concluded that the 200-level experimental group showed the most difference but that they did not fully achieve commitment to or a sense of responsibility for community, as measured by this study's instruments. The 400-level groups showed no statistical difference but, based on their journal entries, the 400-level experimental group had achieved a level of commitment and responsibility.

As a result of this study, several points from the research literature were reinforced and several additional conclusions are suggested. The quality of the placement, the amount of time spent at the service site, and the opportunities for meaningful reflection on the service experience are essential components for positive student outcomes. The design of this study restricted all three of these components, and, as a result, probably did not provide participants with the full realization of what participation in a service-learning experience could achieve. The implication is that future service-learning experiences for occupational therapy students should be designed with these components more fully integrated.

One of the strengths of this study's design was that it sampled a cross section of a population of occupational therapy students. This allowed for a broader view of the developmental process outlined in the SLM and the CSIPI. The attachment of the service component to practice courses was another strength of the study. These types of courses exist in all occupational therapy curricula, and therefore this design could be replicated more easily than one that used unique courses.

Conversely, the design drew participants from only one occupational therapy program. The participants may not be representative of all occupational therapy students. All programs have similar admission standards and certain standards of practice that must be maintained, but this sameness does not necessarily explain or expose potential social, economic, and cultural differences that may occur at other colleges and universities. The relatively small sample size also limits the generalizability of the findings.

The idea that many consider that the outcomes related to service-learning are developmental has considerable implications for curriculum design and the measurement of those outcomes. That is, service that is connected to and integrated into a course or course of study, that meets real community needs, and that provides an opportunity for critical reflection on the service experience and its relationship to the student's studies (American Association of Community Colleges, 1995; Bringle & Hatcher, 1996; Cohen & Kinsey, 1996; Couto, 1994; Enos & Troppe, 1996; Eyler & Giles, 1999; Oates, 1996).

An additional consideration not mentioned in the literature concerning design, and of particular interest to the original purpose of this study, may be to incorporate service-learning developmentally into a curriculum. That is, to design service-learning programs within a curriculum with certain expectations in mind. For example, if the participants are young and inexperienced, perhaps the service-learning expectations should concentrate on developing a more concrete awareness of demographics and resources and only begin to heighten a reflective attitude toward community issues and cultures. If the participants are more experienced, then the service-learning experience could be designed to elicit stronger commitments to issues and sensitivity and understanding of cultural norms and expectations. This study appears to support the latter suggestion. For those curricula, like occupational therapy and other service-oriented professions, that tend to be more lock step, developmental integration would be easier to accomplish. Similarly, the measurement of student outcomes could parallel the developmental levels that the service-learning experience sought to achieve. Using or designing a measurement tool that incorporated the developmental scale put forth by Delve, Mintz, and Stewart (1990) and possibly combining it with Eyler and Giles' (1999) Five Elements of Citizenship could provide a course instructor with valuable formative and summative information as to the success of the service-learning component and where adjustments may need to be made. This could ensure that outcomes meet expectations but would not necessarily deter a student from surpassing expectations.

REFERENCES

American Association of Community Colleges. (1995). *Community colleges and service-learning.* Washington, DC: Corporation for National and Community Service.

American Occupational Therapy Association. (1998). *Standards for an accredited educational program for the occupational therapist.* Bethesda, MD: Author.

Astin, A. W., & Sax, L. J. (1998). How undergraduates are affected by service participation. *Journal of College Student Development, 39*(3), 251-263.

Astin, A., Sax, L., & Avalos, J. (1999). Long-term effects of volunteerism during the undergraduate years. *The Review of Higher Education, 22,* 187-202.

Astin, A. W., Sax, L. J., Korn, W. S., & Mahoney, K. M. (1999). *The American freshman norms for fall 1999.* Los Angeles: Higher Education Research Institute, UCLA.

Batchelder, T. H., & Root, S. (1994). Effects of an undergraduate program to integrate academic learning and service: Cognitive, prosocial cognitive, and identity outcomes. *Journal of Adolescence, 17,* 341-355.

Boyte, H. C., & Kari, N. N. (1996). *Meanings of citizenship.* Excerpt from Building America: The democratic promise of public work. Philadelphia: Temple University Press.

Bringle, R. G., & Hatcher, J. A (1996). Implementing service-learning in higher education. *Journal of Higher Education, 67,* 221-239.

Chambliss, C., Rinde, C., & Miller, J. (1999). *The liberal arts and applied learning: Reflections about the internship experience.* Position Paper, Ursinus College. (ERIC Document Reproduction Service No. ED 399 916).

Cohen, J., & Kinsey, D. F. (1994, Winter). Doing good and scholarship: A service-learning study. *Journalism Educator,* 4-14.

Conrad, D., & Hedin, D. (1981). *Instruments and scoring guide of the experiential education evaluation project.* St. Paul, MN: University of Minnesota, Center for Youth Development and Research.

Corbett, J. B., & Kendall A. R. (1999, Winter). Evaluating service-learning in the communication discipline. *Journalism and Mass Communication Educator,* 66-76.

Couto, R. A. (1994, September). *Teaching democracy through experiential education: Bringing the community into the classroom.* Paper presented at the Annual Meeting of the American Political Science Association, New York, NY. (ERIC Document Reproduction Service No. ED 381 422).

Delve, C. I., Mintz, S. D., & Stewart, G. M. (1990). Promoting values development through community service: A design. *New Directions for Student Services, 50,* 7-29.

Driscoll, A., Gelmon, S., Holland, B., Kerrigan, S., Spring, A., Grosvold, K., & Longley, M.J. (1998). *Assessing the impact of service-learning: A workbook of strategies and methods* (2nd ed.). (ERIC Document Reproduction Service No. ED 432 949).

Driscoll, A., Holland, B., Gelmon, S., & Kerrigan, S. (1996). An assessment model for service-learning: Comprehensive case studies of impact on faculty, students, community, and institution. *Michigan Journal of Community Service Learning, 3,* 66-71.

Engelhardt, H. T. (1977). Defining occupational therapy: The meaning of therapy and the virtues of occupation. *American Journal of Occupational Therapy, 31*(10), 666-672.

Enos, S., & Troppe, M. (1996). *Curricular models for service-learning.* Metropolitan universities, New Brunswick, NJ: Transaction Periodicals Consortium.

Eyler, J., & Giles D. (1999). *Where's the learning in service-learning?* San Francisco: Jossey-Bass.

Fazio, L. S. (2000). *Developing occupation-centered programs for the community: A workbook for students and professional.* Upper Saddle River, NJ: Prentice Hall.

Grabhorn, R. (1998). *Affective experience in a case of group therapy with psychosomatic inpatients. Psychoanalytic Inquiry.* New York: International Universities Press.

Giles, D. E., & Eyler, J. (1994). The theoretical roots of service-learning in John Dewey: Toward a theory of service-learning *Michigan Journal of Community Service learning, 1*(1), 77-85.

Grace, W. (1996, February). *Values, vision, voice, virtue: The 4 "V" model for ethical leadership development.* Paper presented at the Fifth Annual International Conference for Community & Technical College Chairs, Deans, and Other Organizational Leaders, Phoenix/Mesa, Arizona. (ERIC Document Reproduction Service No. ED 394 542).

Gray, M. J., Ondaatje, E. H., Fricker, R. D., Jr., & Geschwind, S. A. (2000, March/April). Assessing service-learning: Results from a survey of "Learn and Serve America, Higher Education" *Change*, 30-39.

Kalata, P. (1996, June). *Generational clash in the academy: Whose culture is it anyway?* Essays by Fellows in the Mid-Career Fellowship Program, Princeton University. (ERIC Document Reproduction Service No. ED 397 874).

Kerlinger, F. N. (1973). *Foundations of behavioral research* (2nd ed.). New York: Holt, Rinehart, and Winston.

Kielhofner, G. (1992). *Conceptual foundations of occupational therapy.* Philadelphia: F. A. Davis.

Kniepmann, K. (1997). Prevention of disability and maintenance of health. In C. Christiansen & C. Baum (Eds.), *Occupational therapy enabling function and wellbeing* (pp. 531-553). Thorofare, NJ: Slack.

Kolb, D. A. (1984). *Experiential learning: Experience as the source of learning and development.* Englewood Cliffs, NJ: Prentice-Hall.

Kolb, D. A., & Fry R. (1975). Towards an applied theory of experiential learning. In C. L. Cooper (Ed.), *Theories of group processes* (pp. 33-58). London: John Wiley.

Lawson, E. D. (1989). Sex-related values and attitudes of college students: A sexism scale vs. the semantic differential. *Psychological Reports, 64*(2), 463-476.

Leder, D., & McGuinness, I. (1996, Summer). Making the paradigm shift: Service-learning in higher education. *Journal for Metropolitan Universities: An International Forum, 7*(1), 47-56.

Markus, G. P., Howard, J. P., & King, D. C. (1993). Integrating community service and classroom instruction enhances learning: Results from an experiment. *Education Evaluation and Policy Analysis, 15*, 410-419.

Nnakwe, N. E. (1999). Implementation and impact of college community service and its effect on the social responsibility of undergraduate students *Journal of Family and Consumer Sciences, 91*(2), 57-61.

Nunnally, J. C. (1978). *Psychometric theory* (2nd. ed.). New York: McGraw-Hill.

Oates, K., (1996, October). *Integration and assessment of service-learning into the curriculum.* Paper presented at the annual conference of the Association for Integrative Studies. Ypsilanti, MI. (ERIC Document Reproduction Service No. ED 403 855).

Osgood, C. E., Suci, G. J., & Tannenbaum, P. H. (1971). *The measurement of meaning.* Urbana, Ill: University of Illinois Press.

Paulins, V. A. (1999). Service-learning and civic responsibility: The consumer in American society. *Journal of Family and Consumer Sciences, 91*(2), 66-72.

Payne, C. A. (1992). *Construction of an instrument to assess the service-learning model: Establishing concurrent validity and internal reliability.* Doctoral Dissertation, University of Northern Colorado. Ann Arbor , MI: University of Michigan.

Payne, C. A. (2001). *Changes in involvement preferences as measured by the community service involvement preference inventory.* Manuscript submitted for publication.

Payne, C. A., & Bennett, E. B. (1999). Service-learning and changes in involvement preferences among undergraduates. *National Association of Student Personnel Administrators Journal, 37*(1), 337-347.

Pew Health Professions Commission. (1998, December). *Recreating Health Professional Practice for a New Century. Fourth Report.* San Francisco: The Center for the Health Professions, University of California Press.

Putnam, R. (1996). The strange disappearance of civic America. *The American Prospect, 7*(24), 34-48.

Reilly, M. (1962). Occupational therapy can be one of the great ideas of 20th century medicine. *American Journal of Occupational Therapy, 16*, 1-9.

Rogers, J. (1983). The study of human occupation. In G. Kielhofner (Ed.). *Health through occupation: Theory and practice in occupational therapy* (pp 93-124). Philadelphia: F. A. Davis.

Sax, L., & Astin, A. (1997). The benefits of service: Evidence from undergraduates. *Educational Record, 78*, 25-32.

Sax, L. J., Astin, A. W., Korn, W. S., & Mahoney, K. M. (1999). *The American freshman: National norms for fall 1999.* Los Angeles: UCLA Higher Education Research Institute.

Stewart, G. (1990). Learning styles as a filter for developing service-learning interventions. *New Directions for Student Services, 50*, 31-42.

Wilcock, A. (1998). *An occupational perspective of health.* Thorofare, NJ: Slack.

Yerxa, E. J., Clark, F., Frank, G., Jackson, J., Parham, D., Pierce, D., Stein, C., & Zemke, R. (1990). An introduction to occupational science: A foundation for occupational therapy in the 21st century. *Occupational Therapy in Health Care, 6*(4), 1-17.

PART IV

THE IMPACTS ON SERVICE-LEARNING PARTICIPANTS

CHAPTER 8

COMMUNITY AGENCY PERSPECTIVES IN HIGHER EDUCATION
Service-Learning and Volunteerism

Andrea Vernon and Lenoar Foster

INTRODUCTION

Research pertaining to service-learning as a viable pedagogy for teaching subject material and civic responsibility continues to expand as higher education institutions nationwide look to service-learning as a means to enhance both community service and student learning. Literature in the field documents the impacts of higher education service-learning on students, faculty, and institutions. What is less clear, however, is the community's perspective on higher education service-learning and volunteer activities, and the perceived impacts that college students have on the needs they are trying to address in the community either as service-learn-

Service-Learning Through a Multidisciplinary Lens
A Volume in: Advances in Service-Learning Research, pages 153–175.
ISBN: 1-931576-81-5 (cloth), 1-931576-80-7 (paper)

ing participants or volunteers. Without an informed understanding about how college student service-learning and volunteer activities impact the community agencies and individuals being served, service-learning programs are overlooking the collaborative ingredient between campuses and communities that is crucial for effective service-learning (Sigmon, 1979). In order to add to the body of knowledge regarding the effectiveness and impacts of service-learning, researchers and practitioners in the field have identified the need to engage in research that examines community-based perceptions of higher education service-learning programs (Chesler & Vasques Scalera, 2000; Cruz & Giles, 2000; Ferrari & Worrall, 2000; Vernon & Ward, 1999; Ward & Wolf-Wendel, 1997).

The purpose of this study was to examine college student service-learning and volunteer activities from the community perspective via data gathered from community agency personnel who work directly with college student service-learning participants and volunteers. The study examined the perceived impacts that college students have at the community agencies where they serve and on the needs of youth their service is addressing. The study concentrated on service to meet the needs of youth because this is the population on which the majority of college students' service-learning and volunteer activities focus (Campus Compact, 1999). College students worked with community agencies to serve youth in a variety of ways including tutoring, mentoring, and coaching. More specifically, the study sought to answer the following research questions:

- How do community agencies form collaborative service-based partnerships with higher education institutions?
- According to agency personnel, what impacts do college student volunteers have at the youth service agencies where they serve?
- What impacts do college student volunteers have on youth through their volunteer service efforts as perceived by community agency personnel?
- What views does the community have about college student volunteers as perceived by community agency personnel?

REVIEW OF LITERATURE

A review of literature pertaining to higher education service-learning was performed to identify the impacts of service-learning on communities. Studies indicate that communities are generally satisfied with student service, that the service is useful, and communities report enhanced university relations (Cohen & Kinsey, 1994; Driscoll, Holland, Gelmon, & Kerrigan, 1996; Ferrari & Worrall, 2000; Foreman, 1996; Gray, Ondaatje, Fricker, & Geschwind, 2000; Nigro & Wortham, 1998). Recent studies in the field highlight the lack of attention paid to the community by service-learning researchers (Chesler & Vasques Scalera, 2000; Cruz & Giles, 2000, Vernon & Ward, 1999; Ward & Wolf-Wendel, 2000). The literature shows the need to identify community impacts of higher education service-learning programs, and the ways in which reciprocal relationships between campuses and communities are formed. Ferrari & Worrall point out that very "little research exists that focuses on the agency's views of the student service provider or the college-partner institution' (p. 35). The past emphasis on campus-centered research prevents campus administrators, faculty, and students from moving beyond a self-serving approach to one that engages the foundational values of effective service-learning and supports collaborative partnerships between campuses and communities.

It is ironic that researchers have continued to overlook the community when examining service-learning impacts because the heart of service-learning lies in the university-community partnership (Corrigan, 2000). In addition, service-learning has been identified by leaders in higher education as a viable tool to civically engage students in community-based work by addressing and helping to solve real life community issues through service (Astin, 1992; Boyer, 1987; Corrigan, 2000). Civic engagement refers to the process of individuals working to create a society that promotes and sustains the common good (Lisman, 1998). It is what we rely on in a civil society to keep a common sense of order and a shared set of norms to guide public action and discord.

Civic engagement, in turn, builds social capital. Social capital theory stems from the belief that social networks bring value to the greater good. Social capital consists of components such as reciprocity, networks of mutual obligations, and cooperation for mutual benefit. It is a web of interrelated structures that assists in maintaining community well-being (Putnam, 1995). One of the primary foundations for service-learning rests on the theory of social capital; therefore, it is important for researchers to examine whether or not college students, who are engaged in service, are actually building social capital for communities by strengthening the ties between higher education resources and community-based efforts designed to address identified needs. Without more research to lend merit to the community voice and identify actual community-based impacts of service, the higher education service-learning movement lacks validity and credibility.

RESEARCH DESIGN

This study examined the impacts of college student service-learning participants and volunteers on the agencies and youth they served via input from community youth service agency personnel. For the purposes of this study, service-learning participants differed from college student volunteers because the service that college student service-learning participants performed was directly connected to course curriculum and intertwined with academic learning. College student volunteers were students who served with organizations as an extra-curricular activity and did not receive course credit.

To address the research questions, a qualitative study was performed, and information from community agency personnel with regard to the impacts of higher education service-learning and college student volunteers was gathered and analyzed. A collective case study model was utilized to perform this research study.

In-person, semi-structured interviews were conducted with 17 personnel from 15 community agencies that utilized college student volunteers to help meet the needs of youth in seven Montana communities. Agencies included programs such as Big Brothers/Big Sisters, Boys and Girls Club, America Reads/America Counts, after school tutoring/mentoring programs, the YMCA, and youth environmental education programs. The agencies utilized college student volunteers and service-learning participants in their programs to work with youth as tutors, mentors, coaches, and/or educators in order to meet identified needs of the youth. The criteria for selecting agencies to participate in the study were based on the presence of a college or university in the community and on an established relationship between the agency and the community service/service-learning/volunteer office on campus.

The interview protocol was designed based on prior results from a pilot study (Vernon & Ward, 1999). The pilot study was a quantitative analysis measuring community perceptions of the benefits and drawbacks associated with college student volunteers and service-learning participants. Sixty-five community agency directors who worked with college students to meet the needs of various constituencies completed questionnaires. Findings from the study revealed several positive and negative factors associated with college student volunteers and service-learning participants and the ways in which agency directors perceived the impacts of their service. The study prompted further inquiry to discover the why and how behind the positive and negative perceptions held by community agencies regarding college student volunteers; hence, the present study ensued.

The interview protocol for the study included pre-formulated, targeted questions designed to obtain baseline data from each respondent. Open-ended questions were included in order to provide respondents with the freedom to communicate their own versions and interpretations of the college students' service. All interviews were tape recorded and later transcribed word for word for analysis.

Data were analyzed using an inductive content analysis described by Strauss and Corbin (1990) as "open coding." This constant comparative method involved a continuous cycle of conceptualizing data, categorizing the information, and defining the properties and dimensions of each concept. Patterns and themes then emerged through open coding and provided the basis for an indepth understanding and explanation of the phenomenon to unfold. The ATLAS.ti computer software program was used to aid in the analysis phase of the study.

AGENCY INFORMATION

Each agency in the study was a community-based or school-based (K-12) agency/organization/program that functioned to help meet the needs of youth. At the time of the study, more than 1670 youth representing ages from 3 to 19 were served by these agencies in the previous two years. In turn, the agencies involved more than 973 college student volunteers and service-learning participants who served to meet the needs of these youth. The percentage of college students who served with these organizations as a service-learning experience versus an extra-curricular activity varied. Nine of the fifteen agencies indicated that the majority of the college student volunteers were serving as part of a class requirement. In these cases, the service-learning participants linked their service experience to specific concepts and theories learned through their coursework. For example, college students from a nursing class served with one of the agencies to perform a health screening fair for youth.

Three agencies indicated that less than half of the college students served as part of a service-learning class, and three agencies were unaware of whether the students were serving as part of a class requirement or for extra-curricular purposes.[1] All of the agencies integrated the college students as typical volunteers within their programs regardless of if the students were there as service-learning participants or not. The type of service the college students performed with the agency and the ways in which they interacted with youth did not differ significantly based on the students' status as a service-learning participant or a volunteer.

Youth served by the programs operated by each of the agencies came from various backgrounds and had numerous needs related to their personal circumstances. Some of the children needed academic tutoring assistance; some needed an additional adult role model in their lives. Others had limited social skills, and many came from low income families where there was a lack of resources available to provide children with a sense of security or a bright future. Children from one organization in particular all had a parent who was incarcerated.

Most of the college student volunteers who worked with children through each agency were in some way attempting to increase the self-esteem levels of the children they worked with as a means to help build the children's resiliency skills and enable them to cope with the challenges in their lives. The volunteers helped build self-esteem through several different types of service activities, including mentoring, tutoring, coaching, teaching, or providing guided supervision for the children. The college student volunteers who served at the agencies were primarily white, middle-class, traditional-aged students.

Respondents in the study agreed to be interviewed and share their thoughts and perceptions based on anonymity. Therefore, agency names were changed to maintain confidentiality.

FINDINGS

The themes that emerged from the open coding data analysis process were organized into groupings based on relationships to each research question and consistency of content among the informants' responses. The open coding process involved distinct phases of analysis to make continual comparisons of information segments and to ask questions about how the information segments related to the phenomenon under study. Four research categories emerged and related to the research questions. The research categories included:

1.   Community agency partnerships with higher education institutions;
2.   College student volunteer impacts on agencies;
3.   College student volunteer impacts on youth; and
4.   Community perceptions of college student volunteerism.

Each research category contained themes that emerged based on informants' collective responses.

Community Agency Partnerships With Higher Education Institutions

This research category focused on identifying how community agencies worked with their local college or university to form partnerships for more effective community service programs, and the ways in which agencies accommodated and supported course-based service-learning activities. Several themes emerged within this research category demonstrating the ways in which colleges collaborate as community partners with organizations to help identify and meet critical needs. The themes within this research category are listed in Exhibit 1, and findings from each theme are discussed.

Campus/community collaboration is an important issue in service-learning. The examination of how higher education institutions collaborate as community partners with organizations to help identify and meet critical needs is a foundational value of effective service-learning (Sigmon, 1979). The findings within this theme revealed several ways in which community agencies partnered with campuses to recruit college students who were interested in extra-curricular volunteer service.

EXHIBIT 1
Community Agency Partnerships With Higher Education Institutions

Research Category:	*Community Agency Partnerships With Higher Education Institutions*
Relevant Themes:	1. Campus/Community Collaboration
	2. Service-Learning Partnerships
	3. Service-Learning Support

The data showed that campuses with an active and well-staffed office for service-learning/community service were perceived by the respondents as being better equipped to collaborate and form partnerships with community agencies. One agency director's comment exemplified this point by explaining, "I think the university, it seems to me, in the last four or five years has put more emphasis on getting the students out to volunteer and help in the community. I think through the Office of Community Service they seem to be more organized campus-wide, which I think is beneficial for groups like ours." This finding supports the best practices literature for effective service-learning programs (Campus Compact, 1999).

Respondents also pointed out the difficulties and frustrations they faced when there are real and/or perceived barriers between them and the campus. Several program coordinators illustrated the problem they encountered when there is staff turnover on campus. At the Big River Mentoring program, the coordinator explained, "If we needed a volunteer we [used] to call Heather and say, 'See what you can do for us.' And I don't know exactly what happened to it. I mean slowly but surely, things just started to dwindle away." Another director went on to explain that there seemed to be an overall willingness on the part of the college to collaborate but without a centralized office or consistent contact person it was difficult to make progress.

> I think from institution to institution we're able to get volunteers generally because somebody knows somebody. Organizational structure-wise, I think there's a lack of linkage and we have the willingness to work with 'whatever' but there isn't a 'whatever' there at the college to work with. So I mean, everyone thinks it's a good idea but then I can't find the right person to be able to set up some formal recruiting, or how students can benefit academically by having this be a part of their education.

The *service-learning partnerships* theme referred to the ways in which community agencies partnered with specific academic units or faculty on campus to develop and implement mutually beneficial course-based service-learning opportunities for students as opposed to extra-curricular volunteerism described previously. Ten of the respondents indicated that they have a fairly significant amount of personal contact with faculty on campus. The agencies targeted departments that they believed had an inherent connection to the services and programs offered by their agency and then forged relationships with faculty who were receptive to the idea of having their students involved. In very few cases, faculty were the ones who initiated contact with the agency.

Once contact was made, and both the agency and faculty member believed the service provided a suitable fit, arrangements were made to accommodate the service-learning experience. In some instances, agency personnel initially gave in-class presentations, provided announcement materials, or e-mailed information to the faculty member to distribute to class participants for recruitment. Depending on the nature of the project, such as if it was a one-time occurrence or if it was ongoing, the program coordinator from the agency sometimes had the opportunity to do training and/or orientation for the students during class time.

Generally, in the instances where the agency person had approached a faculty member and had been positively received, agency personnel perceived the projects and service that ensued as effective and high quality. One respondent representing this point of view stated, "I appreciate the fact that the college gives the students credit...I appreciate that the professors feel like [the service] is worth giving extra credit for, that they'll support us." However, when communication between the agency and professor was not consistent, or the partnership did not have a firm foundation, the situation sometimes ended in disaster. At one campus, professors of a general studies class required students to perform ten hours of community service as part of the course and referred students to a particular organization in town. However, the professors did not notify the organization or arrange for the service to take place, so when 45 students descended on the agency the personnel were not prepared and it caused a lot of disruption for the agency. When the agency attempted to contact the professors to ask about creating a more organized referral structure, they did not want to cooperate. As a result, the agency no longer accepted student volunteers from those courses.

Another program coordinator described how she was attempting to re-build a partnership that had failed in the past.

> I've talked with a new person at the college about the black eye the college received from the involvement [of student volunteers in the program] last year to see if he can do some damage control on his end and talk with the dean of arts and sciences to see if maybe we can prove to the community that that was a one-time deal, because this is a good [service] opportunity for college students. I think what I learned was my responsibility [in the future]

would be to say 'Hey, this is my expectation from you [the college partner], you need to do some supervision. If these guys [student volunteers] can't meet my expectations then it's on you.'

The *service-learning support* theme encompassed activities that organizations perform internally to support and accommodate course-based service-learning activities within their programs. The levels of support for service-learning within the agencies varied among the programs in the study. In most cases, the agencies were very aware of the meaning and role of higher education service-learning within their organization, yet at three of the agencies it was more abstract and the connection was less apparent.

For example, one after-school program coordinator received strong support from his supervisor so it made his job working with college student volunteers a little easier. He explained, "The principal here is a big proponent of service-learning, and so I get a lot of support with service-learning ideas that I have and tying classroom exercises into the community."

At three agencies, the informants had no understanding of service-learning whatsoever. These were agencies where college students were volunteering, and sometimes even as a service-learning requirement, but the agency was completely unaware that it was a course-based experience for students. This called into question the extent to which the campus was a true, collaborative partner with the agency, and whether or not this type of service should be described as service-learning or as community volunteer service. Nonetheless, based on responses from informants at these agencies, the service that students were providing to the agency was perceived as valuable and contributed to the goals and mission of the organization.

There were specific areas in which the organizations tried to support the college student service-learning participants at the agencies where service-learning was a visible attribute. The program coordinator at the Garden City Preschool Program explained how he placed students according to the student's expectations as well as the agency's needs.

Predominantly, [the college students are] going to be placed in the classroom as basically a teacher aid. And, the reason behind that is that is what most of the college students want. They are coming from the education department and social work and the psychology department and they want to be in there to see how the kids are acting so it helps them understand more concretely what they are doing overall in school.

All of the agencies involved in this study acknowledged that college students were a unique category of volunteer within their organization, regardless of their status as a service-learner or as an extra-curricular volunteer. The agencies realized the demands of school and that the academic year contained pockets of time when students were simply not available. Several of the agencies adapted to these quirks in order to make the most effective use of college student volunteers. One informant exemplified this finding by explaining, "Yeah, one of our first questions is 'When is spring break and when is finals week?'" She realized, "If it is finals week or anything I'm doing that falls right into some really big time for them, they are unavailable and they are unavailable unilaterally, like don't even go there." At several of the mentoring programs, agency personnel forewarned parents about the times when the college student volunteers would not be available. One informant said that when students "leave for the summer, we put those matches on hold and then just reopen them when they come back in the fall."

College Student Volunteer Impacts at the Agencies

The agencies included in this study engaged in a variety of activities in order to measure and ensure the quality and effectiveness of the service that college student volunteers provided. Quality management activities included screening, training, and supervising volunteers. Programs utilized national service resources through AmeriCorps and VISTA as a means to ensure high quality and effective volunteer-based programs. Agencies measured the quality and effectiveness of volunteer service through formalized evaluation procedures, such as pre- and post-test analysis, and informal mechanisms, like observations of staff and feedback from teachers and parents. Agency personnel were able to explain the impacts of the college students' service both at the agency and on the youth served based on their programs' activities related to ensuring and measuring the quality and effectiveness of college student volunteers' service. Three themes that emerged from the data related to the college student volunteer impacts at agencies research category are outlined in Exhibit 2.

EXHIBIT 2
College Student Volunteer Impacts at Agencies

Research Category:	College Student Volunteer Impacts at Agencies
Relevant Themes:	1. Programmatic Impacts
	2. Positive Attributes of College Student Volunteers
	3. Negative Attributes of College Student Volunteers

The *programmatic impacts* theme revealed the ways in which college student volunteers contributed to program operations at each of the agencies. The majority of respondents were overwhelmingly positive about the types of impacts college student volunteers had at the agency where they served. The college student volunteers had become valuable human resources for the organizations to broaden and expand the services they offer and reach more youth. One program director highlighted findings in this theme by explaining the following.

> It was nice for me because I was...basically trying to do it all myself. And, I was able to give some programs to a college student and let them make the schedule and make the calls and recruit in the school so it freed me up time wise just cause its an after-school program, and I was running around with my head cut off there for awhile trying to do it all.

The use of college student volunteers as human resources allowed two of the programs to be able to expand and garner additional funding as well. One respondent explained program expansion in the following statement.

> We're one of the fastest growing programs in Montana and that's because of the college students, because we have that source of volunteers. We're ranked in the top 10 percent of programs across the United States in terms of the number of children served per capita. Our grants that come in from the state, the United Way, the school program, you know it all ties in one way or another to the fact that we have excellent volunteers which come from the university.

When asked how their programs would be different without college student volunteers, informants stated that their programs would be greatly reduced and the number of children served would decrease. Responses related to this finding included, "It's the mainstay of my volunteer base so I don't think that I would have much of a program"; "It wouldn't be as full of a program in the sense of being an educational program"; and "There would be no way we could do half of the stuff that we are doing in this community without the college students."

In addition to the overall benefits that college student volunteers provided for program operations, respondents in the study also pointed out specific *positive attributes of the college students* that they viewed as beneficial for the agency. One of which was energy. A program director exemplified this finding by explaining that college students are "energetic, they are willing to try just about anything. They haven't got preconceived notions as to what is going to be in the program and they come with some different ideas." Other directors also pointed out that the volunteers' energy level helps to provide a boost for staff at the agency who are suffering from burnout.

Among the respondents there was a lot of discussion about how college students are the right age for working with youth. Traditional-aged college students were viewed by the informants (as well as the youth and the community which will be elaborated in further sections) as being cool. Informants explained that youth are more willing and able to make a connection with them because of the traditional college students' ages. One respondent summed this up by stating, "In the school-based program, especially in the middle schools, those kids want to be cool, and it's cool to have a college mentor, it's not cool to have someone who is 40 years-old."

Some respondents perceived the college students as committed volunteers, while others identified commitment as a negative factor. Positive comments regarding the students' level of commitment included, "A lot of the college volunteers take it very seriously, this volunteer business, and they are busy, but boy when they come into it, we can't get better volunteers'; "We have [some] college volunteers that are just outstanding people that go way above and beyond, stay with their children for years and years on end, and develop incredible relationships with them"; and "I think we have a better rate of retention with college students as far, I think, if I did the percentages, I think there are more college students [than community volunteers] returning next year."

Not all agencies had such positive perceptions about the commitment level that college student volunteers were willing to make. This was one of the areas outlined in the *negative attributes* theme for this research category. One program director explained, "I think with college students we experience that there is a higher degree of initial interest with waning commitment. And, that may have to do with age or the fact that they are busy and have academic commitments." He went on to explain that the agency tried to circumvent the problem by "helping people decide to bail prior to contact" with the youth.

The academic year and annual school breaks presented scheduling challenges for the agencies. One respondent explained that, "May sneaks up so fast and the [K-12] students are still in dire need of the attention and the help either emotionally or academically and, you know, a lot of these well intended college students are out of here." A different program coordinator said, "You know its sort of a general issue with college volunteers, they are very much in their own college world which has a different pace and a different set of deadlines than the other world that the community has." Another respondent described the toll that scheduling inconsistencies take on the youth being served.

> The schedule is hard just because they have a month off, and so sometimes it's kind of wearing on the kids. When they can't...some of the younger kids especially can't conceptualize vacation or break or when they're [the volunteers] coming back and why they are going...So I think its hard on the kids sometimes when there's a long break or when they wind up ending the school year earlier than the kids do. That's a little bit of a struggle and so there is kind of an unknown, and every college student has a different kind of class schedule at the end of the year. So, some college students leave earlier and some leave later and the kids see other [college student] mentors coming all the way through June and they are like, "What happened to my person?" So that's a stress, I think. The scheduling can be hard.

Findings from this study pertaining to the positive and negative attributes of college student volunteers support conclusions from a previous research study that found students' age and energy were especially beneficial while their lack of commitment and scheduling inconsistencies created detriments (Vernon & Ward, 1999).

In light of all the drawbacks associated with working with college student volunteers, informants in the latter half of the study were asked if it was worth it. All of the directors who were asked the question responded positively. One director summed up this sentiment when she explained, "Even if 80 percent of them [the volunteers] failed, the fact that these 20 percent have these successes that completely change [children's] lives, to me it's worth it. If you keep trying, eventually they'll get it to work out."

College Student Volunteer Impacts on Youth Served

This research category encompassed information about the ways in which college student volunteers impact the youth they are serving. The scope of this study did not include any youth as informants. Therefore, in order to answer questions in this research category, respondents drew upon their program evaluation data and personal observations related to how youth who are served are impacted by college student volunteers. Three main themes emerged related to this category and are illustrated in Exhibit 3.

Data regarding *youth perceptions of college student volunteers* were gathered by asking each of the agency informants what, in their opinion, the children thought of the college student volunteers. Responses had one consistent answer—the children would say that the college students were cool. The cool factor played heavily in the minds of the youth being served according to the informants as indicated by the following responses.

- "I think they [the youth] would think they [college students] were cool because they're younger and they are cool. You know what I mean, they are cool, they are interested, and they're entirely focused.

EXHIBIT 3
College Student Volunteer Impacts on Youth Served

Research Category:		*College Student Volunteer Impacts on Youth Served*
	1.	Youth Perceptions of College Student Volunteers
Relevant Themes:	2.	General Benefits to Youth
	3.	Impacts on Youth

They basically think they're cool and they think they're funny and they get real attached."

- "I think they look at them as kind of a cooler, older peer, someone they can relate to that's not an adult figure yet."

Another informant explained the children's reactions this way.

They would say all sorts of funny things. As I said, [the college students] are "Gods" to them. They are adults but they are not parents and it's what they want to grow up to be. Everyone I've worked with that's worked well, the children when they see them their faces just light up. The elementary and the middle school kids start jumping up and down. The older middle school kids of course don't care about anything because they are too cool. But you see the faces light up, they are jumping up and down and its like, it's not even time to go to class, and they want to come in off the playground and go into class. And that to me is, if they want to give up playground time to go and be with this person, that is pretty impressive.

The overwhelmingly positive perceptions that children had of the college student volunteers alluded to the types of *general benefits* youth received from their service and made up the second theme in this research category. Self-esteem was an area in which college students were really able to make a difference for youth, as indicated by a director who explained that the teacher of a student being mentored by a college student volunteer noticed that "she's a lot more confident, a lot more social, a lot less introverted. So, its gone beyond the academic thing which most of the tutor/mentor matches did." Another director pointed out, "You could see that self-esteem in the kids. How they thought they were pretty cool because these pretty cool college kids thought they were cool."

Another benefit identified by informants involved improved academic performance. One director explained that results from their program evaluation were "just staggering. We just presented to our board that 79 percent [of youth served] are getting along better in school, 50 percent have improved grades." The ability to bond and connect with another caring, adult figure in their lives was another benefit identified by informants. One director summed up this finding as follows.

I think just the opportunities that that child is having with that volunteer maybe to go out to the river and fish might be something that that little boy has never done, but now that he has a [mentor] he has someone that can take him out to do that. Or the girl who is having a hard time adjusting to her parents' divorce and have that [mentor] there just to spend time with her and talk with her about how things are going and can kind of relate to that.

Informants also added that sometimes the college student volunteers were able to provide a sense of future or a new perspective for children through their service. For example, a program director representing this point of view stated, "I think the best impact on the kids is seeing that there are adults who can run and order their lives without drugs and alcohol, and in a manner that is ethical."

The various ways in which the youth benefited from the volunteers was further illustrated by data contained in *the impacts on youth* theme. This theme was made up of stories that reflected the types of positive and negative impacts that college student volunteers had on youth they served. The instances in which volunteers negatively impacted youth primarily involved situations in which a college student dropped out of the program with little or no notice. Several of the informants expressed concern over the fact that the college students needed to be fully aware of the consequences their actions had on the children when they did not show up at their scheduled time or dropped out unexpectedly. One director summed this up by explaining that when youth have "somebody who they're expecting to come and see them after school, it's very important for the volunteers to be there." Because many of the youth served by these programs come from low income or unstable home environments it places an even greater importance on the role of the volunteer in their life, whether it is a tutor, mentor, or a coach. One director explained that it would not be uncommon to hear youth in his program say, "They [the volunteer] visited me once and once again they never came back, they abandoned me." He said, "It really hurts a lot when the college student decides they think they want to do it and then they just blow it off."

The following stories from respondents reflect the positive outcomes that occurred when the college student volunteers were committed and followed through on their responsibilities.

- "There's one that stands out just the fact that this female from the college volunteered for the tutoring/mentoring program and basically established a family relationship with the match and it went to that next level. It was a university student and the high school student was kind of in need of a sister, and a role model, had come from rural Montana and was kind of struggling with the big city life, Green Valley being the big city, but this girl just kind of went beyond the call of duty and became this awesome mentor and tutor and then also just became her friend and they're doing stuff this summer. Like they're going on trips and vacations together, and this college student is taking her back to Wisconsin and its just like it went to this next level and they became sisters in the true sense of sisters. You know there was permission from the parents and the parents were super open to having this university student at their house and it was all kind of checked out by phone calls and good communication, and it was just neat to watch that develop. And the university student made such an impact in this girl's life, confidence-wise, and socially, but also academically."

- "These kids will remember them [the volunteers] forever. How somebody finally believed in them and how somebody finally helped them with a test or how somebody finally showed them how to, 'Oh that's all it was!' Lots of times that's it. 'You mean that's all I had to do was put the negative sign on the other side of the equation? Oh, my God!'"

Community Perceptions of College Student Volunteers

Community perceptions of college student volunteers were measured based on the perceptions of respondents in the study. Community was defined for informants to include other agency staff, partner organizations, parents, teachers and other people who were involved with the children and knew that a college student was serving the children in some manner. The respondents' perspectives validly reflected community perceptions because the respondents based their perceptions on the evaluative measures their programs had in place to receive feedback and information from community members about the services they provided. Responses to the questions related to this category were grouped into three themes and are outlined in Exhibit 4.

EXHIBIT 4
Community Perceptions of College Student Volunteers

Research Category:	Community Perceptions of College Student Volunteers
Relevant Themes:	Perceptions of Volunteer Motives
	Community Characterization of College Student Volunteers
	Community Perceptions of Service Provided

Approximately half of the respondents believed that community members think the *motive for college students to volunteer* is because they are required to for course credit. A director illustrated this by stating, "I imagine a lot of them feel that the volunteers volunteer because they have to, because they need credits." Another added, "People in the community think it's part of the whole college experience, they need to volunteer to know about the world out there and to volunteer as part of a class."

The following quotations from informants demonstrated that they believed many of the students volunteer because of religious or moral reasons. "They [college students] want to do something, they want to be able to help somebody and to give something back and they're not in a financial position to do so, this is their way of doing it"; "Some people might think it is because of religious reasons, some people might think it's because they were abused as a kid so they have a passion."

Another perception included the notion that college students volunteer in order to feel like a part of a community. This finding was reflected in the following comment, "I think the people would say that many of them are away from home, away from families, and this is a good opportunity for them to get involved in the community, a good way for them to meet people...it's a way for them to make this their home if they are away from their families."

Informants from two agencies expressed their concern, and they believed other community members shared this concern, regarding the lack of motivation that is present for some service-learning students who are only serving because they are required to by a professor in order to pass a class. These directors pointed out that when the only motive or reason that students serve is because they have to, then it reflects in the type of service they provide. One director summed up this finding by stating, "The handful of college students that were gaining credit for doing it were doing it because that's what motivated them. 'Okay at the end of the semester I'm getting credit for this, that's why I'm showing up.' Well, kids can tell, parents can tell, program coordinators can tell and that's frustrating."

Agency directors pointed out a variety of ways in which the *community characterizes the college students* who perform volunteer service. The descriptors they identified were overwhelmingly positive and reflected a very supportive and satisfied view of the students as service providers. Comments included, "They are fun, energetic, and intelligent"; "They were reliable and able to manage the students and follow all the rules"; and "They are quality kids [college students] with quality futures and quality ideas."

The informants believed general *community perceptions of the service* provided by students were typically very supportive and positive. Within this theme, all of the agencies in the study pointed out positive benefits the community receives as a result of college students volunteering with youth. And, based on these benefits the community is supportive of the service they provide and believe that it generally makes a positive difference for youth. Responses included, "I know that the organizations that we are dealing with are seeing that it is great, they are excited"; "I think the community sees it as a pretty positive asset"; and, "They know that a lot of things that go on here would not happen without the [volunteers]."

Negative community perceptions were identified by two informants and related to two separate issues. The first pointed out that he and others in the community perceive college student volunteers as not being entirely effective because they are not serving to meet the most critical needs of youth. He explained this in the following statement.

It's just that we think, that there are other valuable volunteer activities that could really impact people's lives and that discussion [between the campus and community] is not happening. That community needs assessment is not happening. I don't know at what level that happens, but we're not participating in it and I think we and others should be.

The other director pointed out that community partners she works with tend to be focused on the failures they have had with college student volunteers and, as a result, tend to view their service as ineffective. She explained, "People seem to focus so much on the failures. You might have ten volunteers, two of them fail, eight of them are wonderful and the next year they'll say, 'Well, two of them failed I don't want to do this anymore.'"

CONCLUSIONS AND RECOMMENDATIONS

Research data from this study revealed several key findings associated with each of the research questions. These findings play an important role in the field of higher education service-learning and volunteerism because they represent the voices of community agencies where college student volunteers are utilized. The informants in the study provided information based on their experiences, feedback from community partners and other constituents, and their own opinions regarding college student volunteerism and service-learning. Without identifying and addressing the successes and challenges that community agencies experience as a result of having college student volunteers, higher education service-learning and volunteer programs are overlooking some of the most important ingredients for collaborative and effective program operations. Conclusions based on the findings from this study are outlined as follows.

1. *Community youth service agencies overwhelmingly appreciate and support the service provided by college student volunteers.* The informants in this study had very positive perceptions of the college students and the service they provide for youth. This finding supports the notion that higher education service-learning and volunteer programs are conduits for building social capital in a community. When resources such as student volunteers and faculty members from colleges and universities form collaborative partnerships with community-based organizations to address identified needs, the sense of reciprocity and cooperation for mutual benefit of others is apparent. Respondents pointed out that when college students connect with youth they are very effective and positively impact their lives. However, the results can be disastrous when a college student volunteer fails to maintain responsibility for

his/her commitment to the child by dropping out of a program unexpectedly.

2. *Agencies believe that traditional-aged college students make easier and stronger connections with youth because they are viewed by youth as cool.* Informants continually emphasized the age of college students as an important factor in their effectiveness working with youth. Because traditional-aged college students are young adults, youth perceive them as being more cool and have more in common with them, such as similar tastes in music, clothing, and recreational activities, than with older adults who are perceived by youth as parental figures.

3. *Agencies are not always supportive of service-learning requirements.* In some cases, informants explained their wariness when college students approach the agency and explain that they have to volunteer as part of a class requirement. Some involved in the nonprofit sector generally are more willing and eager to want to work with volunteers who express a heartfelt desire to serve rather than being required to serve.

4. *Due to the vulnerability of the youth being served, agencies want a stronger commitment from college students and protocols for campuses to follow to increase retention and responsibility levels among volunteers.* Many informants described situations in which the child being served by a college student volunteer was left feeling devastated and deserted when the volunteer dropped out of the program early or unexpectedly. As a result, agencies want campuses to hold students more accountable for their service commitments when the students are volunteering as part of a service-learning class.

Based on these conclusions, the following recommendations are offered for campus-based service-learning and volunteer programs and community agencies in order to increase effectiveness and strengthen programs.

1. *Campuses must designate a specific unit and/or faculty and staff who are responsible for operating and supporting the service-learning and volunteer activities for students.* Agencies residing in communities in which the campus had no consistent office or person to contact as a means to facilitate service-learning and volunteer activities were consistently more frustrated and unsatisfied with the impacts and effects of college student volunteers. Campuses that are committed to the values and actions of civic engagement need to designate the appropriate resources, both financial and human, in order to work collaboratively with the community to make it happen.

2. *Professors who teach service-learning courses need to hold students accountable for the service they are providing.* Several informants expressed their concern about the low levels of accountability that students are held to by their professors. In some cases, informants were very frustrated by the fact that students could drop out of programs and fall short of their

service responsibilities and have little, if any, consequences imposed by professors. In order to properly address the very real issue of the vulnerability of the youth served in these programs, professors should have clear-cut guidelines for students to follow that outline the responsibilities and expectations of them as service-learning participants.

3. *Colleges need to be more aware of college students' motivations for volunteering.* Several informants pointed out that they believe one of the motivations for college students to volunteer with youth is because the students miss their families and through volunteerism they are seeking familial settings. This is an aspect of service-learning and volunteerism that is rarely discussed in the research. If campus programs are better able to identify student motives for volunteering there may be other avenues to tie in students' community volunteer experience with personal development and growth experiences on campus, such as residential life programs or leadership development programs.

4. *Campus service-learning professionals need to work with community agencies to overcome the negative connotation that required volunteerism sometimes holds.* Campuses need to communicate better with agencies and students to educate them about the academic goals of service-learning. Some of the informants in the study pointed out that they had negative gut reactions toward students who admitted they were only volunteering because they had to for a class. If students and agencies alike were better informed and educated about the fundamental learning goals on which service-learning experiences should be focused, there might be a more positive reception both from students and agencies.

5. *Campuses need to do better outreach to community agencies to explain service-learning.* Three of the informants in the study had very little understanding of what service-learning is. Their lack of understanding did not seem to have detrimental effects on their perceptions of the college student volunteers, but these instances point out that collaboration is not occurring between agencies and campuses. Under these circumstances one must question whether or not it should be called service-learning even if the students are serving as part of a class.

6. *Agencies need to develop and implement a strong infrastructure of resources to support and sustain a strong volunteer base.* When the agencies' actions related to quality and effectiveness of the service were less consistent or non-existent, there was a clear distinction in the levels of satisfaction that agencies had with college student volunteer service. For example, agencies that had fewer resources available to provide ongoing supervision and/or supplemental training of volunteers had more negative experiences with college student volunteer service as compared to agencies in which there was a strong infrastructure to support high-quality, effective volunteer service.

7. *Agencies should implement more consistent and stringent program evaluation measures.* Findings from the study indicate there was a disparity in the

types of program evaluation implemented by each agency. Most programs had quantitative and qualitative mechanisms in place to measure the quality and effectiveness of college student volunteer service, while a few relied solely on anecdotal feedback from program participants. With the overwhelming number of hours that college student volunteers provide at these agencies, it is apparent that more stringent program evaluation would benefit both the agencies and higher education service programs by offering valid evidence of the impacts the service is having. This evidence could be used to create stronger levels of support, both human and financial resources, for service-based partnerships between campuses and community agencies.

8. *Increased collaboration between agencies and campuses needs to occur in order to identify the most effective way of utilizing college student volunteers.* Some community agencies believe college student volunteers are not serving to meet the most critical needs of youth in the community. Therefore, the effectiveness of their service is perceived by the community as diminished and insignificant. This was most apparent in rural communities where there was not an abundance of resources for the community to draw from.

Findings and recommendations from this study open doors for future research in higher education service-learning and volunteer programs. For instance, will the influx of non-traditional aged college students change community perceptions of the effectiveness of their service with youth? How do the youth who are being served and their parents or guardians perceive college student volunteers and the service they provide? What motivates college students to volunteer in the first place? How can campuses better integrate volunteerism and student development?

While much has been accomplished in the field of higher education service-learning and volunteerism in the past decade, there are still many areas that need to be expanded and explored in order to further refine and strengthen the way in which programs are operated and implemented. The findings from this study help to shed light on the valuable perspectives that community agencies have related to college student volunteers and service-learners. Higher education service-learning must continue to examine and assess this side of the service equation if those in the field wish to accurately represent the true nature of collaborative service-based partnerships between campuses and communities.

NOTE

1. In order to maintain consistency, the term "college student volunteer" is used predominantly throughout the remaining text. This term refers to college

students who are volunteering at the agencies either as part of a service-learning class or as an extra-curricular activity. In circumstances where it was important to note the difference between extra-curricular volunteers and service-learning participants, the author has made the distinction for readers.

REFERENCES

Astin, A. W. (1992). *What matters in college? Four critical years revisited.* San Francisco, CA: Jossey-Bass.

Boyer, E. (1987). *College: The undergraduate experience in America.* New York: Harper & Row, Publishers.

Campus Compact. (1999). *Service matters.* Providence, RI: Campus Compact.

Chesler, M., & Vasques Scalera, C. (2000). Race and gender issues related to service-learning research. *Michigan Journal of Community Service Learning,* (Special Issue 2000).

Cohen, J., & Kinsey, D. (1994, Winter). 'Doing good' and scholarship: A service-learning study. *Journalism Educator, 12.*

Corrigan, R.A. (2000, April). Keynote address presented at the Western Campus Compact Consortium Third Annual Continuums of Service Conference. University of Washington, Seattle, Washington.

Cruz, N. I., & Giles, D. E. (2000). Where's the community in service-learning research? *Michigan Journal of Community Service Learning,* (Special Issue 2000).

Driscoll, A., Holland, B., Gelmon, S., & Kerrigan, S. (1996). An assessment model for service-learning: Comprehensive case studies of impact on faculty, students, community, and institution. *Michigan Journal of Community Service Learning, 3.*

Ferrari, J. R. & Worrall, L. (2000). Assessment by community agencies: How "the other side" sees service-learning. *Michigan Journal of Community Service Learning, 7.*

Foreman, C. W. (1996). *Service-learning in the small group communication class.* Paper presented at the Annual Meeting of the Speech and Communication Association, San Diego, CA.

Gray, M. J., Ondaatje, E. H., Fricker, R. D., & Geschwind, S. A. (2000). Assessing service-learning, results from a survey of "Learn and Serve America, Higher Education." *Change,* March/April.

Lisman, C. D. (1998). *Toward a civil society: Civic literacy and service learning.* Westport, CT: Bergin & Garvey.

Nigro, G., & Wortham, S. (1998). Service-learning through action research. In R.G. Bringle & D.K. Duffy (Eds.), *Collaborating with the community: Psychology and service-learning.* Washington, DC: American Association for Higher Education.

Putnam, R. D. (January, 1995). Bowling alone: America's declining social capital. *Journal of Democracy, 6*(1), 65-77.

Sigmon, R. (1979). Service-learning: Three principles. *Synergist, 8*(1).

Strauss, A., & Corbin, J. (1990). *Basics of qualitative research.* Newbury Park, CA: Sage Publications.

Vernon, A., & Ward, K. (1999). Campus and community partnerships: Assessing impacts and strengthening connections. *Michigan Journal of Community Service Learning, 3.*

Ward, K. (1996). Service-learning and student voluntcerism: Reflections on institutional commitment. *Michigan Journal of Community Service Learning, 3.*

Ward, K., & Wolf-Wendel, L. (1997, November). A discourse analysis of community-based learning: Moving from "doing for" to "doing with." Paper presented at the annual meeting of the Association for the Study of Higher Education, Albuquerque, New Mexico.

Ward, K., & Wolf-Wendel, L. (2000). Community-centered service-learning: Moving from doing for to *doing with. American Behavioral Scientist.*

CHAPTER 9

MOTIVATING ENVIRONMENTALLY RESPONSIBLE BEHAVIOR THROUGH SERVICE-LEARNING

Beth A. Covitt[1]

Motivational theories from psychology were applied to conduct a preliminary examination of the role that fulfillment of personal goals plays in the relationship between environmental education programs (service-learning and field trips) and intentions to engage in environmentally responsible behaviors. SAS PROC MIXED, a type of statistical analysis, was used to test the hypothesis that motive fulfillment mediates the impact of environmental education experiences on intentions. The evidence for motive fulfillment as a mediator was mixed. Service-learning programs negatively affected or did not affect motive fulfillment. Field trips led to a high level of motive fulfillment. Evidence for a strong relationship between motive fulfillment and intentions was supported. When the relation between program treatment and motive fulfillment was strong, motive fulfillment played a mediating role in the effect of program treatment on intentions. These preliminary results

Service-Learning Through a Multidisciplinary Lens
A Volume in: Advances in Service-Learning Research, pages 177–197.
Copyright © 2002 by Information Age Publishing, Inc.
All rights of reproduction in any form reserved.
ISBN: 1-931576-81-5 (cloth), 1-931576-80-7 (paper)

suggest that fulfillment of personal goals plays a significant role in whether or not students will report intentions to engage in helping behaviors after their environmental education experience. Consequently, service-learning program developers and facilitators who consciously strive to help students fulfill their goals may achieve greater success in fostering prosocial and pro-environmental behaviors.

INTRODUCTION

In recent years, service-learning has become an increasingly popular pedagogical method among environmental educators (Ward, 1999). This increase is likely due to the close match between environmental education (EE) goals and service-learning goals. The primary goal of EE is to provide people with the awareness, knowledge, attitudes, skills, and motivations to solve environmental problems (Tblisi Intergovernmental Conference on Environmental Education, 1978). Outcomes sought through service-learning include enhancing learning, promoting personal development of values and self-efficacy, fostering civic responsibility, and serving communities (Waterman, 1997). Thus, EE and service-learning share not only the cognitive goal of promoting learning and knowledge, but also the behavioral goal of fostering prosocial and pro-environmental actions.

Research over the past decade has provided growing bodies of evidence that service-learning can positively influence prosocial, or civic, outcomes. Studies have found that students who participate in service-learning may develop higher levels of civic responsibility and willingness to become involved in community service (e.g., Furco, 2002; Melchior & Bailis, 2002; Weiler, LaGoy, Crane, & Rovner, 1998). Studies of environmental service-learning and similar environmental education programs that emphasize real world environmental problem solving have also found positive outcomes for increasing environmental responsibility and commitments (e.g., Holt, 1988; Lieberman & Hoody, 1998; Ramsey, Hungerford, & Tomera, 1981; Ramsey, 1987).

Because service-learning programs may vary greatly in design and implementation, studies that focus solely on the outcomes of service-learning may not provide program developers and practitioners with sufficient information for creating and improving their programs. Fewer studies have focused on the important questions of how and why service-learning influences civic outcomes. In a recent book chapter, Melchior and Bailis (2002) suggested that researchers should focus on program design and implementation as well as considering the outcomes fostered through service-learning.

It is also instructive to consider the mechanisms (or mediating variables) through which these characteristics influence service-learning outcomes. An understanding of mediating mechanisms can provide a guide for determining which combinations of service-learning program characteristics will be most successful for fostering positive outcomes. One mediating factor that may help explain how service-learning influences civic outcomes is motive fulfillment, or the extent to which students are able to achieve their personal goals associated with positive psychological functioning through their service-learning experiences (e.g., Clary, Snyder, & Stukas, 1998a; Clary, Snyder, Ridge, et al., 1998b).

Motive fulfillment is a good candidate for mediating the relationship between service-learning programs and service-learning outcomes for several reasons. First, a consideration of standards for quality service-learning demonstrates that there are many connections between service-learning best practices and psychological motives including competence, autonomy, and social affiliation. For example, the service-learning standard that students should be involved in planning service-learning activities (Alliance for Service-Learning in Educational Reform, [ASLER], 1995; Toole, 1999) connects with the psychological goal of autonomy (e.g., Allen, Kuperminc, Philiber, & Herre, 1994; Deci & Ryan, 1980; Stukas, Snyder, & Clary, 1999). Establishing autonomy is thought to be a central process of adolescent development (Allen et al., 1994).

In addition to evidence that quality service-learning standards relate to students' motives, there is also theory and research supporting that motive fulfillment is related to civic outcomes. Studies in both personality and cognitive psychology suggest that one key factor for fostering environmentally and socially responsible behaviors is a consideration of the personal goals or motives that individuals fulfill through engaging in these behaviors (Clary et al., 1998b; Kaplan, 2000).

Although motive fulfillment is a good candidate to mediate the effect of service-learning programs on civic outcomes, little research has directly tested this mediation pattern (e.g., Allen et al., 1994). Therefore, this study, through an evaluation of a middle school environmental service-learning program, addresses the proposition that education programs designed to foster environmentally responsible behaviors (ERBs) will be more successful to the extent that they support individuals' personal goals related to positive psychological functioning and well-being.

The context for this study is an evaluation of the Chesapeake Bay Foundation's (CBF's) middle school education programs. CBF is a nonprofit environmental organization headquartered in Maryland that conducts restoration of and education about the Chesapeake Bay. As part of their education program offerings, CBF provides three types of Bay learning experiences for middle school teachers and students. These include:

1. CBF staff-run field trips;
2. Curricular materials and teacher training; and
3. CBF-supported environmental service-learning programs.

This study places particular emphasis on the relative ability of CBF environmental service-learning and other environmental education programs to fulfill students' personal goals, and subsequently, to foster intentions to engage in ERBs.

TWO THEORIES RELATING MOTIVES AND PROSOCIAL BEHAVIORS

One way to consider the role of personal motivation in fostering ERB is presented in social psychologists Clary and colleagues' (1998b) functional approach to motivations for volunteering. The functional approach suggests that individuals engage in service behaviors because service fulfills multiple and differing psychological functions (or goals) for different individuals (Clary et al., 1998b). Fostering service behaviors is particularly applicable to the topic of service-learning, which is concerned with students' continuing prosocial or pro-environmental behaviors after they complete a service experience. A major predictive postulate of the functional approach is that motivation will be enhanced to the extent that persuasive appeals and/or service experiences match participants' goals (Clary et al., 1998b).

Through studies of individuals engaging in service (e.g., Chapman & Morley, 1999; Clary et al., 1998b; Omoto & Snyder, 1995), researchers have identified six motivational goals served by volunteerism. These goals include values, understanding, social, career, protective, and enhancement (Clary et al., 1998b). Clary and colleagues (1998b) measured these six goals with the Volunteer Functions Index scale. They assessed the reliability and validity of their scale through exploratory and confirmatory factor analyses and through cross-validation with multiple populations. The postulate that motivation will be enhanced to the extent that persuasive appeals and/or service experiences match participants' goals has been supported by several studies (e.g., Clary, Snyder, Ridge, Miene, & Haugen, 1994; Stukas et al., 1999). Although there are many similarities and connections, no studies have examined the functional approach to motivation in the context of service-learning.

Kaplan (2000) presents another perspective concerning fostering environmentally responsible behavior in his evolutionary/cognitive/motivational reasonable person model. Kaplan (2000, p. 497-98) suggests that, "...by recognizing human inclinations and the circumstances that are supportive of human motivations, it may be easier to get people to behave in environmentally responsible ways without calling on guilt or sacrifice." Kaplan and Kaplan (1989) identify three basic human motives which, if supported, may help to foster ERB. These include motivation to "understand what is going on," and to avoid confusion, motivation to be a self-directed learner and explorer, and motivation to be an active participant rather than a helpless person in the world (Kaplan, 2000).

This description of the reasonable person theory sheds light on how the theory can relate to environmental service-learning. First, it is possible to highlight how service-learning pedagogy matches the reasonable person theory. For example, by combining academic learning with community service, service-learning emphasizes both understanding and participation. In addition, the reasonable person theory can provide insight into how service-learning programs can be intentionally structured to support basic motives. For example, preference for self-guided learning can be supported with some level of exploration or role autonomy in service-learning experiences, and preference for participation can be supported through engaging students in meaningful rather than menial service roles.

The goal of fostering civic outcomes is not easy to achieve, as evidenced by some service-learning programs that demonstrated no civic improvements (e.g., Ford, 1995). If environmental educators and service-learning practitioners are to achieve this difficult goal, they will need a deep understanding of the processes by which these educational programs and pedagogies lead to positive outcomes (Allen et al., 1994). In the functional approach to motivation and the reasonable person model, we find two approaches with direct relevance to service-learning and EE.

By testing predictive postulates from the functional approach to motivation and the reasonable person model in a service-learning context, it is possible to explore the relationship between intentions to engage in prosocial behaviors and motive fulfillment. This understanding can then be applied to structuring and implementing service-learning programs that are sensitive to the motives and personal goals held by students.

METHOD

Participants

Sixth, seventh, and eighth grade students (n = 2365) and teachers (n = 37) in Maryland and Virginia participated in this study. Teachers, trained in the use of CBF curricula or service-learning projects, were recruited through a combination of mail and phone calls. Teachers were placed in treatment "conditions" based on the educational programs that they had independently, or because of district or school requirements, decided to use in their classrooms. Although teachers were not randomly assigned to conditions, student placement in different programs did not reflect a bias in which students self-selected into program groups. Middle school students generally do not have the option of selecting a school or classroom.

Chesapeake Bay Foundation Education Programs

The students and teachers in this study participated in various combinations of CBF one-day field trips, curricular activities, and the *Bay Grasses in Classes* (*Grasses*) service-learning project. Some also participated in service-learning projects other than *Grasses*.

One-Day Field Trips

CBF one-day field trips take place in diverse locations around the Bay and provide students with the opportunity to learn first-hand about ecology, history, and environmental issues related to the Chesapeake Bay.

Curricular Programs and Materials

CBF's curricular materials are designed to help teachers integrate Bay-related activities into their classroom instruction. To receive the materials, teachers must participate in CBF professional development workshops. The curricular guides include a variety of learning activities as well as suggestions for Bay-related service-learning projects. Teachers are encouraged to, but may not implement a service project as part of a Chesapeake Bay learning unit.

Bay Grasses in Classes Program

CBF developed the *Grasses* program in response to a combination of factors including the implementation of a state service-learning requirement in Maryland and feedback from teachers that they did not have sufficient materials or knowledge to introduce Chesapeake Bay service-learning projects into their classrooms without assistance. Teachers who participate in the program must attend a training workshop where they receive all materials and equipment needed to grow underwater grasses in the classroom. Components of *Grasses* include a simple aquaculture system set up by students, an interdisciplinary classroom curriculum, and a hands-on field experience that includes planting the grasses within the Chesapeake Bay watershed.

Non-CBF Bay Service-Learning Projects

To provide additional opportunities for comparison, teachers and students who participated in a CBF curricular program and a service-learning project other than *Grasses* were also included in the study. Examples of non-CBF service-learning projects that these teachers and students developed and completed included: individual student projects such as small-scale habitat enhancement or Bay-related information campaigns and class projects such as building and installing bluebird boxes, coordinating school recycling programs, planting trees, or growing and releasing yellow perch.

No Service-Learning Students

To provide a comparison group, this study also includes students and teachers who used CBF curricular activities, but who did not participate in any service-learning. Thirty-five percent of the 912 students in this no service-learning group also went on a CBF field trip. This group of no service-learning students provided a baseline against which the *Grasses* service-learning students and the non-CBF service-learning students could be compared.

Instruments

Instruments for this study included student pre-tests and post-tests. Measures of intentions to engage in ERBs were adapted from survey instruments that were used in a previous study and found to be reliable (Zint, Kramer, Northway, & Lim, 2002). The intentions to help the Bay index (Exhibit 1) was an average of responses to six items (each measured on a 5-point scale). The reliability (alpha) of the index was .82.

EXHIBIT 1
Index of Intentions to Help the Bay

Post-test Alpha = .82, (1-5 Scale, Very unlikely to Very likely)
In the next six months I intend to . . .

Protect the Bay by conserving water at home.
Tell others about ways that they can protect the Bay.
Plant trees to help the Bay.
Clean up or care for a local stream.
Join Student BaySavers.
Participate in a Student Bay Savers workday.

Measurement scales for motive fulfillment constructs were developed based on past research and preliminary qualitative and quantitative research. Based on relevant literature (e.g., Clary et al., 1998b; Kaplan, 2000; Stukas et al., 1999) a preliminary set of motives was identified. Through qualitative individual and group interviews with students (n = 60) attending a CBF student workday, motives expressed by young people helping the Bay were identified. A scale of motive measures was then developed and pilot tested with seventh grade students (n = 92) in Michigan. Based on results from this pilot, a post-test scale with items addressing the fulfillment of the proposed motive constructs described in Exhibit 2 was developed and implemented.

Based on previous research, it was expected that factor analysis would reveal a cognitive structure in which measures of motives would separate into three factors representing understanding/competence, social affiliation, and autonomy.[2] However, an unforced Principle Axis Factor analysis including items proposed to measure these three facets of motivation yielded a one-factor solution. Therefore, the eight measures that were included in the Factor Analysis were averaged to form an index reflecting one motive fulfillment construct (Exhibit 3). The reliability (alpha) of this index was .87.

EXHIBIT 2
Motive Constructs for Index of Motive Fulfillment

Motive	Description	Source(s)
Competence and Understanding	Reflects a desire to know what is going on and what to do.	Kaplan (2000); White (1959)
Social Affiliation	Reflects a desire to belong to a group, establish friendships, intimacy, or a sense of community. Social affiliation goals have been found to influence students' attitudes about school and achievement.	Maslow (1954); Wentzel (1991),
Participation	Individuals are motivated to play a role in what is going on around them. Learning about problems without being able to help solve them is unpleasant, and can even lead to a sense of helplessness. Participation is not just taking action, but taking action that is satisfying or meaningful in some way.	Kaplan (2000)
Autonomy	When decisions are made externally for students, the result can be a decrease of interest in and sense of personal relevance of what they are learning about. This does not suggest that students always desire to be completely self-directed, just that some level of choice and autonomy has been found to increase motivation.	Brehm & Brehm (1981); Deci & Ryan (1985)

There was some evidence that the lack of separation of factors may have reflected the developmental stage of the study participants. Separate factor analyses conducted for sixth, seventh, and eighth grade students with pre-test motive importance rating measures revealed that a two-factor

EXHIBIT 3
Index of Motive Fulfillment

Post-test Alpha = .87, (1-5 Scale, Strongly disagree to Strongly agree)	
While studying about the Chesapeake Bay (and working on a project to help it) . . .	*Factor**
I developed new skills. (Und./Comp.)	.73
I learned how to help solve some of the problems that the Bay faces. (Und./Comp.)	.67
I discovered some things that I am good at doing. (Und./Comp.)	.67
I learned things that are important to my life. (Und./Comp.)	.67
I was able to do hands-on learning about the Bay, instead of just reading or hearing about it. (Und./Comp.)	.70
I had opportunities to work with my friends. (Soc. Aff.)	.67
I worked as part of a team to help the Bay. (Soc. Aff.)	.71
I was able to make my own choices about important aspects of the project. (Aut.)	.55

*An unforced Principle-Axis Factor Analysis yielded a one-factor solution with these loadings

motive importance structure was more distinct (i.e., had less double loading measures and less non-loading measures) for seventh graders as compared to sixth graders. In addition, the factor analysis model of motive importance ratings for eighth graders yielded a three-factor solution. This suggests that what older students consider to be separate motives, may not be well differentiated in the minds of younger adolescents. Further work in this area will likely lead either to additional evidence that young adolescents do not have a high degree of cognitive differentiation for the motives explored in the study, or to better validated items and indices for measuring the constructs.

Procedure

Teachers administered pre- and post-tests to students before and after their CBF learning experiences. Groups for the analysis included the combinations of field trips and service-learning projects shown in Exhibit 4. All students, even those who did not engage in service or go on a field trip, participated in CBF curricular learning activities in their classrooms. Thus, analyses test for any effect of service-learning or field trips in addition to that found for participating in classroom curricular activities about the Bay. The length of time between pre- and post-tests varied from one week to 17 weeks. The mean time between pre-tests and post-tests was nine weeks.

EXHIBIT 4
Number of Students in Six Service-Learning and Field Trip
Treatment Groups

	CBF Field Trip		No CBF Field Trip	
	n	%	*n*	%
Grasses	405	17	518	22
Non-CBF Bay Service Project	194	8	336	14
No Service-Learning	317	14	595	25

Data Analysis

The SAS PROC MIXED data analysis technique was used in this study. PROC MIXED provides analysis options similar to ANOVA or regression with the added benefit of fitting hierarchical models (e.g., students nested within classrooms) (Singer, 1998). The random effect of classroom was included in all models in this study.

In the analysis, some of the limitations of quasi-experimental design were addressed by controlling for pre-existing covariates. The models control for gender and pre-test levels of past behaviors and intentions to help the Bay. Covariates that were not significant predictors (and which were thus removed) included grade level, public/private school, race, and urban/suburban/rural community.

Experimental Hypotheses

Through completing a quasi-experimental design pre- and post-test study with middle school classrooms using CBF programs, the following primary research question was addressed. Does students' motive fulfillment mediate the effect of treatment (i.e., field trip and service-learning) on reported intentions to engage in ERBs? Based on the functional approach to motivation (Clary et al., 1998b), it was hypothesized that motive fulfillment would play a mediating role in the effect of all of the treatment programs on students' intentions to help the Chesapeake Bay. In addition, some specific hypotheses about individual relations among the variables in the mediation model were also made.

Because of *a priori* knowledge about *Grasses*, it was predicted that this program would not have a positive influence on students' levels of motive fulfillment and their intentions to help the Bay. *Grasses* was developed in response to Maryland teachers' needs for a service-learning program that would be easy to implement within their classrooms. After service-learning was mandated as a graduation requirement for Maryland students in 1992 (Finney, 1997), CBF found that an increasing number of teachers expressed difficulty in integrating environmental service-learning into their lesson plans. Therefore, CBF developed *Grasses* with the goal of providing a service-learning package that would be easy for teachers to implement. The potential downside of this pre-packaged form of service-learning is that in such programs, students may not have opportunities to be involved in planning service-learning projects. Thus, it was hypothesized that students in this program would not report high levels of autonomy motive fulfillment. Also, although *Grasses* is intended to take place both in the classroom and in the field, it was known that as many as half of the participating students generally did not go into the field to plant the grasses. This could limit students' motive fulfillment related to gaining competency skills.

Hypotheses about the effect of the non-CBF service-learning programs on students' motive fulfillment and intentions were less certain. These programs were implemented individually by teachers, so the characteristics of these programs were not fully known to the researcher. However, based on general guidelines for effective service-learning programs that match many of the hypothesized motives in the study (ASLER, 1995; Toole, 1999), it was thought that positive effects on motive fulfillment and intentions would be found for the non-CBF service-learning students.

The hypothesized effect of field trips on students' motive fulfillment and intentions was also uncertain. EE research has suggested that one time exposure to programs is generally not successful for changing student behaviors (Hungerford & Volk, 1990). Because field trips are one-day programs, one would not expect a sizable change in students' intentions and behaviors. However, field trips may support many of students' motivational goals because students often find the outside learning environment to be exciting and engaging. CBF field trips, though short, provide opportunities for hands-on exploration of the Bay, finding out about Bay problems and solutions, and working together with other students. Based on positive affective responses found in previous studies of CBF field trip programs (Zint et al., 2002), it was thought that field trips would positively influence motive fulfillment. However, because the experiences only lasted one day, they were not predicted to have a large positive effect on students' intentions to help the Bay.

RESULTS

In order to emphasize the mediating role that motive fulfillment plays in the relationship between treatment and intentions to help the Bay, the results for the main effects of *Grasses* service-learning, non-CBF service-learning, and field trips are presented. [3]

Grasses

Exhibit 5 below presents three models. Compared with the curriculum only treatment, *Grasses* had a negative effect on motive fulfillment (effect = -.20, p ≤ .01) (Model 2). Motive fulfillment had a positive effect on intentions (effect = .29, p = < .001) (Model 3). And *Grasses* changed from a nonsignificant negative to a nonsignificant positive predictor of intentions when motive fulfillment was controlled for (in Model 1, effect = -.02, p = .63; in Model 3, effect = .03, p = .42). Although *Grasses* was not significantly affecting intentions differently from curriculum activities only (no service condition), motive fulfillment was playing a mediating role in the model (Sobel test statistic = -3.25, p = .001) (Preacher & Leonardelli, 2001). The negative effect of *Grasses* on motive fulfillment probably reflects the fact that the *Grasses* program does not follow several important standards for quality service-learning.

Non-CBF Service-Learning

Non-CBF (or teacher created) service-learning did not have a different effect on motive fulfillment than the no service-learning treatment (effect = .08, p = .27) (Model 2). Because this relation was not significant, motive fulfillment did not play a mediating role in the relation between non-CBF service-learning and intentions to help the Bay (Sobel test statistic = 1.14, p = .25) (Preacher & Leonardelli, 2001). The finding that non-CBF service-learning did not predict motive fulfillment was probably caused by the lack of cohesiveness of this treatment. Teachers in this group created service-learning projects that reflected a range of quality in terms of following service-learning best practices. Therefore, a difference in motive fulfillment between these students and students who did not engage in service-learning was not demonstrated, and motive fulfillment did not play a mediating role.

Field Trips

Compared with the curriculum only treatment, participation in a CBF field trip led to a positive effect on students' motive fulfillment (effect =

EXHIBIT 5: MODELS
MODEL 1
Fffects of *Grasses*, Non-CBF Service, and Field Trip on Intention and Intention Least Square Means

	Effect	*Std. Error*	*P-Value*	*Mean** *(On 1-5 Scale)*	*Std. Error*
Grasses Service	-.02	(.05)	.63	2.19	(.03)
Non-CBF Service	.11	(.06)	.06	2.33	(.05)
No Service	0	-	-	2.21	(.04)
CBF Field Trip	.08	(.04)	.04	2.28[a]	(.03)
No Field Trip	0	-	-	2.21[a]	(.03)

Notes: *The pre-test mean for the entire sample for intention to engage in ERB was 2.19 (.77). The post-test mean for the entire sample for intention was 2.22 (.78).
[a] Means are significantly different at p = .05 level.

MODEL 2
Effects of *Grasses*, Non-CBF Service, and Field Trip on Motive Fulfillment and Motive Fulfillment Least Square Means

	Effect	*Std. Error*	*P-Value*	*Mean** *(On 1-5 Scale)*	*Std. Error*
Grasses Service	-.20	(.06)	<.01	$3.18^{a,b}$	(.04)
Non-CBF Service	.08	(.07)	.27	3.46^{a}	(.06)
No Service	0	-	-	3.38^{b}	(.04)
CBF Field Trip	.56	(.05)	<.001	3.62^{c}	(.04)
No Field Trip	0	-	-	3.05^{c}	(.03)

Notes: * The mean for the entire sample was 3.26 (.91).
[a,b,c] Means are significantly different at p = .05 level.

MODEL 3
Effects of *Grasses*, Non-CBF Service, and Field Trip on Intention with Motive Fulfillment as Predictor and Intention Least Square Means

	Effect	*Std. Error*	*P-Value*	*Mean** *(On 1-5 Scale)*	*Std. Error*
Motive Fulfillment	.29	(.02)	<.001	-	-
Grasses Service	.03	(.04)	.42	2.21	(.03)
Non-CBF Service	.09	(.05)	.07	2.27	(.04)
No Service	0	-	-	2.18	(.03)
CBF Field Trip	-.09	(.03)	<.01	2.17[a]	(.03)
No Field Trip	0	-	-	2.27[a]	(.02)

Notes: *The pre-test mean for the entire sample for intention to engage in ERB was 2.19 (.78). The post-test mean for the entire sample for intention was 2.22 (.78).
[a] Means are significantly different at p = .05 level.

.56, p ≤ .001) (Model 2). Because field trips had a positive effect on motive fulfillment, and motive fulfillment had a positive effect on intentions to help the Bay, motive fulfillment was a significant mediator in this case (Sobel test statistic = 8.86, p = 0) (Preacher & Leonardelli, 2001). Controlling for motive fulfillment, the effect of field trips on intentions was negative (effect = -.09, p ≤ .01) (Model 3). Because the relation between field trips and motive fulfillment was strong, and the relation between motive fulfillment and intentions was strong, motive fulfillment had a powerful influence in this case, changing the effect of field trips on intentions from a significant positive relation to a significant negative relation.

Summarizing these results, the two service-learning programs examined in this study did not have consistent effects on motive fulfillment or significant effects on intentions. Motive fulfillment, however, had a consistently strong relation with students' intentions to help the Bay. This suggests that although motive fulfillment is a promising mediator for understanding how and why educational programs may lead to civic outcomes, the broad category of *service-learning program* may not be specific enough to capture the essence of what is leading to motive fulfillment and intentions.

DISCUSSION

If the overarching category of *service-learning program* is not sufficiently narrow to predict differences among students' intentions, it may be helpful instead to focus on specific service-learning design and implementation characteristics to examine how they relate to motive fulfillment and intentions. The most instructive case from this study may be the *Grasses* program. The characteristics of *Grasses* that relate to program design are relatively easy to consider in the context of motive fulfillment and intentions. Also, some additional data that were gathered about the program lend further explanatory evidence to understanding why this program had a negative effect on students' motive fulfillment relative to the no service-learning group.

One element of *Grasses* design that may have negatively impacted students' motive fulfillment and led to the lack of effect of the program on intentions is the fact that it is a pre-packaged program. Because the program is very specific and structured in its content, many participating students do not have the opportunity to be involved in project planning in a meaningful way. Furthermore, the structured program does not provide sufficient opportunities for students to interact with and develop a collegial relationship with adults other than their teachers. Previous research has suggested that student decision making and student-adult relationships are important aspects of educational programs like service-learning. An experiential education study by Conrad and Hedin (1981) demonstrated that experiences that fostered student autonomy promoted personal growth attributes such as self-esteem. Conrad and Hedin also found that experiences that fostered collegial relationships with adults led to social outcomes including increased sense of responsibility.

The pre-packaged content of the program may also negatively affect the extent to which students feel the program is relevant to their lives and provides them with knowledge and skills that will be useful in their lives. In work with young urban environmental activists, Habib (1996) found perceived relevance to their own lives and communities to be a major reason why urban youth became involved in environmental actions. When a service-learning project covers limited and specific content areas and offers limited and specific participatory roles, opportunities for students to choose topics that interest them, independently explore the problem space, and devise their own solutions for addressing the problem are not provided. The results of this study suggest that the very characteristics that make *Grasses* easy to implement, and thus desirable to many teachers, may be negatively related to the aspects of service-learning that are most promising for supporting the fulfillment of students' personal goals and motives.

There is also evidence that implementation of the program may have contributed to the lower level of motive fulfillment reported by many *Grasses* students. For example, 15 percent of students who were in classes participating in *Grasses* did not know that their class was engaged in this project. A further 26 percent reported that they were not involved in growing and testing the grasses that were in their classrooms. Furthermore, although planting grasses is intended to be a culminating experience in *Grasses*, few students actually participated in this aspect of the program. Only 44 percent of *Grasses* students went on a Chesapeake Bay field trip while participating in the program, and of the students who did go on a field trip, only 44 percent reported that they actually planted grasses.

Although this evidence of reduced participation in *Grasses* reflects implementation problems, it also relates to program design. *Grasses* was designed to help teachers in a variety of schools, including those in public schools with multiple classrooms and many students. The packaged format of the program was intended to make it easier to use for many CBF teachers who are responsible for four or five classes and upwards of 150 students. Although it is relatively easy to implement and highly regarded by teachers, the *Grasses* program may simply not provide sufficient opportunity for meaningful student participation. This type of trade-off, where many students are nominally involved in a service-learning project, but few students actively participate in meaningful service (e.g., by growing, monitoring, and planting grasses), is likely to lead to poor results. In a chapter concerning program quality, Eyler and Giles (1997) report that doing meaningful work and making a contribution during service-learning were important program elements for fostering outcomes including learning, personal growth, and social responsibility.

Whereas *Grasses* had a specific array of characteristics associated with it that allowed for an examination and some *post hoc* understanding of the mediation pattern that was found for this program, the non-CBF service-learning treatment was not sufficiently specific to provide this type of information. Because the non-CBF service-learning treatment reflected a range of service-learning design and implementation characteristics that were described in more and less detail by different teachers, it is not possible to gain a great deal of insight into the results that were found. At most, one may report that the spectrum of Bay-related service-learning programs implemented by these teachers did not influence students' levels of motive fulfillment or intentions to help the Bay differently from the programs implemented without a service-learning component.

Several observations about the current state of service-learning in Maryland and Virginia and recommendations for future service-learning research and practice may be drawn from these results. One observation is that this study reflects environmental service-learning as it is currently being implemented in schools in Maryland and Virginia. As is evidenced by this study, not all service-learning currently being implemented follows standards for quality service-learning (ASLER, 1995; Toole, 1999). Because these quality practices support students' personal goals and motivations that relate to their intentions to engage in civic behaviors, many service-learning programs that are currently in use may not be achieving the level of outcomes that are expected and desired of them.

The importance of quality service-learning program design and implementation calls into question the wisdom of creating service-learning mandates in schools where teachers may not have the training or support needed to implement effective service-learning. Teacher responses in this study suggest that many teachers face a variety of barriers to using effective service-learning with their classes. For instance, 66 percent of the overall sample of teachers who participated in the study (N = 54) [4] disagreed with the statement that they had adequate preparation time to conduct Chesapeake Bay service-learning projects with their classes. Sixty-four percent disagreed with the statement that they had adequate monetary resources, and 49 percent disagreed with the statement that they had adequate transportation to implement Chesapeake Bay service-learning. Given these constraints, service-learning mandates such as the requirement in the state of Maryland (Finney, 1997) may lead to teachers implementing service-learning of compromised quality. And, unfortunately, this study suggests that when service-learning is not implemented in a manner that models best practices, it may actually have negative impacts on students' motivations and no impact on their civic outcomes.

With regard to service-learning research, the findings reported in this study point to several promising paths. First, because motive fulfillment was related to the intentions outcome while service-learning programs were not, it will be instructive in the future to focus on specific service-learning program and design characteristics to examine how they relate to motive fulfillment and outcomes such as students' civic behavior intentions. The importance of understanding the relation between program inputs and outcomes has also been emphasized in related service-learning studies including Melchior and Bailis' (2002) recent chapter examining the impact of service-learning on civic outcomes, and the article by Allen et al. (1994) examining the effectiveness of autonomy and relatedness supporting program characteristics for preventing problem behaviors in adolescents.

A decade ago, service-learning researchers struggled to demonstrate that service-learning could have positive impacts on student outcomes (Howard, Gelmon, & Giles, 2000). This research was intended to encourage districts, schools, and teachers to integrate service-learning into their curricula. Now that this goal has been achieved, and service-learning has been integrated into many schools across the United States (Chapman, 1999), it is important to provide evidence concerning the program design and implementation characteristics that will be most effective in achieving various desired outcomes. Without such evidence, it may be difficult to convince schools and teachers that the program characteristics that can be difficult or intimidating to implement at the outset are also likely to be key to the success of a program.

Finally, one suggestion concerning the way in which various program design and implementation characteristics are examined may be instructive. Although relevant results are not presented here, another pertinent finding of this study was that students' perceptions of service-learning program characteristics (e.g., their reports of whether they had a choice about their projects or opportunities to reflect) were strongly related to their intentions. In contrast, teachers' reports of whether or not they used reflection activities with students and whether or not they provided students with choices about their service-learning projects were not related to students' intentions.

This suggests that student ratings of program characteristics may not always match the program facilitators' beliefs about program characteristics. Thus, student reports alone may not be adequate indicators of program characteristics. This is a concern that was also raised by Allen et al. (1994, p. 636). They state, "...it is possible that measures of autonomy and relatedness at a site reflect students' status rather than influence it . . . Obtaining measures from multiple informants and including items sensitive to both student and facilitator behavior lessens this possibility, but does not eliminate it." Another effective way to address this issue would be to conduct experimental or quasi-experimental design studies that specifically compare the effectiveness of various program characteristics. Interactions among program characteristics may also be examined through experimental design studies. These types of intensive studies will be necessary to separate program design inputs from students' perceptions of programs. Independent measures of these constructs will lead to a deeper understanding of the mechanisms through which service-learning program characteristics influence desired outcomes.

The study presented here describes preliminary findings demonstrating how motivation theory may be applied to EE and service-learning research, program design, and implementation. Although results concerning the effect of treatment on intentions were not strong, evidence was presented to support that motive fulfillment is strongly related to students' intentions to engage in ERBs. Through continuing research directed toward refining motivation measures, understanding developmental differences in adolescent motivation, and exploring the relation between program design and motive fulfillment, we may gain a better understanding of how to increase both positive psychological functioning in students and positive actions on behalf of our environment and society.

NOTES

1.   This research was supported by the Chesapeake Bay Foundation, the Corporation for National Service, and the Maryland Student Service Alliance. I thank my co-researcher Anita Kraemer and my advisor Dr. Michaela Zint for their work with me on this project. Also, thanks to Ken Guire for his assistance with SAS PROC MIXED analysis. Correspondence concerning this article should be addressed to Beth Covitt, School of Natural Resources & Environment, University of Michigan, 430 East University, Ann Arbor, MI 48109. Electronic mail may be sent to bcovitt@umich.edu.

2.   Participation measures were not used for analyses because they were only included in instruments completed by service-learning students. Although not reported in this study, analyses that focused specifically on service-learning students suggest that participation is also a motivational goal with important implications for fostering commitments to ERBs.

3.   A few notes on the analyses and results are provided here. The SAS PROC MIXED output provides effects relative to no treatment condition. Reported effects are analogous to unstandardized beta weights in regression. Field trip by service-learning interactions were tested and found not significant for the first and third models. There was a relatively small, but significant interaction in the model examining the effect of treatment on motive fulfillment. In order to simplify interpretation, and because the interaction effect did not alter the relations among the groups (i.e., field trip students had significantly higher levels of motive fulfillment than non-field trip students for all three service-learning conditions), the additive model was reported. When appropriate, a Bonferroni Adjustment was used in the comparison of multiple least square means.

4.   The N = 54 reported reflects that although they were not included in the analyses reported here, this study also included a group of teachers and students

who only participated in CBF field trips and a group who did not participate in any CBF programs.

REFERENCES

Allen, J. P., Kuperminc, G., Philiber, S., & Herre, K. (1994). Programmatic prevention of adolescent problem behaviors: The role of autonomy, relatedness, and volunteer service in the Teen Outreach Program. *American Journal of Community Psychology, 22*(5), 617-638.

Alliance for Service-Learning in Educational Reform. (1995). *Standards for school-based and community based service-learning programs.* Alexandria, VA: Close Up Foundation.

Brehm, S. S., & Brehm, J. (1981). *Psychological reactance: A theory of freedom and control.* New York: Academic Press.

Chapman, C. (1999). *Youth service-learning and community service among 6th through 12th grade students in the United States: 1996 and 1999.* Washington DC: National Center for Education Statistics.

Chapman, J. G., & Morley, R. (1999). Collegiate service-learning: Motives underlying volunteerism and satisfaction with volunteer service. *Journal of Prevention & Intervention in the Community: Special Issue: Educating Students to Make a Difference: Community-Based Service-Learning, 18*(1-2), 19-33.

Clary, E., Snyder, M., & Stukas, A. (1998a). Service-learning and psychology: Lessons from the psychology of volunteers' motivations. In R. Bringle & D. Duffy (Eds.), *With service in mind: Concepts and models for service-learning in psychology* (pp. 35-50). Washington, D.C.: American Association for Higher Education.

Clary, E. G., Snyder, M., Ridge, R. D., Copeland, J., Stukas, A. A., Haugen, J., & Miene, P. (1998b). Understanding and assessing the motivations of volunteers: A functional approach. *Journal of Personality and Social Psychology, 74*(6), 1516-1530.

Clary, E. G., Snyder, M., Ridge, R., Miene, P., & Haugen, J. (1994). Matching messages to motives in persuasion: A functional approach to promoting volunteerism. *Journal of Applied Social Psychology, 24,* 1129-1149.

Conrad, D. E., & Hedin, D. (1981). National assessment of experiential education: Summary and implications. *Journal of Experiential Education, 4*(2), 6-20.

Deci, E., & Ryan, R. (1985). *Intrinsic motivation and self-determination in human behavior.* New York: Plenum.

Eyler, J., & Giles, D. (1997). The importance of program quality in service-learning. In A. Waterman (Ed.), *Service-learning: Applications from the research* (pp. 57-76). Mahwah, NJ: Lawrence Erlbaum Associates, Inc., Publishers.

Finney, M. (1997, October). Service-learning in Maryland: Making academics more relevant. *NASSP Bulletin.*

Ford, L. (1995). *Active Citizenship Today: Final Evaluation Report,* unpublished report.

Furco, A. (2002). Is service-learning really better than community service? A study of high school service program outcomes. In A. Furco & S. H. Billig (Eds.), *Service-learning: The essence of the pedagogy, Vol. 1, Advances in service-learning research* (pp. 23-50). Greenwich, CT: Information Age Publishing.

Habib, D.L. (1996, Winter/Spring). Youth spirit rising: Urban environmental activ-
    ists. *Race, Poverty & the Environment.*
Holt, J. G. (1988). *A study of the effects of issue investigation and action training on char-
    acteristics associated with environmental behavior in non-gifted eighth grade students.*
    Unpublished research paper, Southern Illinois University at Carbondale.
Howard, J., Gelmon, S., & Giles, D. (2000, Fall). From yesterday to tomorrow: Stra-
    tegic directions for service-learning research. *Michigan Journal of Community Ser-
    vice-Learning,* (Special Issue 2000), 5-10.
Hungerford, H. R., & Volk, T. L. (1990). Changing learner behavior through envi-
    ronmental education. *Journal of Environmental Education, 21*(3), 8-21.
Kaplan, S. (2000). Human nature and environmentally responsible behavior. *Jour-
    nal of Social Issues, 56*(3), 491-508.
Kaplan, S., & Kaplan, R. (1989). The visual environment: Public participation in
    design and planning. *Journal of Social Issues, 45,* 59-86.
Lieberman, G., & Hoody, L. (1998). *Closing the achievement gap: Using the environment
    as an integrating context for learning.* San Diego: State Education and Environ-
    ment Roundtable.
Maslow, A. (1954). *Motivation and personality.* New York: Harper.
Melchior, A. & Bailis, L. (2002). Impact of service-learning on civic attitudes and
    behaviors of middle and high school youth: Findings from three national eval-
    uations. In A. Furco & S. H. Billig (Eds.), *Service-learning: The essence of the peda-
    gogy, Vol. 1, Advances in service-learning research* (pp. 201-222). Greenwich, CT:
    Information Age Publishing.
Omoto, A. M., & Snyder, M. (1995). Sustained helping without obligation: Motiva-
    tion, longevity of service, and perceived attitude change among AIDS volun-
    teers. *Journal of Personality and Social Psychology, 68,* 671-686.
Preacher, K. J., & Leonardelli, G. J. (2001, April). Calculation for the Sobel test: An
    interactive calculation tool for mediation tests [Computer software]. Retrieved
    13 June 2002 from http://quantrm2.psy.ohio-state.edu/kris/sobel/sobel.htm
Ramsey, J. (1987). *A study of the effects of issue investigation and action training on char-
    acteristics associated with environmental behavior in seventh grade students.* Unpub-
    lished doctoral dissertation, Southern Illinois University.
Ramsey, J., Hungerford, H. R., & Tomera, A. N. (1981). Effects of environmental
    action and environmental case study instruction on overt environmental
    behavior of eighth grade students. *Journal of Environmental Education, 13*(1),
    24-29.
Singer, J. D. (1998). Using SAS PROC MIXED to fit multilevel models, hierarchical
    models, and individual growth models. *Journal of Educational and Behavioral Sta-
    tistics, 24*(4), 323-355.
Stukas, A. A., Snyder, M. & Clary, E. G. (1999). The effects of "mandatory volunteer-
    ism" on intentions to volunteer. *Psychological Science, 10*(1), 59-64.
Tblisi Intergovernmental Conference on Environmental Education. (1978). *Toward
    an action plan: A report on the Tblisi conference on environmental education. A paper
    developed by the FICE Subcommittee on Environmental Education.* Washington, D.C.:
    U.S. Government Printing Office, Stock No. 017-080-01838-1.
Toole, P. (1999). *Essential elements of service-learning.* Roseville, MN: National Ser-
    vice-Learning Cooperative.
Ward, H. (1999). Why is service-learning so pervasive in environmental studies pro-
    grams? In H. Ward (Ed.), *Acting locally: Concepts and models for service-learning in*

environmental studies (pp. 1-12). Washington D.C.: American Association for Higher Education.

Waterman, A. (1997). An overview of service-learning and the role of research and evaluation in service-learning programs. In A. Waterman (Ed.), *Service learning: Applications from the research* (pp. 1-11). Mahwah, NJ: Lawrence Erlbaum Associates, Inc., Publishers.

Weiler, D., LaGoy, A., Crane, E., & Rovner, A. (1998). *Executive summary: An evaluation of K-12 service-learning in California: Phase II final report.* Emeryville, CA: RPP International with the Search Institute.

Wentzel, K. (1991). Social and academic goals at school: Motivation and achievement in context. In M. Maehr & P. Pintrich (Eds.), *Advances in motivation and achievement: A research annual* (Vol. 7, pp. 185-212). Greenwich, CT: JAI Press Inc.

White, R. W. (1959). Motivation reconsidered: The concept of competence. *Psychological Bulletin, 104,* 36-52.

Zint, M., Kraemer, A., Northway, H., & Lim, M. (2002). An evaluation of the Chesapeake Bay Foundation's Conservation Education Program. *Conservation Biology, 16*(3), 1-9.

CHAPTER 10

SERVICE-LEARNING AND ACADEMIC OUTCOMES IN AN UNDERGRADUATE CHILD DEVELOPMENT COURSE

Kari Knutson Miller, Shu-Chen Yen, and Nicole Merino

In this chapter, one model for integrating service-learning into an undergraduate child development course is described. Two research questions related to this integration are addressed. First, do undergraduate students who participate in this service-learning experience have a greater understanding of course content than students who do not? Second, of what value is the service provided to the service recipient? Outcomes related to content knowledge and application of conceptual understanding as well as perception of service-value are reported. Finally, challenges associated with measurement of the relationship between service-learning and academic outcomes are discussed and recommendations for future service-learning experiences are provided.

Service-Learning Through a Multidisciplinary Lens
A Volume in: Advances in Service-Learning Research, pages 199–213.
ISBN: 1-931576-81-5 (cloth), 1-931576-80-7 (paper)

INTRODUCTION

Background

Service-learning is a promising pedagogical approach intended to benefit equally both the provider and the recipient of service (Furco, 1996). Service-learning typically takes place in the context of an academic course where students may identify opportunities to provide high quality service in collaboration with community partners and course instructors. In this context, learning should enhance service and service enhance learning. The practice of service-learning is supported theoretically by constructivist principles recommending that students have an active role in learning where tasks introduced represent challenges encountered outside of the classroom.

In the fields of Human Development and Developmental Psychology, the concept of Developmentally Appropriate Practice (DAP) is examined frequently. Practices, programs, and approaches are considered DAP when they address age trends, individual differences, and cultural differences and facilitate positive outcomes in various developmental domains including the physical, cognitive, socio-emotional, and moral (Hyun, 1998). Service-learning is a "rich," pedagogical approach that has the potential to impact developmental outcomes in several domains. From a theoretical standpoint, service-learning would appear to facilitate not only academic achievement, but also critical thinking, character development, social relationships, self-esteem, citizenship, and cultural awareness. Service-learning experiences may be modified based on age or developmental levels of the participants involved and offer opportunities for individual choice in site selection or theme of service-learning project.

Literature Review

Data analyzed to date have shown a consistent, positive relationship between participation in service-learning experiences at the college level and outcomes such as social responsibility and civic engagement (e.g. Stanton, 1991; Batchelder & Root, 1994; Giles & Eyler, 1994; Roschelle, Turpin, & Elias, 2000). The relationship between service-learning and academic outcomes is less clear, however (Furco, 2000; Gray, Ondaatje, & Zakaras, 1999). Although investigations conducted by Hardy and Schaen (2000); Batchelder and Root; Reeb, Sammon, and Issackson (1999); and Markus, Howard, and King (1993) demonstrated positive effects on academic learning, questions remain due to measurement or design issues. In the

Hardy and Schaen (2000) article, for example, academic outcomes were assessed through student self-report, while Osborne, Hammerich, and Hensley (1998) and Batchelder and Root focused on cognitive complexity, rather than mastery of specific content-related learning goals.

Reeb, Sammon, and Issackson (1999) investigated the relationship between service-learning and academic achievement in an abnormal development course. Although they reported a positive relationship between service-learning and academic outcomes as measured by course examinations, generalizability of these findings is somewhat unclear since students self-selected a service-learning or non-service-learning option. Markus et al. (1993) also reported a positive relationship between service-learning and academic outcomes. In this study, although lectures and exams were consistent across courses, discussion sections were facilitated by different individuals and mastery of course content focused on an understanding of students' roles as citizens in a representative democracy, the conduct of political campaigns, and important policy controversies. While subjects in this study did not knowingly choose to participate in service-learning, questions remain regarding the impact of the instructor on course outcomes. It is also unclear whether results could be generalized to courses where learning objectives focus on other discipline-specific concepts, theories, and principles.

Investigations conducted by Shastri (2001) and Strage (2000) focused on academic outcomes in educational psychology and child development courses, respectively. In the Shastri study, instructor and course content were held constant across two sections of an educational psychology course. Students in the first section were required to write two 7 to 10 page papers while students in the second section completed a service project. Students enrolled in the service-learning section completed a minimum of 20 hours at a designated field site, maintained reflective journals, and submitted a final reflection paper. Although Shastri found the mean of total course points achieved by the service-learning group was 10 points higher than the non-service-learning group, this difference was not statistically significant.

Strage (2000) studied the relationship between academic outcomes and service-learning in an undergraduate child development course. As in the Shastri (2001) study, instructor and examinations were consistent across sections. In the non-service-learning sections, students completed brief observations, took notes on these observations, and prepared a summary of their findings. Students in the service-learning sections, in contrast, were required to spend 20 hours working with children at a school site and reflecting on their experiences in journal entries. Strage compared student performance on three examinations which all had both multiple-choice and essay components. While students in the service-learning group achieved a greater number of points on the first exam, group differences were not significant. Group differences were significant on the second and final examinations. Further analysis of the second exam revealed that service-learning students achieved higher scores on the essay, but not the multiple-choice components. Strage suggested differences between service-learning and non-service-learning sections may appear later in the semester as it takes time for the academic advantages of service-learning to manifest themselves. Strage also suggested differences were more likely to be seen on narrative assessments than multiple-choice questions.

The literature reviewed here suggests there is further need to clarify the relationship between service-learning and academic outcomes. Furthermore, this review indicates it is important to consider the following when investigating the relationship between service-learning and academic outcomes:

a. Random assignment of students to service-learning and non-service-learning conditions;
b. Consistency of content, assessment, and instructor between conditions;
c. Operational definition of learning or achievement; and
d. Characteristics of chosen assessment measures.

In the present research investigation, students registered for six sections of a child development course on a random basis. Sections of this course taught during the spring 2001 semester were not designated "service-learning" until the registration process was completed. Course content, assessment, and instructors were consistent across sections. Academic outcomes, in this case, were represented by mastery of course-specific learning goals and were measured by performance on two multiple-choice examinations and one applied course project. Based on results reported in previous research studies (e.g., Strage, 2000), group differences on the applied course project were expected. Because students frequently rate service-learning experiences highly and report that they benefit from them (Hardy & Schaen, 2000; Fenzel, 2001), it was hypothesized that group differences on multiple-choice examinations would also be revealed.

In addition, quality of service was evaluated in this investigation. Gelmon (2000) reported that studies of service-learning outcomes to date focus primarily on its general impact on students as individuals and on student learning. The impact of service-learning on the recipients of service has not been studied to the same degree. Weah, Simmons, and Hall (2000) as well as Vernon and Ward (1999) recommended future investigation attend to the voice of service recipients in order to assess the impact of service-learning on the community served. In this study, service recipients were asked to evaluate the value of service received and to make recommendations for future collaborations. In this context, the value-added as well as the degree of balance between learning and service outcomes may be examined.

METHOD

Service-Learning Participants

Participants included 194 students enrolled in an upper division, undergraduate child development course during the fall 2000 (n = 103) and spring 2001 (n = 91) scmcsters. The majority of the subjects were female (n = 189) and all were Child and Adolescent Development majors. Participants enrolled in six sections of this course on a random basis. Three sections of the course were taught during the fall 2000 semester prior to the integration of service-learning and were designated non-service-learning sections. During the spring 2001 semester, service-learning was integrated into three sections of this course. Service-learning participants enrolled in these sections were not aware of service-learning requirements prior to the first day of class.

Service-Recipients

Participants also included 32 undergraduate student tutors from the America Reads and Counts (ARC) Program. These undergraduate students received work-study funds for tutoring second through fifth graders needing assistance in reading and math at local elementary and after-school program sites during the spring 2001 semester. The ARC tutors were the designated service-recipients in this investigation.

Course Description

At the beginning of each semester, course requirements were introduced. Course content, examinations, assignments, and textbook were consistent across sections. Two faculty members taught both service-learning (spring 2001) and non-service-learning (fall 2000) sections of the course. Each course section met for 90-minutes per week in class; in-class activities consisted primarily of lecture and discussion related to physical, cognitive, socio-emotional, and moral development in middle childhood (ages 6 to 12). Learning goals for this course included demonstration of knowledge of normative and atypical development in middle childhood, individual differences and environmental contexts influencing developmental changes, and developmental theories and their implications. Achievement of these learning goals was assessed through midterm examinations, final examinations, applied course projects, and final course grades. Midterm and final examination questions required analysis of contextual situations and application of course themes in a multiple-choice format. For the applied course project, students were required to identify a theme relevant to middle childhood, read scholarly articles on the topic, and identify an audience for whom they would summarize their under-standings. Students summarized the results of their literature reviews and generated suggestions for developmentally appropriate practice for the designated audience in written formats. Sample formats included newslet-ters, handbooks, resource guides, and brochures. Finally, all students com-pleted reflections based on the course project. In these reflections, students were asked to describe their rationale for choosing project themes as well as the extent to which they shared their project with individuals out-side of class. It was expected that the process of developing projects based on course themes to meet needs articulated by a real, as opposed to a hypo-thetical or potential, adult audience would increase the authenticity of the exercise and contribute to greater levels of engagement in course activi-ties.

Service-Learning Integration

Service-learning was integrated into three sections of the child develop-ment course during the spring 2001 semester. Efforts were made to estab-lish an on-campus partnership between academic faculty and student affairs personnel in order to facilitate a service-learning experience for stu-dents in this course. Initial discussion sessions attended by the two course instructors, student affairs personnel, and campus service-learning coordi-nators revealed a match between learning goals of the child development course and needs of the ARC program. It was agreed that students in the child development course would:

a.   Prepare materials in which they would integrate discussion of chil-dren's developmental characteristics and recommendations for prac-tice (suggestions for effective tutoring); and
b.   Disseminate these materials to ARC tutors at a monthly training ses-sion.

At the beginning of the spring 2001 semester, students enrolled in the child development course were introduced to the pedagogy of ser-vice-learning and were provided with an overview of the ARC Program by student affairs personnel. The instructors of the child development course designed a needs-assessment survey that corresponded to course themes to be completed by ARC tutors. ARC tutors were surveyed at their initial semester training session and child development students analyzed the results in order to identify tutors' informational and resource needs. The child development students then brainstormed potential course projects based on these needs. Students submitted a project proposal to the course instructor indicating project topic, format, and plan for integrating information on relevant developmental trends and practice recommendations. This process ensured that both the needs of the service recipients, the ARC tutors, and the course learning goals were taken into account. Child development students then developed their approved projects and disseminated them to ARC tutors at a monthly training session.

To assess quality of service, ARC tutors were asked to reflect on the value of information prepared and disseminated by service-learning participants. Tutors were also asked to discuss the way(s) in which they integrated the information provided in subsequent tutoring sessions. Lastly, tutors were asked whether they would recommend future collaborations between the ARC program and child development students.

In summary, the service provided by students in the child development course involved processing surveys received by ARC tutors, determining relationships between needs articulated by the tutors and course themes, and developing projects based on these themes for distribution at ARC training sessions. Students in both service-learning and non-service-learning sections developed applied course projects for a designated audience. While students in non-service-learning sections developed these projects for "potential" or imaginary adult audiences, service-learning participants determined the content of course projects after reviewing needs articulated by the ARC tutors.

Measures and Analysis

Academic outcomes were assessed through midterm examinations, final examinations, applied course projects, and final course grades. In addition, all child development students completed end-of-semester reflections based on their application projects. In these reflections, students were asked to discuss their rationales for choosing project themes. Students were also asked to discuss whether they had shared their projects with individuals outside of class. Group differences on outcome measures were analyzed quantitatively, while student reflections were analyzed through qualitative content analysis. This qualitative analysis of student reflections was used to evaluate the impact of the "real" vs. "hypothetical" audience on student completion and dissemination of course projects. It was expected that service-learning participants and non-participants would differ in these regards due to the authentic nature of the service-learning experience.

ARC tutors were asked to discuss the way(s) in which they integrated the information provided in subsequent tutoring sessions. Tutors were also asked whether they would recommend future collaborations between the ARC program and child development students. Tutor reflections were analyzed through qualitative content analysis in order to examine the degree to which the information disseminated by the child development students was valued by the tutors and the extent to which tutors were able to use this information to improve their tutoring effectiveness. Finally, overall recommendations related to future collaborations were examined.

RESULTS

First, group means on measures of academic outcomes were evaluated to identify trends. Students in the non-service-learning sections had slightly higher means than students in the service-learning sections on each outcome measure. Means and standard deviations are displayed in Exhibit 1.

While the direction of mean trends indicated that students enrolled in the non-service-learning sections of the child development course achieved slightly higher scores on examinations, applied course projects, and final grades, group differences were not statistically significant. Multivariate analysis of variance (MANOVA) results were as follows:

a.   Exam I, $F = .19$, $p = .66$;
b.   Exam II, $F = .32$, $p = .57$;
c.   Applied Project, $F = 2.78$, $p = .1$; and
d.   Final Grade, $F = 1.37$, $p = .24$.

These data are summarized in Exhibit 2. Furthermore, these findings were consistent across instructors ($F = .28$, $p =. 84$).

Student reflections on applied projects were examined through qualitative content analyses. The investigators reviewed all reflections, identified themes that emerged, and categorized responses individually according to type (inter-rater reliability = .90). The following response categories emerged from the analysis of reflections related to rationale for project themes: personal interest (e.g., "It interested me"; "I chose the topic based

EXHIBIT 1

Means and Standard Deviations for Measures of Academic Outcomes by Section Type

	Exam I		Exam II		Applied Project		Final Grade	
	M	SD	M	SD	M	SD	M	SD
Service-Learning (N = 91)	62.4 2	8.2	61.5 5	6.9 1	61.53	7.33	182.4 9	17.1 9
Non-Service-Learning (N = 103)	62.8 9	6.7 5	62.0 9	6.5 6	63.29	7.36	188.2 8	15.9 5

EXHIBIT 2
Group Differences on Measures of Academic
Outcomes; MANOVA Results

Variable	df	F	p
Exam I	1, 192	0.19	0.66
Exam II	1, 192	0.32	0.57
Applied Project	1, 192	2.78	0.1
Final Grade	1, 192	1.37	0.24

Note: p > .05.

on experiences in my life"; "I chose the topic because of personal issues"); focus on practical issues (e.g., "I picked a similar topic in another class"; "It seemed simple and straight to the point"); listing of project theme (e.g., "Rewards and ability"); relevance to future work contexts (e.g., "Teachers need to know about ADHD"; "Teachers need to know how to motivate children"); and general statement (e.g., "Children seem to have problems with maintaining motivation"; "Children need to develop better reading habits"). The percentages of students in service-learning and non-service-learning sections demonstrating each response type are displayed in Exhibit 3. Percentage comparisons indicated that students in the non-service-sections were somewhat more likely to choose topics on the basis of personal interest than students in the service-learning sections (75.5% vs. 59.7%). Service-learning participants were more likely to choose topics on the basis of contextual relevance (improvement of teaching) than students in the non-service-learning sections (14.6% vs. 3.7%).

EXHIBIT 3
Rationale for Choosing Theme for Applied Course Project, Student
Response Type By Section

	Personal Interest	Practical Issue	Listed Project Theme	Relevance to Future Work Context	General Statement
Service-Learning (N = 91)	59.7 %	18.3 %	1.2 %	14.6 %	6.1 %
Non-Service-Learning (N = 103)	75.5 %	14.6 %	2.4 %	3.7 %	3.7 %

Student reflections on the extent to which they had shared or intended to share projects with individuals outside of class were also examined through qualitative content analyses. The following response categories emerged from the analysis: affirmative (e.g., "Yes, I have"); qualified affirmative (e.g., "Yes, I will if..."); perhaps (e.g., "Maybe, if..."); negative (e.g.,

"No," "Not likely"); response not relevant (e.g., "Good to take this class"); and no response. The percentages of students enrolled in service-learning and non-service-learning sections demonstrating each response type are displayed in Exhibit 4. When asked if they intended to share their projects and knowledge gained as a result of completing their projects with individuals outside of class, 64 percent of students enrolled in the *non-service-learning sections* responded in the affirmative. An additional 23 percent of students in non-service-learning sections said they would if the audience was interested.

EXHIBIT 4
Likelihood of Sharing Applied Project with Individuals Outside of Class;
Student Response Type by Section

	Affirmative	*Qualified Affirmative*	*Perhaps*	*Negative*	*Response not Relevant*	*No Response*
Service-Learning (N = 91)	47.6 %	29.3 %	8.5 %	12.2 %	0.0 %	2.4 %
Non-Service-Learning (N = 103)	62.2 %	23.2 %	8.5 %	1.2 %	1.2 %	3.7 %

On initial needs assessment surveys, ARC tutors indicated they would find particularly useful information related to child development and instructional strategies, individual differences and learning, and motivation. Written materials were then prepared and distributed by child development students at tutor training sessions. The ARC tutors were asked to evaluate the service they received and discuss ways in which they would implement strategies suggested by the child development students. All 32 tutors indicated that they found the information valuable and helpful. Specifically, tutors noted that "problems faced in everyday tutoring situations were addressed," "the information provided will help us communicate with children and enhance their learning," and "the topics presented deal with students we work with...I'm eager to implement the strategies". Many tutors (47%) identified specific strategies they intended to use to improve their effectiveness in future tutoring sessions. Strategies discussed included methods for encouraging intrinsic motivation and helping children express anger appropriately, for example. Tutors were also asked if they would recommend future collaborations between child development students and ARC personnel. All 32 responses were affirmative and future collaborations were highly recommended (e.g., "I would definitely recommend this collaboration," "The knowledge and input is very useful").

DISCUSSION

Connor-Linton (1995) discussed service-learning models that integrate more and less direct forms of service. When engaged in indirect service-learning, students learn about the community, apply course knowledge to create a service or product designed to meet community needs, and analyze course content through this application (Connor-Linton). The service-learning component integrated into this child development course would best be characterized as indirect. In this indirect service-learning experience, child development students learned about the ARC program and evaluated the needs of participating tutors. The child development students then analyzed the relationship between the needs articulated by the ARC tutors and course learning goals. Finally, students integrated information relevant to child development into applied projects and disseminated these projects to ARC tutors. Academic outcomes, however, were not significantly different for students who engaged in indirect service-learning in this context and students in non-service-learning sections of the child development course.

Based on results reported in previous research studies (e.g., Strage, 2000), it was expected that service-learning participants would receive higher scores on applied course projects than non-participants. It was anticipated that child development students completing course projects for authentic audiences would be more engaged in this process than students in non-service-learning sections. Optimistically, this deeper level of engagement would transfer to other aspects of the course, thus contributing potentially to higher levels of interest, motivation to achieve course learning goals, and enhanced academic outcomes as measured by multiple-choice examinations and course grades.

Contrary to expectations, students in the non-service-learning sections of the child development course prepared projects for real, not hypothetical, audiences. When asked if they intended to share their projects and knowledge gained as a result of completing them with individuals outside of class, the majority of students in the non-service-learning sections replied that they would or that they already had. Furthermore, students in the non-service-learning sections appeared to have slightly higher levels of personal interest in their projects as evidenced by patterns emerging from course reflections. Qualitative analyses of reflections submitted by students in the non-service-learning sections suggested that like students in the service-learning sections, they completed projects for a real audience. Academic outcomes as measured by the course project were similar for students in service-learning and non-service-learning sections of the child development course.

The primary beneficiary of this indirect service-learning experience appeared to be the service-recipients. In submitted reflections, ARC tutors reported that the information developed and disseminated by the service-learning participants was very valuable. Tutors noted that the information was related to challenges faced everyday in tutoring sessions and that the provided suggestions helped them to communicate more effectively with children and enhance their learning. When asked if they would be interested in future collaborations between ARC personnel and child development students, all tutors replied in the affirmative.

Limitations

This investigation involved random assignment of students to service-learning and non-service-learning conditions and consistency of content, assessment, and instructor between conditions. Generalizability is limited, however, due to the possibility of semester effects, academic outcome measures selected, and characteristics of the service-learning experience. In addition, students in both the service-learning and non-service-learning sections submitted reflections based on applied course projects at the end of the academic term. In this context, reflections connecting course themes to service-learning experiences were minimal. Further investigation of the relationship between service-learning and academic outcomes might include systematic attention to characteristics of the service-learning experience and the role of reflection in the learning process.

Recommendations

The results obtained here suggest instructors consider carefully the potential impact of direct vs. indirect service on the achievement of course learning goals. As discussed previously, the primary beneficiary of this indirect service-learning experience appeared to be the service-recipients. Service-learning is intended to benefit the provider and the recipient of service equally. Although indirect service may impact learning positively in other academic contexts, more direct forms of service may enhance learning to a greater degree in fields such as psychology, sociology, and education.

All participants in this study were upper-division Child and Adolescent Development majors. The majority of these undergraduate students intend to seek employment in early childhood education, elementary education, special education, counseling, and social work. It is likely, therefore, that these students share a "service-orientation." This orientation was suggested in student reflections on applied course projects. Students shared course projects with real audiences regardless of section designation. In order to achieve balance between service and learning in this context, as well as value-added, direct service-learning is recommended. In a child development course, for example, students may themselves tutor elementary school children, as did participants in the Strage (2000) investigation. Students may also complete their service-learning experiences at nonprofit agencies that serve children. In these settings, students have opportunities to work directly with children, reflect on their experiences, and connect their experiences to course themes. This provides a learning opportunity that is qualitatively different from that associated with a traditional lecture/discussion oriented, campus-based course.

Like in previous research investigations (e.g., Strage, 2000; Shastri, 2001), no consistent, positive effects of service-learning on academic outcomes were found on multiple-choice examinations. The indirect service experience described here did not appear to change inherently the characteristics of the child development course. While this type of service-learning project was valued highly by the ARC tutors, it appeared to neither enhance nor detract from learning the content of the child development course.

Objective-type examinations including multiple-choice questions are used commonly to measure achievement at all levels of education. It is therefore suggested that the relationship between service-learning and academic outcomes as assessed through these measures be studied further. Specific characteristics related to the service-learning experience that may promote academic outcomes in this context should be explored and identified. Both the type of service-learning experience and the role of reflection in promoting understanding of course themes may impact academic outcomes. Recommendations related to the provision of direct service experiences have been addressed. The second issue to consider here then is degree of alignment between reflections on service-learning experiences and course learning goals.

In this investigation, all child development students completed reflections related to the applied project. This form of reflection was minimal in terms of intensity and duration. It is therefore suggested that the impact of service-learning on academic outcomes be studied further in contexts where students participate in direct service-learning and complete structured reflections based on related experiences. The frequency of connections between service activities and course themes may determine the extent to which these activities facilitate the understanding of content related goals (Astin, Vogelesang, Ikeda, & Yee, 2000). Furthermore, the completion of structured reflections, where service experiences are connected deliberately to specific course themes, may enhance understanding of course content (Ikeda, 2000).

Instructors may need to design specific assignments and prompts for reflection that require students to link service experiences and course themes. Open-ended reflections or general narrative discussions based on service-learning experiences may not correspond to learning goals assessed through other outcome measures. With more structured reflection prompts, on the other hand, students link service-learning experiences to course content assessed in other measures. In a child development course, for example, the ability to analyze and classify children's social status is often expected and "tested." A structured reflection prompt would ask students to consider examples of children observed through their service activities that would be classified as having popular, rejected, neglected, or controversial social status. Students would also be asked to provide a rationale for their classifications. When students complete more structured reflections, there is greater potential for alignment between service-learning experiences and course learning goals. In this context, we may see value-added in terms of enhanced academic outcomes as measured by traditional forms of examination.

REFERENCES

Astin, A. A., Vogelgesang, L. J., Ikeda, E. K., & Yee, J. A. (2000). *Executive Summary: How service learning affects students.* Los Angeles, CA: Higher Education Research Institute. (ERIC Document Reproduction Service No. ED445577).

Batchelder, T. H., & Root, S. (1994). Effects of an undergraduate program to integrate academic learning and service: Cognitive, prosocial cognitive, and identity outcomes. *Journal of Adolescence, 17,* 341-355.

Conner-Linton, J. (1995). An indirect model of service-learning: Integrating research, teaching, and community service. *Michigan Journal of Community Service Learning, 2,* 105-111.

Fenzel, L. M. (2001, April). *Enhancing the benefits of service-learning in undergraduate psychology courses.* Paper presented at the annual meeting of the American Educational Research Association, Seattle, WA.

Furco, A. (1996). Service-learning: A balanced approach to experiential education. *Expanding Boundaries: Serving and Learning* (pp. 2-6). Washington, DC: Corporation for National Service.

Furco, A. (2000, October). *Service-learning in teacher education: A review of the research.* Paper presented at the Connections: Infusing service-learning into teacher preparation meeting sponsored by the California State University Office of Community Service Learning, Los Angeles, CA.

Giles, D. E., Jr., & Eyler, J. (1994). The impact of a college community service laboratory on students' personal, social, and cognitive outcomes. *Journal of Adolescence, 17,* 327-339.

Gelmon, S. B. (2000). How do we know that our work makes a difference? Assessment strategies for service-learning and civic engagement. *Metropolitan Universities: An International Forum, 11*(2), 28-39.

Gray, M. J., Ondaatje, E. H., & Zakaras, L. (1999). *Combining service and learning in higher education.* Santa Monica, CA: RAND Corporation.

Hardy, M. S., & Schaen, E. B. (2000). Integrating the classroom and community service: Everyone benefits. *Teaching of Development, 27*(1), 47-49.

Hyun, E. (1998). *Making sense of developmentally and culturally appropriate practice (DCAP) in early childhood education.* New York: Peter Lang.

Ikeda, E. K. (2000, April). *How reflection enhances learning in service-learning courses.* Paper presented at the annual meeting of the American Educational Research Association, New Orleans, LA.

Marcus, G. B., Howard, J. P. F., & King, D. C. (1993). Integrating community service and classroom instruction enhances learning: Results from an experiment. *Educational Evaluation and Policy Analysis, 15*(4), 410-419.

Osborne, R. E., Hammerich, S., & Hensley, C. (1998). Student effects of service-learning: Tracking change across a semester. *Michigan Journal of Community Service Learning, 5,* 5-13.

Reeb, R. N., Sammon, J. A., & Issackson, N. L. (1999). Clinical application of the service-learning model in development: Evidence of educational and clinical benefits. *Journal of Prevention & Intervention in the Community, 18*(1-2), 65-82.

Roschelle, A. R., Turpin, J., & Elias, R. (2000). Who learns from service-learning? *American Behavioral Scientist, 43*(5), 839-847.

Shastri, A. (2001, March). *Examining the impact of service-learning among preservice teachers.* Paper presented at the annual meeting of the American Association of Colleges for Teacher Education, Dallas, TX.

Stanton, T. K. (1991). Liberal arts, experiential learning and public service: Necessary ingredients for socially responsible undergraduate education. *Journal of Cooperative Education, 27*(2), 55-68.

Strange, A. A. (2000). Service-learning: Enhancing student learning outcomes in a college-level lecture course. *Michigan Journal of Community Service Learning, 7,* 5-13.

Vernon, A., & Ward, K. (1999). Campus and community partnerships: Assessing impacts and strengthening connections. *Michigan Journal of Community Service Learning, 6,* 30-37.

Weah, W., Simmons, V. C., & Hall, M. (2000). Service-learning and multicultural/multiethnic perspectives. *Phi Delta Kappan, 81*(9), 673-675.

PART V

FUTURE DIRECTIONS IN SERVICE-LEARNING RESEARCH

CHAPTER 11

SUPPORTING A STRATEGIC SERVICE-LEARNING RESEARCH PLAN

Shelley H. Billig and Andrew Furco

This chapter addresses the need for more and better research in the field of service-learning. After a brief profile of the current K-12 and higher education service-learning research, the authors outline challenges for attracting more funding and more researchers to the field and provide multiple strategies to address the challenges.

INTRODUCTION

The popularity of service-learning as an educational reform strategy is growing. According to the National Center for Education Statistics (NCES, 1999), service-learning in K-12 education is practiced in half of all public high schools and one-third of all public schools. Private school participation is estimated to be even stronger, with nearly 80 percent implementing service-learning (Pritchard, 2002). In higher education, it is estimated that

Service-Learning Through a Multidisciplinary Lens
A Volume in: Advances in Service-Learning Research, pages 217–230.
Copyright © 2002 by Information Age Publishing, Inc.
All rights of reproduction in any form reserved.
ISBN: 1-931576-81-5 (cloth), 1-931576-80-7 (paper)

over 40 percent of all colleges and universities in the United States now offer service-learning experiences to their students (Campus Compact, 2001).

However, as was mentioned at the beginning of this volume, the research base remains "soft." While there is a body of evidence that supports positive impacts for participating students, schools, and communities, (Billig, 2000; Eyler, Giles, Stenson, & Gray, 2001), the research base contains few studies that would qualify under the new federal definitions of 'scientifically-based evidence.' This is especially true for service-learning research focused on K-12 issues. Criticisms of service-learning research include issues surrounding lack of standardized definitions, over-dependence on self-reports and anecdotes, too few experimental and quasi-experimental studies, over claiming, lack of depth in the analysis, and too few longitudinal studies (Billig, 2002).

The need for high quality research is reaching a critical stage. Those who are unfamiliar with service-learning would like to see evidence of its effectiveness before they decide to adopt it in their schools or districts. Those who are current practitioners demand research on "best practices" so they know how to improve their service-learning approaches. Some advocates are concerned about sustainability of service-learning without appropriate data to show its efficacy. Many want to know how educational context affects particular program designs and impacts. Still others call for finer grained studies to understand how service-learning affects which students on what types of academic achievement, civic responsibility, career choice, and social-emotional growth. In their assessment of the importance of service-learning research, Howard, Gelmon, and Giles (2000, p. 7) state, "...Developing the knowledge and practice bases in service-learning [is] essential to advancing the service-learning agenda..."

As shown by the First Annual International K-H Conference on Service-Learning Research, there are a substantial number of researchers who are willing and eager to conduct research on K-12 service-learning, though the need to attract more researchers to the field is clear. Over the past year, the level of interest has increased as evidenced by submissions to the 2002 conference, the number of publications in the field, and the number of dissertations being written that address a broad range of service-learning issues.

CHALLENGES

There are substantial barriers to the conduct of service-learning research in K-12 and higher education settings. First, there is currently no funding stream to support small- and large-scale studies of service-learning. While several organizations represent 'natural' sources of funding, notably the

Corporation for National and Community Service (CNCS) and the U.S. Department of Education, neither has placed a priority on service-learning research. Until recently, CNCS primarily funded evaluation, and only funded research through its Fellows. The U.S. Department of Education funded the 1999 NCES surveys, but little else.

Likewise, foundations have not been forthcoming with research dollars. While the W. K. Kellogg Foundation (WKKF), for example, generously funded a research component for the K-12 *Learning In Deed* initiative, it expressly did not fund the conduct of any new research within the component. The Pew Charitable Trust has expressed preliminary interest in funding a small service-learning study but financial support is not a certainty. Few other private sources (e.g., other foundations, businesses, and the nonprofit sector) have identified service-learning research as an item on their funding agendas. The lack of funding inhibits research performed by high quality research organizations and highly qualified researchers who rely on outside funding to support their work.

A second major challenge is attracting large numbers of highly qualified researchers from colleges and universities to the field. The lack of motivation to conduct research is partially explained by lack of funding, but also has its roots in two other challenges: few peer-reviewed, high quality journals and other venues in which to publish service-learning research and, until recently, no dedicated venue for presentation and networking. Tenure and promotion decisions are based on publications and presentations, thus it makes sense that faculty would seek to work in a field that enables them to progress within their chosen profession. While the annual K-H Service-Learning Research Conferences begin to address this issue, much more is needed.

A third challenge is that even when research is performed, it is rarely replicated, leaving the field with a series of disparate, unconnected studies. Without a dedicated venue, those who do perform research in the field tend not to build a body of research because they orient their studies to a particular content area. This means that, for example, individuals who research service-learning from a developmental perspective are most likely to present their findings at a research conference or in a journal that is associated with psychology. A researcher who is interested in service-learning that involves seniors or the homeless may present at a sociology conference. Those who study service-learning as a pedagogy may submit a paper at an education conference. While this phenomenon can lead to more presentation venues, it inhibits replication of studies and the building of a stronger and well-known research base that is widely disseminated to practitioners. In addition, this phenomenon makes it difficult for service-learning to become a part of the lexicon of mainstream, academic research that can garner substantial funding and attract highly qualified researchers.

A fourth challenge is the lack of coordination of research information and activity. As Furco (2000, p. 130) suggests, "No organization collects information exclusively on service-learning research, and certainly not in any comprehensive or exhaustive manner." The organizations that do serve as repositories for service-learning research are resource centers rather than research centers. Without an organization that monitors the development, progression, and quality of service-learning research, the ability to produce high quality research is severely compromised.

RESEARCH PRIORITIES

In K-12 education, the overriding theme today is accountability. The most common and, in some cases, required way of operationalizing accountability in schools is to demand that any school-based practice prove itself through the generation of increased test scores and/or by presenting "scientifically-based evidence" of its worth. Thus, for service-learning to survive as a school-based practice, the most pressing need is to design, implement, and widely disseminate a longitudinal quasi-experimental study that documents the impact of well-designed, high quality service-learning experiences of sufficient duration and intensity on various key stakeholders including participating students and teachers, schools as organizations, and communities. For students, it is imperative to understand academic outcomes. Schools exist to help young people acquire knowledge and skills related to particular content, and service-learning needs to prove that it contributes to cognitive development in order to remain viable as a school-based phenomenon.

The impact of service-learning is not as likely to be shown immediately in gross measures of academic performance, such as state assessments, though impact is likely to be seen in particular subtests or item clusters that measure skills such as problem solving, analysis, evaluation, transfer of knowledge to authentic settings, and other more complex thinking skills which contribute to an increase in overall scores. (Determining the precise areas of impact would require disaggregation of scores at the item cluster level.) Instead, service-learning research in K-12 education should use finer-grained measures such as those that address cognitive complexity, ability to generate multiple solutions to a problem, understanding connections between nested systems, for example, the relationship between local events or experiences and social organizations, transfer of knowledge and skills from one domain to another, and so on. Such measures frequently include pre-/post-essays that are scored for multiple traits using well-established rubrics, performance assessments, and untimed problem solving exercises. An alternative is to measure a mediating factor to school achievement, such as engagement or motivation to learn. The research literature suggests that service-learning impacts would be very high on these dimensions.

In higher education, service-learning is used to serve a variety of educational and institutional purposes including improving teaching and learning, advancing the institution's civic mission, building learning communities, and improving town/gown relationships (Furco, 2002). Like service-learning in K-12 education, higher education seeks to determine the effects of service-learning on students. In fact, most of the service-learning research conducted on higher education issues has focused on student impacts (Eyler, Giles, Stenson, & Gray, 2001). However, the higher education service-learning field has few common academic impact measures and too few studies that build upon the knowledge generated by the few studies that exist. While the need for "proof of concept" of service-learning in terms of academic achievement is very different in higher education than in K-12 education, better measures of academic outcomes are still needed for higher education if service-learning is to remain a viable teaching and learning strategy.

The research literature strongly suggests that service-learning has a multitude of other impacts on participating students, particularly with regard to civic engagement, interpersonal and social development, and career exploration (Billig, 2000; Eyler, Giles, Stenson, & Gray, 2001; Furco, 2002; Melchior, 1999). The service-learning research field in higher education has also investigated the role of specific programmatic issues such as reflection (Eyler & Giles, 1999, Freidus, 1997), service as a requirement (Stukas, Snyder, & Clary, 1999), and issues of institutionalization (Bell, Furco, Ammon, Muller, & Sorgen, 2000; Bringle & Hatcher, 2000; Furco, 2002).

The civic outcomes of service-learning are particularly intriguing since so little is known about the best ways to reconnect seemingly alienated young people to larger societal institutions. Multiple studies, such as those by Kahne and Westheimer (2001), Scales, Blyth, Berkas, & Kielsmeier (2000), and Morgan and Streb (1999), have been initiated to understand political participation, skills and habits of citizenship, the roots of activism, and other forms of civic participation. The literature suggests that social capital is built, especially with regard to the nature of the relationship of service-learning participants and their communities and particular institutions within their communities. However, while a few well-designed studies exist in this arena, too few are known and too little can be said with confidence. Given the current emphasis on the civic mission of schools, research on this topic could fill what is becoming an important need in a time when there is a window of opportunity.

The interpersonal and social outcomes of service-learning on student participants, while better established, are not always linked well to theory. Thus the research appears to be able to document effects without being able to say with certainty why the effects occur. The failure to link with theory inhibits the ability of practitioners to understand how quality can be enhanced and the parameters for program design can maximize outcomes.

Student outcomes related to career exploration are documented in the literature. However, while the higher education research has explored longer term changes in career aspirations based on students' involvement in service-learning (Astin, Sax, & Avalos, 1999), this issue has only been superficially investigated in the K-12 service-learning literature.

Finally with regard to student outcomes, too few studies examine longer term effects of service-learning. The studies that examine students for just two years show that effects of service-learning are sometimes gone after a year (e.g., Melchior, 1999). In their study of undergraduate students, Astin, Sax, and Avalos (1999) found that nine years after graduating college, individuals' level of volunteering was correlated with the amount of service they performed in high school. Still, too little is known about how service-learning experiences can be designed to have longer term effects and indeed, exactly what the longer term effects are on dispositions, attitudes, and behaviors.

There is a paucity of studies on the impact of service-learning on other key stakeholders such as faculty, educational institutions, and community members and agencies. While several studies have begun to examine these effects (for example, Berkas, 1997; Billig & Conrad, 1997; Bringle & Hatcher, 2000; Furco, 2002; Melchior, 1999; and Weiler, LaGoy, Crane, & Rovner, 1998) these studies are simply suggestive of hypotheses that bear critical and substantive investigation.

OTHER PRESSING RESEARCH NEEDS

There are two other areas that warrant serious attention. The first is the need for practitioners to understand the program design variables that are critical to developing quality and maximizing impact. A review of the research suggests that the most pertinent variables include student voice, choice, and leadership; direct contact with service recipients; content of reflection activities; placement quality; duration and intensity of service; alignment with specific learning goals; and instructional conversations (Billig, 2000; Eyler, Giles, Stenson, & Gray, 2001). However, there are too few rigorous studies that have examined these hypotheses in detail, and there is little linkage (other than to constructivism) to theories to explain how and why these variables are of importance. Key issues such as the relative merits of mandatory service also require attention.

In addition, there is a glaring lack of research attention to issues that have plagued the field of service-learning and little study of its phenomenal growth. The research on innovative practice, for example, shows that certain factors need to be in place if service-learning is to grow and flourish as a field (Fine, 2001). These include:

- Distinct identity: clear, differentiated, and recognized activities.
- Standard practice: activities that occur within recognized parameters that are known to be linked with desired outcomes.
- Knowledge base: cumulative evidence linking activities and content to desired outcomes.
- Leadership and membership: identifiable individuals and organizations that advance practice, serve as spokespeople, credential practitioners, and ensure successive generations of leaders.
- Information exchange: dependable and well-known communication vehicles to disseminate knowledge.
- Resources: structures and organizations that provide dependable funding and facilitate collaboration.
- Critical mass of support: enough people and organizations to sustain activities and ensure continued growth.

STRATEGIES FOR IMPLEMENTING THE RESEARCH AGENDA

Given the vastness of the research needs and the challenges that are currently serving as impediments, the research community and its supporters need to become strategic in their actions to further the field. The following represents one road map for achieving desired research goals.

Strategy 1: Convey a sense of urgency, responsibility, and efficacy through a well-designed communication and social marketing campaign.

It is important to tap into the deep convictions of the practitioners and supporters in the field and launch an ambitious campaign to support the research agenda both in terms of attracting key people to it and finding resources to fund it. The nation is at a time of readiness for this activity. There is a strong call for well-designed research in education at the national level as evidenced by the priority being placed on scientifically-based research and practice. There is strong visibility for K-12 service-learning as a school-based practice thanks to the work of the National Commission on Service-Learning and the specific credibility of Senator John Glenn ad other well-known and highly regarded Commissioners. There are organizations, such as the National Service-Learning Partnership, SEANet, the American Youth Policy Forum, and the Education Commission of the States, serving as vehicles for advocacy. In higher education, the work of Campus Compact, the American Association of Higher Education, a growing number of discipline-based professional organizations (e.g.

American Psychological Association), American Association of Community Colleges, and the Council of Independent Colleges continue to expand their support for the advancement of service-learning in higher education.

The nation, having experienced a terrible tragedy, has recognized and strongly responded to the need for service among all populations. There is bipartisan support, a sense of growing knowledge that individuals can and do make a difference, and an increasing belief in the ethic of service.

These conditions converge to create a unique opportunity, but the opportunity will present itself for a short period of time, only until the next issue arises. Therefore, it is urgent that action be taken now. Key messages about urgency, responsibility, and efficacy are needed to build and sustain social and fiscal capital.

Strategy 2: Consolidate a network of key researchers and add both 'star power' and a strong group of younger scholars to the network mix.

Right now, there is a loose confederation of service-learning researchers who investigate service-learning as a primary or ancillary area of study. The researchers tend to be located in universities and colleges and in a few research and evaluation organizations. Nearly all of the individuals active in the field conduct service-learning program evaluations. Most of the rest explore service-learning activities associated with campus projects.

The research agenda will serve to stimulate the field and provide the means for looking beyond the limited parameters of program evaluation or campus activities. Funds attract more prominent researchers, though many will not come to a 'new' field unless the research connects to their already developed expertise. Thus, prominent researchers who study cognitive development, democracy, diversity, community engagement, and career exploration, for example, may be relatively easy to attract to the field through the provision of funds. Others who are interested in less easily connected areas of investigation will be harder to attract. Therefore, it is important to help researchers currently in the field to expand their activities and then to supplement their activities through the use of well-known researchers in related fields who may or may not sustain their involvement in service-learning research. By involving well-known researchers to supplement current researchers and deepen and extend knowledge, but not counting on these outside researchers to sustain their involvement, the field will grow, and interest is more likely to be sustained as initial funds are expended.

In addition, strategies need to be put into place to encourage younger scholars (those who are graduate students, assistant professors, or research associates) to become interested in the study of service-learning. This can be accomplished through specialized sessions for such individuals at con-ferences, endowed scholarships, and construction of research to involve multiple sites and mentorships. Another alternative here is to establish a stronger Fellowship program, such as the Dissertation Fellow program sponsored by the Spencer Foundation. These programs have the dual goals of supporting high quality educational research and creating a cadre of skilled researchers who stay in the field. Scholars who receive these fellowships are expected to convene regularly to present their work and share issues as a small, hands-on group, often joined by a handful of highly-respected advisors or mentors.

Over time, it will become important to solidify the network into an organization. The organization can then assume responsibility for annual research conferences, peer reviewed journals, annual books, newsletters, and other communication designed to attract researchers to a credible, highly regarded venue for communication and dissemination. However, at this point, there are not enough funds to support service-learning research or a network, and there are strong cautions in the field to build the network slowly through the existing research conference. Current researchers believe that it will be important not to affiliate the emergent organization with any given university since it is important for multiple universities and colleges to be included and to develop visibility and derive credibility through the sponsorship of the annual International K-H Service-Learning Research Conference. The researchers simultaneously feel that it is important to have permanent staff for the conference to ensure smooth operations and continued fundraising so that the profits from the conference can eventually be used to sustain the organization and the staff. It is anticipated that it will take 3 to 5 years to build the organization. However, once built, the organization should be self-sustaining.

An alternative to the network is to form a National Center for Service-Learning Research. A National Center would help provide easier access to service-learning research, coordinate service-learning research information and activity, and explore ways to connect service-learning to broader research efforts (Furco, 2000). The National Center could be established through a collaborative of institutions of higher education and/or research organizations or as an independent 501(c)(3) organization.

There are strong arguments to be made for the development of such a Center in each of several forms. In general, a centralized structure with a director and staff is likely to be sustained over time if a regular source of funding can be found. Expertise can be gathered more effectively and efficiently, and on a regular basis. However, if the Center is located at one university, faculty from other universities may perceive themselves as being excluded and thus undermine the potential success of the Center. If the Center consists of a collaborative, it will be perceived as more inclusive but may be unwieldy from a management standpoint. If the Center is independent, it may have more difficulty in attracting stable funding unless the

Center is endowed and initially finds funds for researchers from multiple institutions. The configuration of the National Center for Service-Learning Research should be "based on the field and the research questions posed in the various service-learning research agendas that exist" (Furco, 2000, p. 132). As Furco (2000) suggests, the establishment of a National Center would help provide a more systematic approach for studying service-learning, ultimately bringing greater strength and recognition to the service-learning field.

Strategy 3: Attract funders through a strategic plan that involves leveraging resources.

Currently, the private funders who are most interested in service-learning such as the W. K. Kellogg Foundation, the Surdna Foundation, Pew Charitable Trusts, Atlantic Philanthropies, and the Carnegie Foundation, are not funding service-learning research, though they do fund evaluation. The Corporation for National and Community Service appears to be shifting its interest and is ready to fund research, but it has limited funds that can be devoted to the research and multiple programs that demand research attention. The U. S. Department of Education currently has few, if any, funds devoted to the study of service-learning. The same is true of the U.S. Departments of Labor, Justice, and Health and Human Services. Some smaller private funders may be interested, but they have too few funds to support a large-scale study, and many are loath to fund any research that involves public schools, or colleges and universities. Therefore, it is important to begin a leveraging strategy or to take a 'menu-driven' approach to funding.

The leveraging strategy involves starting with a few funders who are willing to support small, collective planning grants and are willing to match dollars with other funders for implementation of the study. Thus, for example, the Corporation for National and Community Service may fund $100,000 to an organization or consortium to design multiple studies, and then match funds with the U. S. Department of Education through an intergovernmental partnership (IERI program) or Mobuis grant to fund a portion of a longitudinal study that is also supported by several private funders. If each partner contributes $300,000 to $500,000, the estimated $2.5 million for the quasi-experimental, longitudinal, multisite, national three-year study could be accomplished.

A second possibility is to use a 'menu driven' approach. In this strategy, the entire research agenda for K-12 service-learning (Billig & Furco, 2002) and the Campus Compact National Research Council Service-Learning Research Agenda (1999) are 'shopped around.' Private sources that have an interest in one aspect of service-learning, such as possibly the Pew Charitable Trust whose interest is in civic engagement, could be asked to support one piece of the research agenda. Others would be contacted to support other studies of interest, but each study would be linked through the research agenda, and an expectation to communicate with other researchers working on the agenda would be explicit. In this way, a body of evidence and a set of replicable studies and instruments to be shared could be developed. While research would be conducted independently, the researchers could be linked via the research network organization described previously.

Strategy 4: Develop valid and reliable tools for the study of service-learning.

The Compendium of Assessment and Research Tools (CART), developed by RMC Research, and a new volume by Bringle (forthcoming), which identifies well-tested instruments to measure outcomes of service-learning students, are a good start for gathering measures that can be used to study service-learning. However, too few of the authors of the measures allow permission to use the tools without substantial cost, and too few of the tools have been validated.

This strategy calls for the development of valid and reliable measures for student, teacher, school, and community outcomes in the form of survey scales at no cost to the user. The development of such tools will allow replication of studies, extending knowledge, and hypothesis testing. The tools could be housed at the National Service-Learning Clearinghouse, ERIC, and multiple other sites and could be widely distributed through the research conference. Qualitative measures could also be included.

In addition, sample research designs could be shared to help younger researchers in their studies. Information on human subjects protection and how to seek institutional review board approval (IRB) or Office of Management and Budget (OMB) approval could also be provided. Researchers who use the same tools could be advised of each other's results and urged to publish collectively.

Strategy 5: Develop communication and technical assistance vehicles for linking research to practice.

Practitioners need to be able to help researchers define research needs for the field and need to use research results to improve practice. Researchers need to become aware of research priorities, need to access sites for study, and need to make their research results accessible to practitioners. Over the past few years, loose confederations have begun to develop. The communities of K-12 service-learning researchers and practitioners exchange information at a few venues, such as during sessions of the National Service-Learning Conference, through the National Clearinghouse on Service-Learning, through the International K-H Service-Learning Research Conference, and through newsletters from and web sites of various organizations. In addition, research collaboratives on service-learning are being formed at various discipline-based professional organizations such as the American Psychological Association. However, more formal linkages need to be established.

These linkages could be accomplished through the provision of sessions, information, and summaries to SEANet, the National Service-Learning Clearinghouse, Campus Compact, the American Association for Higher Education, National Service-Learning Partnership, and the Technical Assistance Exchange; by specific annual convenings of representatives of the research network and key constituent groups; or by multiple other means such as the requirement of dissemination by each of the CNCS technical assistance providers. The most efficacious way of determining the best formal strategy for this is to convene key leaders from the research and practice communities to develop a plan.

CONCLUSION

There is a sense of urgency to implementing the strategies called for in this paper. The 'window of opportunity' is now, the interest is palpable, and the need is enormous. Capitalizing on the current momentum, interest in, and visibility on the field should yield great return on investment. To guarantee the future of service-learning, to affect young people in life-changing ways, and to transform education, we must act now.

REFERENCES

Astin, A. W., Sax, L. J., & Avalos, J. (1999). Long-term effects of volunteerism during the undergraduate years. *Review of Higher Education, 22*(2), 187-202.

Bell, R., Furco, A., Ammon, M. S., Muller, P., & Sorgen, V. (2000, July). *Institutionalizing service-learning in higher education: Findings from a study of the Western Region Campus Compact Consortium.* Bellingham, WA: Western Region Campus Compact Consortium.

Berkas, T. (1997, February). *Strategic review of the W. K. Kellogg Foundation's service-learning projects, 1990-1996.* Battle Creek, MI: W. K. Kellogg Foundation.

Billig, S. H. (2000, May). Research on K-12 school-based service-learning: The evidence builds. *Phi Delta Kappan, (81)*9, 658-664.

Billig, S. H. (2002). Studying service learning. Challenges and solutions. In S. H. Billig & A. Waterman, (Eds.), *Studying service-learning*. Mahwah, NJ: Lawrence Erlbaum Associates, Inc.

Billig, S. H., & Conrad, J. (1997). An evaluation of the New Hampshire service-learning and educational reform project. Denver, CO: RMC Research Corporation.

Billig, S. H., & Furco, A. (2002). Research agenda for K-12 service-learning: A proposal to the field. In A. Furco & S. H. Billig (Eds.), *Service-learning: The essence of the pedagogy, Vol. 1, Advances in service-learning research* (pp. 271-279). Greenwich, CT: Information Age Publishing Inc.

Campus Compact. (2001). Campus Compact annual survey statistics – 2001. Providence, RI: Author.

Eyler, J., Giles, D. E., Jr., Stenson, C. M., & Gray, C. J. (2001). *At a glance: What we know about the effects of service-learning on college students, faculty, institutions and communities, 1993-2000* (3rd ed.). Nashville, TN: Vanderbilt University. Retrieved online at http://www.compact.org/resource/aag.pdf (5 June 2002).

Fine, M. (2001). *What does field-building mean?* Prepared by Melinda Fine, Ed.D., Fine Consulting. New York: Academy for Educational Development.

Freidus, H. (1997). Reflection in teaching: Development plus. Paper presented at the Annual Meeting of the American Educational Research Association, Chicago, IL.

Furco, A. (2002). Institutionalizing service-learning in higher education. *Journal of Public Affairs, 6,* 39-67.

Furco, A. (2002). Is service-learning really better than community service? A study of high school program outcomes. In A. Furco & S. H. Billig, (Eds.), *Service-learning: The essence of the pedagogy, Vol. 1, Advances in service-learning research* (pp. 23-50). Greenwich, CT: Information Age Publishing Inc.

Furco, A. (2000). Establishing a national center for research to systematize the study of service-learning. *Michigan Journal of Community Service Learning,* (Special Issue 2000), 129-133.

Howard, J. P., Gelmon, S. B., Giles, D. E., Jr. (2000). From yesterday to tomorrow: Strategic directions for service-learning research. *Michigan Journal of Community Service Learning,* (Special Issue 2000), 5-10.

Kahne, J., & Westheimer, J. (2001, April). *The limits of efficacy: Active citizens in a democratic society.* Paper presented at the meetings of the American Educational Research Association, Minneapolis, MN.

Melchior, A. (1999). *Summary report: National evaluation of Learn and Serve America.* Waltham, MA: Center for Human Resources, Brandeis University.

Morgan, W., & Streb, M. (1999). How quality service-learning develops civic values. Bloomington, IN: Indiana University.

National Center for Education Statistics. (1999). *Service-learning and community service in K-12 public schools.* Report Number NCES-1999-043. Washington, DC: Author.

Pritchard, I. (2002). Community service and service-learning in America: The state of the art. In A. Furco & S. H. Billig (Eds.), *Service-learning: The essence of the pedagogy, Vol. 1, Advances in service-learning research* (pp. 3-21). Greenwich, CT: Information Age Publishing Inc.

Scales, P. C., Blyth, D. A., Berkas, T. H., & Kielsmeier, J. C. (2000). The effects of service-learning on middle school students' social responsibility and academic success. *Journal of Early Adolescence, 20*(3).

Stukas, A. A., Snyder, M., & Clary, E. G. (1999). The effect of "mandatory volunteerism" on intentions to volunteer. *Psychological Science,* 10(1), 59-64.

Westheimer, J., & Kahne, J. (2000). Report to the Surdna Board-D.V.I. New York: Surdna Foundation.

Weiler, D., LaGoy, A., Crane, E., & Rovner, A. (1998). *An evaluation of K-12 service-learning in California: Phase II Final Report.* Emeryville, CA: RPP International with the Search Institute.

ABOUT THE AUTHORS

Mary Sue Ammon is Staff Research Associate for Research and Evaluation at the Service-Learning Research & Development Center at the University of California, Berkeley. Dr. Ammon has spent over 30 years at Berkeley conducting research, teaching, and writing on service-learning, children's cognitive, language, and literacy development, parent involvement in education, and teacher development. She was the lead researcher for SLRDC on its recently-completed three-year evaluation of California's K-12 service-learning initiative.

Shelley H. Billig, Ph.D., is Vice President of RMC Research Corporation in Denver, Colorado. She co-edited *Service-Learning: The Essence of the Pedagogy* with Andrew Furco, co-edited *Studying Service-Learning* with Alan Waterman, and directs multiple service-learning and educational reform projects at the national, state, and local levels.

Beth Covitt is a Ph.D. candidate at the University of Michigan studying Environmental Education and Conservation Psychology. She holds a BA in Government and Spanish from Dartmouth College and a MS in Resource Policy and Behavior from the University of Michigan School of Natural Resources and Environment. Ms. Covitt's work focuses on understanding

Service-Learning Through a Multidisciplinary Lens
A Volume in: Advances in Service-Learning Research, pages 231–234.
Copyright © 2002 by Information Age Publishing, Inc.
All rights of reproduction in any form reserved.
ISBN: 1-931576-81-5 (cloth), 1-931576-80-7 (paper)

and fostering individuals' motivations to engage in environmentally responsible behaviors. Recently, she has collaborated on an evaluation on the Chesapeake Bay Foundation's middle school level environmental education and service-learning programs.

Janet Eyler is Professor of the Practice of Education at Vanderbilt University where she teaches graduate programs in Human Resource Development and in Higher Education as well as in the undergraduate Human and Organizational Development program. She has conducted research and consults in service-learning in higher education.

Peggy Fitch, Ph.D. is an Associate Professor of Psychology at Central College in Pella, Iowa, whose research interests include service-learning, student intellectual development, and cultural awareness. She uses service-learning in her developmental psychology courses and currently serves as the Chair of Central's Diversity Task Force.

Lenoar Foster is an associate professor in the Department of Educational Leadership and Counseling at The University of Montana–Missoula, where he teaches graduate courses in Education Leadership and Higher Education. His research interests and publications are in the areas of educational leadership, the secondary school principalship, school reform, distributed learning in higher education administrative and faculty issues. As of fall 2002, Foster will be an associate professor in the Education Leadership Department at San Diego State University.

Andrew Furco is the founding director of the Service-Learning Research and Development Center at the University of California–Berkeley, where he serves on the Graduate School of Education faculty. Since 1994, he has led more than 20 studies of service-learning in K-12 education, teacher education, and higher education. He is currently serving a four-year term as a Campus Compact Engaged Scholar and is a member of the Campus Compact Research Advisory Board, Kellogg *Learning In Deed* Research Advisory Committee, the AAHE Service-Learning Consulting Corps, the National Service-Learning Partnership Executive Committee, and the National Review Board for the Scholarship of Engagement. He holds a masters degree in Education from UCLA and received his doctorate in the area of Educational Administration from UC Berkeley.

Chris Johnson, Ph.D. is Director of the Center for Vocational Reflection at Gustavus Adolphus College in Saint Peter, Minnesota, where he also teaches religious studies and ethics. He actively promotes service-learning through involvement in national professional associations and regional initiatives. At the time of this study, he was at Buena Vista University in Storm Lake, Iowa.

Janice McMillan is a lecturer in adult education at the University of Cape Town, South Africa. She gained her MPhil from the University of the Western Cape in 1997 and is currently registered for her Ph.D. degree. Her doctoral research is focused on understanding the relationship between the university and community knowledge in service-learning.

Nicole Merino is a graduate of California State University Fullerton (CSUF) who completed her undergraduate major in Child and Adolescent Development. She facilitated service-learning activities as a teaching assistant in the child development course. Her interest in research on service-learning was supported by the McNair Scholarship Program. She will be attending graduate school at the University of California Santa Barbara in fall 2002.

Kari Knutson Miller is an Assistant Professor in the Department of Child and Adolescent Studies at California State University Fullerton (CSUF). Her research activities focus on specific pedagogical alternatives that facilitate academic achievement as well as other positive developmental outcomes. She is a service-learning liaison at CSUF and in this capacity provides support to colleagues interested in integrating service-learning into existing courses and participates in service-learning advisory board and strategic planning activities.

Pamela Steinke, Ph.D. is an Associate professor of Psychology at Central College in Pella, Iowa, whose research focuses on cognitive outcomes of service-learning. She uses service-learing in her cognitive and research courses and previously coordinated the program responsible for the experiential component Central's core curriculum.

Andrea Vernon is the director of the Office for Civic Engagement at The University of Montana. Vernon administers several programs including AmeriCorps, VISTA, American Humanics, and academic service-learing. In addition, she teaches a service-learing course through the Davidson Honors College and the social work department. Her research and publications focus on higher education service-learing, student development, higher education leadership, and campus-community partnerships.

Fredric Waldstein, Ph.D. holds the Irving R. Burling chair in Leadership and is Professor Political Science at Wartburg College in Waverly, Iowa. He has been the principal investigator on several service-learing grants and has been instrumental in the development of Iowa Campus Compact.

Rhonda A. Waskiewicz is the chairperson/program director of the occupational therapy department at the University of Scranton, Scranton, Pennsylvania. She received her BS in occupational therapy from Tufts

University, her MS in health administration from Kings College, Wilkes-Barre, PA, and her Ed.D. in education administration from Temple University. She has practiced as an occupational therapist in a variety of settings since 1973. Her research and education interests include community-based health care delivery and curriculum design.

Adrian Wurr is a recent graduate of the University of Arizona, where the present study was conducted as part of his dissertation research. He currently is an Assistant Professor at UNC Greensboro, where he teaches courses in applied linguistics and composition. His research interests include TESOL, service-learning, and literacy instruction. He is currently collaborating on an ESL Composition book that will be published by Lawrence Erlbaum Associates.

Shu-Chen Yen is an Assistant Professor in the Department of Child and Adolescent Studies at California State University Fullerton (CSUF). Her research interests include service-learning and academic outcomes, goodness-of-fit models, and children's temperament. She received a CSUF mini-grant in order to integrate service-learning into a child development course.